YOU BET

YOU BET

THE BETFAIR STORY:
HOW TWO MEN CHANGED
THE WORLD OF GAMBLING

COLIN CAMERON

HarperCollins*Publishers*

HarperCollins*Publishers*
77–85 Fulham Palace Road,
Hammersmith, London W6 8JB

www.harpercollins.co.uk

First published by HarperCollins*Publishers* 2009

1 3 5 7 9 10 8 6 4 2

Extract from Betfair forum on pp88–91, 93: Betfair.com Forum.
© The Sporting Exchange Limited

Excerpts from Net Line on pp94–95: © GamCare (Registered Charity
No. 1060005). Used with permission. All rights reserved.

A catalogue record of this book is
available from the British Library

HB ISBN 978-0-00-727701-8
PB ISBN 978-0-00-731187-3

Printed and bound in Great Britain by
Clays Ltd, St Ives plc

Mixed Sources
Product group from well-managed
forests and other controlled sources
www.fsc.org Cert no. SW-COC-1806
© 1996 Forest Stewardship Council
FSC

FSC is a non-profit international organisation established to promote the
responsible management of the world's forests. Products carrying the FSC
label are independently certified to assure consumers that they come
from forests that are managed to meet the social, economic and
ecological needs of present and future generations.

Find out more about HarperCollins and the environment at
www.harpercollins.co.uk/green

To Emily and Lois

ACKNOWLEDGEMENTS

With thanks: to all those who gave their time towards this book's content, including those who do not feature in the final text but nevertheless provided invaluable briefings and guidance; to Jonathan Taylor and everyone at Harper Collins; to Alan Byrne for his forensic eye; to Shaun Phillips for the roots of this book; and to Peter Straus, master of his domain.

CONTENTS

AN INTERESTING WHEEZE

During breaks from the writing of this book, any general conversation about the subject matter usually fell into two categories. On one hand plenty wanted to know how, as the subtitle of *You Bet* suggests, two men changed the world of gambling and in the process – and this was the real hook – became multimillionaires. Equally some others wanted to consider the ethics of setting up a company that promotes betting.

Immoral or amazing? An 'interesting wheeze' was one description of Betfair. After reference to the dictionary definition of 'wheeze' – *a cunning plan* – this was refined to 'interesting concept'. As a business endeavour, Betfair is at very least that. To the more enthusiastic the company's progress represents a breathtaking corporate tale of all-conquering growth culminating in market domination and handsome profit.

To me, the story of Betfair, which forms the first part of this book, is a compelling narrative of individuals giving up often assured and substantial incomes in return for pursuing an idea in the spirit of true entrepreneurship, of which there is currently a substantial need, worldwide. As a winner, twice, of Queen's Awards for Enterprise, Betfair has the endorsement of the highest levels of government, and the head of state, Herself.

As for the ethics of Betfair, a negative view on the morality of person-to-person betting probably reflects a position on gambling established before the company was even launched. Moreover, if you were against the activity, in whatever form, before 2000, I would suspect your view of Internet betting of any kind is that this simply brings the unwanted vice of gambling into the home. The world of Internet betting in which Betfair sits very central makes 'it much easier, regrettably, for enormous sums to be spent unthinkingly', said Andrew Langdon, court recorder in the case of Bryan Benjafield. The 23-year-old book-keeper was sentenced in 2008 to five years in prison having gambled over £1 million of a Dorset construction company's holdings with online casino websites, in all around one tenth of his employer's annual turnover.

An old friend from university is not hostile to gambling. A bet just leaves him cold. A few years ago, when he worked in London's financial sector, he went to Goodwood at the invitation of a City client. On each of the afternoon's seven races he placed bets of £10 and was left pondering that even in those contests where proceedings culminated in the closest of photo finishes his heart and pulse rates hardly deviated from normal. Yet, like me, he, too, found the Betfair story intriguing, (possibly even more so than the hedge fund he ran, before quitting to embark on a degree in English, twenty years after graduating from

Cambridge in the Sciences). If you have reservations of the morality in Betfair's core endeavour, I hope that what to me is an historic story of contemporary innovation can still raise your pulse for reasons other than anger.

Of course, whatever your opinion, for consenting adults Betfair is legal. The company went to great lengths and expense to establish this. Betfair cannot be denied on those grounds the host of commendations for creating jobs and general wealth since the company's launch in 2000. After spending many months dealing with Betfair, it is easy for me to see the basis for the civil reception – recorded in Part Two of this book – that the company received in Whitehall and at the Treasury. Betfair, itself, is, by and large, an open, up-front operation. Bar a reluctance to make available the contact details of one original investor, whom in any case I was able to source, independently, I cannot fault the accommodation I was afforded.

And bookmakers, generally? On an individual basis, and discounting that, as publicly quoted companies, there is a limit to what information could be made available to me, I equally could find little to fault the willingness with which they granted me time and co-operated in answering inquiries often implicitly critical. In my experience, if betting is a business you consider immoral, you might find objections harder to sustain when you are sitting across the table from those who make up the corporate entities with whose trade you take issue.

As well as the subject of betting in a broad sense, I write about a whole range of pleasures such as matters of style to wine and cigars. I am lucky to do so. That said, racing and betting represent, to me, a most welcoming village which, though a non-resident, I am always delighted to be received back as a guest. Likewise, neighbouring towns with interests, which touch on matters relating to Betfair and Internet gambling. The support cast of this book was largely receptive to being interviewed and forthcoming. As for those who were initially reticent, they did at least leave themselves open to persuasion. Please note that none, Betfair, bookmakers, or otherwise contributed in any way to the cost of publication.

If you are a dedicated gambler you will most likely already appreciate how the world of betting can grab you. I hope very much that this book, which should have obvious appeal, serves to give you fresh insight into a pastime that you already savour actively. Beyond this, as this is a story that involves society as a whole, if you are not predisposed to take an interest in betting or have fundamental reservations, please excuse me for suggesting you might nevertheless still want to gamble on this book proving most compelling. Why not take a punt?

COLIN CAMERON, MARCH 2009

PART ONE
THE BETFAIR STORY

INTRODUCTION

'There was an old fellow from Ealing
Who had a peculiar feeling.
He read on the door,
Don't spit on the floor.
So he lay down and spat on the ceiling'

'That kind of sums up me'

– Andrew 'Bert' Black, creator of Betfair

Ed Wray was born in 1968. He has a thirst for all sports
though he admits to no great ability at any. Comfortably
over six feet tall, he often finds himself in houses where
the ceiling is a general threat to his wellbeing. Andrew
Black was born five years before Wray in 1963. He is
passionate about horseracing. Indeed, having been taken,
aged eight, to Goodwood by his father, Tony, a property
developer, one imagines that he could be sustained by
this alone (though he does have a near encyclopaedic

knowledge of past Wimbledon winners and their paths to the final).

Apart from the decade of their births and physical scale – actually Black has even more to fear from ceilings than Wray – the pair would appear to have little of substance in common. Maybe also the card game, bridge. Wray, if not quite as sharply dressed as Gordon Gekko in the movie *Wall Street*, has the look of a seasoned City man, with well over a decade of high-wire finance to his name. Black's wardrobe is eclectic. He once collected an entrepreneur's award at a black tie event in his trainers – candidly acknowledged on his Internet blog – having forgotten to change into the more accepted patented style. Black's employment record is the antithesis of Wray's, whose focus and drive carried him up to Vice President rank at financial giants, J.P. Morgan, which he joined straight from university.

The CVs of Black and Wray are perhaps the most striking contrast of all. Black, or Bert, as his best friends know him – reputedly, at King's College, Wimbledon, a teacher mistakenly referred to him by this name – lists golf caddy, professional bridge player, and a spell at the government spooks and spy centre, Government Communications Headquarters (GCHQ), among his jobs since leaving university. Unlike Wray, he also stacked shelves at B&Q.

Until 1998, the pair, despite significant shared family ties, were at best acquaintances, a state easily explained by the lack of a substantive common denominator between the two. In truth, they only came together meaningfully as a result of a conversation that year. The thirtysomethings were at a garden party of Ed Wray's brother, Jeremy, a bridge partner of Black's, which was the principal overlap in the families. On this occasion, Ed Wray – no common nickname, the schoolmasters at Tonbridge being less prone to memory lapses – and Black spoke for perhaps a little longer than normal for two men who knew each other through an extended family network.

There did exist the slenderest of common threads, that of gambling. This probably sustained their social chat into overtime. Wray, who describes himself as an 'enthusiastic punter', mentioned to Black that he was disappointed with the amount of money he had won recently betting on a particular horse. Black remarked back that, in the future, on the basis of an idea he had for Internet gambling, he could expect a better return for his money. 'Tell me more,' invited Wray, whose brother had previously mentioned that his bridge partner and best friend had been thinking about an idea that might amount to something in the gambling world. So Black, sensing growing serendipity, explained; offer gamblers the chance to bet with each other, directly, via the Internet.

Today, as a consequence of this conversation, both Black and Wray are multimillionaires. Betfair, the company they set up in 2000 now stands proudly on the north bank of the Thames, just down from Hammersmith, home to nearly 1,000 of Betfair's global workforce of 1,350. The company is worth in excess of £1.5 billion, a valuation based on the sale in 2006 for £355 million of 23 per cent of the company. The valuation since has gone up. What's more, as a result of this unlikely pair collaborating and colluding, attitudes towards betting, horseracing, sport everywhere, and the stance of governments worldwide, have changed immeasurably.

There is a new global culture of gambling and a growing constituency, worldwide, that bets as a form of leisure.

There has also been a corresponding change in government attitudes to betting with a raft of measures deregulating the industry since 2000. A reflection of this is that across Europe, the names of bookmakers – indeed many of them Internet-based – grace the sports shirts of a steadily increasing number of professional clubs in a range of disciplines. In Britain, where betting topped £91.5 billion in 2006 and was estimated to have exceeded £14 billion with William Hill and Ladbrokes alone in 2007, gambling has, from September 2007, been advertised on mainstream TV and radio for the first time. It has never been easier to play roulette, either, through the many websites – including Betfair – offering the game online to casinos themselves.

Betfair has been at the forefront of betting's transformation from a sleazy, illicit habit into a mainstream pursuit. The Internet is the growing method of betting in countries ranging from Afghanistan to Zambia (just two of the eighty-plus countries in which Betfair boasts clients, using ten different currencies to bet via Betfair.com, available in seventeen different languages). In Britain, nearly one in ten of the population, according to Gambling Commission – a body created in 2005 to regulate the industry – bet regularly in 2007 using remote devices from Internet to mobile phone. But Betfair has done more than simply meet growing demand in a relatively fresh, new market. The world of information has been permanently altered by the emergence of Google, and rival search engines. The website, eBay, has changed the way we buy and sell personal possessions. Because of Amazon we purchase books, CDs, and DVDs differently. And Betfair has changed how many gamble and bet. In simplest terms, an eBay for gamblers, sharing the stock market's ability to aggregate buyers and sellers, has changed its own world, and in the process ones beyond.

What is revolutionary about Betfair? The website enables gamblers to cut out completely the middleman, otherwise known to those in Britain as the bookmaker, so that effectively gambler deals directly with gambler, via Betfair.com. What Black and Wray developed is a concept handling in 2008, the company claims, five million transactions daily – more than all of Europe's stock markets combined – that a new breed of worldwide gambler seeks to place round the clock. The significance of this is that Andrew Black and Ed Wray have enfranchised the world's gamblers. Simply this allows betting on your own terms. What's more this is betting at high speed, in tune with the pace at which many live their lives in today's high-tempo world.

By way of illustration, take a football match. During the ninety minutes, Betfair markets constantly fluctuate reflecting the precise state of play at any time – even in which half the ball is. Say that Manchester United are 2–0 down after ten minutes but you still fancy them to come back and win. Someone else logs on to Betfair who believes the opposite and offers you odds against your prediction. You take the odds on offer, then watch your screen as others enter the market offering different assessments with every subsequent throw in, free kick, corner, yellow and red card, save, near miss, and goal. At any stage you can bet again on the same outcome, or offer odds yourself and take – or, as a bookmaker would say, lay – a bet. At the same time, you could bet on what horseracing is taking place. The odds on that are traded as soon as the runners are known, right up to the last few yards of the final furlong. The market fluctuates with every stride until the field is in the shadow of the winning post. Betting-in-running; a different risk altogether.

This is also betting that is much more acceptable, both socially and to governments. The latter are happy to sanction freely consenting adults betting with each other. Eliminated from proceedings is an element that to many represented not only a middleman, but – with apologies to all respectful bookmakers – a pretty unreliable, unsavoury type, with doubtful ethics and a reputation for dishonesty, topped by a pork pie hat. Using Betfair.com, I bet with you, you bet with me. Or I make the odds – again, lay the bet – for you to take, or you make the odds and I bet. An altogether more civilised means of staking – and of course, potentially losing your shirt. Or as Betfair's marketing campaign of 2008 maintained, *betting as it should be.*

For all the concept's simplicity – Betfair takes up to 5 per cent of winnings as commission, shades of 'neither a lender or borrower be, be a broker and take your fee' – this is betting but not as we had known it before the millennium. Clean and fresh, person-to-person. You start with, say £50, and you can churn this amount through a day of gambling, taking bets, making bets, engaging with your fellow speculators. Meanwhile, a man – statistically that is overwhelmingly likely – walks into a betting shop with the same £50, or enters a parimutuel (mutual betting) café in France, or a TAB-licensed bar in Australia. He has a bet. And waits. He either wins or loses. Eventually, if he wins and once he has been paid out, he might have another bet. Or he might have to go to the bank cashpoint first. Win or lose, the process is pedestrian by comparison. And with the British betting shop in mind, even allowing for home improvements, all in an environment which is rightly deemed inappropriate for minors.

But if you don't bet (apart from the Grand National, of course, or the Melbourne Cup if based in Australia, also in the grip of Betfair, as we will see) so what? Let us leave aside for a moment the scale of trade for which Betfair is responsible. On their own, annual revenues of £239 million for a company only eight years old should command interest from even those prejudiced against the nature of the business. To many, Betfair's true significance over and above offering an alternative way to gamble is how the operation has proved to be able to affect both its own industry and beyond. As well as being part of what has been a huge upheaval in betting since 2000, what Black and Wray created has been more than simply a reflection of the Internet age superseding an otherwise largely Luddite world. Betfair has driven market changes since 2000, as well as met growth in demand as a result of the global spread of affluence, credit crunch and recession notwithstanding. Much of what has been reformed or altered by the power of the market has been as a result of Betfair, a catalyst for broader changes affecting gambler and non-gambler alike. A company capable of this demands attention.

Of course, Betfair is most relevant to those who do bet. Customers of betting industries from Britain to Australia have been directly affected by Betfair. In Britain, for example, where betting giants such as Ladbrokes have enjoyed nearly fifty years of relatively unchallenged domination, Betfair, with a model that takes retail overheads out of the market, cuts into profits. Existing giants of the betting world were motivated to introduce betting-in-running and improve web access to counter this, and to consider revamping licensed premises on high streets, nationwide. As far as Britain is concerned, with about 8,000 betting shops, some of them beyond restoration, you may not have noticed a change yet. But a revolution began in 2000. The latest generation of gamblers are as likely to enter an Internet café as a betting shop.

However, you don't bet. You may even live in a remote location, and have no high street to speak of that is changing, nor enjoy spending time on a computer. You may, though, follow sport. That has changed as a result of Betfair, from the sponsorship of shirts. Betfair's deal with Fulham for the 2002–03 Premier League season opened up the possibility of betting organisations taking space across players' chests previously denied them because of fears of corruption. There have been Memorandums of Understanding, (MOUs). These were originally agreements that Betfair made with sporting bodies to facilitate exchange of information in suspected cases of corruption. Ultimately the government in Britain legislated to make the custom of cooperation universal, meaning that sports bodies are now intimate with betting, in the past more a shadow than enlightening. Indeed, in Britain, the government, which had previously taken the view that betting was a potential social evil that needed to be strictly supervised, changed its attitude. It began, thanks to Betfair, to see person-to-person betting as an acceptable pursuit offering opportunity for gainful employment and legitimate revenue stream. Betfair was the first-ever betting operation to win a Queen's Award for Enterprise.

However closed you are to betting, you are still touched by Betfair. Only if you don't bet, vote, ignore sport and take no interest in the worlds of business and commerce can you rationally feign disinterest. Indeed this is true globally. As the company has grown in Britain, so it begins the same journey of expansion in Australia, starting from Tasmania. Likewise in Malta (a corporate outpost), Italy, Germany, and Austria, where Betfair is formally licensed. Meanwhile, in the world beyond the giant kingdoms of betting and sport, Betfair has been inspiration, even as a template, for new innovations.

An extreme example is the market for gold. Bullion-Vault.com was set up in 2005 to allow traders to bypass the traditional market for gold and speculate directly, leaving brokers redundant. The creator of BullionVault was also an investor in Betfair, which yielded both handsome dividends on an initial stake that bankrolled the set up, and the idea to adapt to other markets. What's more Betfair has inspired others. The business model is increasingly being successfully adapted. You may indeed not bet, but Betfair has touched the lives of many beyond its core endeavour.

This book is the story of Black and Wray from 1998 to the present day, the story of the path Black and Wray took to unimagined wealth by tapping into the changing landscape of global betting, and how exactly they were the catalyst for many changes the world over – both related directly to betting or otherwise.

The basis for Betfair's success is that in Britain the company offers a huge improvement on what was the traditional smoky interior of the high street betting shop (and, it being an Internet outfit, better value free from expensive overheads). You are in charge. Elsewhere in the world, the service for consumers is preferable to state-run monopoly pool betting which, because of high tax and duty levels, offers an even poorer return on winning bets and successes.

What's more, with Betfair, the pace of gambling is faster and more furious, more commensurate with the modern age. Betfair clients hammer away on their keyboards making bet after bet after bet at a speed which makes the process of filling in a betting slip and taking it to the betting shop counter, or even placing a bet on the phone, seem pedestrian. During the 2003 Rugby World Cup, a French-based gambler, trading in stakes that meant liabilities were never greater than £400 a time, was personally responsible for turnover of over £116,000 in less than two hours. Since then, the pace has only quickened.

Betfair grabs those for whom old-style gambling was simply too sedate. For example, the speed of trade that Betfair facilitates has meant that betting-in-running has a growing following by any of those who may previously have opted not to bet on an event but now seek to enhance their experience of live sport by taking out a financial interest. This trade can then be graphed to show how the market fluctuated from starting stalls to winning line, from kick off to final whistle. Football, rugby, cricket, American sports like baseball, and F1 all lend themselves to this type of betting; namely sustained and, during high drama, frantic. Equally, a five-furlong horse race, over in less than a minute, can now sustain any number of bets during the sixty seconds the race takes to run, and not just before the start.

This cyber pursuit's popularity means that growing numbers of serious, full-time gamblers – like shoppers who skip visits to the supermarket by ordering provisions online – no longer bother actually to attend race meetings, the greyhounds, and major sports events other than for company. Likewise, spectators previously enthralled only by the game itself, also stay away. For them betting with Betfair while watching the game at home greatly enhances their enjoyment. Satellite coverage of sport means that you can glean pretty much everything via telecommunications then trade through the web. If you have been able, lately, to get a ticket for the big games, it may be because, along with satellite television, Betfair's appeal has freed up a seat.

From start to chequered flag, first ball to stumps, round one bell to knock out, Betfair handles literally millions of bets, with a financial turnover into tens of millions. This is a stock market for gamblers. Actually, many players derive as much pleasure from simple vindication as they do from outright financial gain. In today's affluent society, being right is as much valued as being even more rich. Betfair offers a chance to test your theories and expectations against the beliefs of others, betting with them directly on anything from the Grand National to the Eurovision Song Contest. With no middleman, betting is hand-to-hand. Protagonists gather in the Betfair Forum chat room both to boast of successes and to unite against injustices outside their own empowered world. For those who think there is something nerdy about Internet betting, time in the Betfair Forum should dissuade you of the notion. This is not a cyberspace for retiring types. Nor the faint-hearted.

The idea that enabled this range, scale, and rate of trade was Andrew Black's, originally. The thought occurred to him while he endured another boring evening after a day's work at GCHQ, in Cheltenham. Away from his friends and family for another working week, Black had time to think and after a few hours had what seemed, not uncommon for him, a reasonable enough notion. The difference with this thought was that, the following morning, the idea still seemed a good one. At the same time, Ed Wray was rooted in J.P. Morgan's prestigious and rewarding debts and capital markets division. Wray was committed to the Square Mile. The City was equally committed to him, and paid accordingly. Black's plan was good enough for him to break completely the ties with all that he had known professionally and draw him away to another world (he even abandoned a cookery course). Then with Wray's help, Black's idea became a reality.

Today, the pair are partners and co-founders of one of the greatest modern success stories of the current business age. Betfair is the multibillion dollar gambling world's own version of Google based on a solid business foundation that will endure long after other web gaming operations have imploded. If Google is the number one ranked Internet enterprise, Betfair claims top-ten status by the yardsticks of growth rate, revenue, and profit. By value, some reckon that of the globe's digital start-up success stories there are only two others worth more of which you have probably heard: Wikipedia and Facebook. All this in less than a decade.

Black and Wray originally teamed up because both have a taste for making money. Wray has always been particularly thirsty for a profit. He saw the potential of Betfair and, after venture capitalists snubbed him – most just couldn't understand the idea that Betfair allowed gamblers to bet with each other, directly and legally – simply invited favoured colleagues to bankroll start-up costs.

A sign that those who invested would be rewarded by being part of a successful business was in the reaction to Betfair of traditional bookmakers. While continuing to attack Betfair on the grounds that allowing punters to take as well as have a bet is a deregulation too far, a steep improvement in shop comforts was not entirely a coincidence. Above that, bookmakers then looked more to the web to shore up a business encumbered by having a portion of retail outlets in poorly-sited inner-city locations. Indeed, for new bookmakers, the Internet is now a point of departure. The web has advantages. For starters, once up and running the overheads are lower. Plus the anonymity allows women, previously put off gambling by the old-style, testosterone culture of the traditional casino and betting shop, to become major players and, in some cases, when finally happy to go public, millionaires and poker world champions. In addition, the Internet allows players to gamble at their convenience. The web is always wide open with broadband. Blackberrys and WAP phones enabling gamblers to bet on the move. Companies like Betfair never close, which in turn is great for business.

According to figures published by the International Federation of Horseracing Authorities, betting on the sport alone reached €89 billion in 2008, up 3 per cent on the previous twelve months. Gambling has experienced extraordinary growth in recent years, and Betfair has been both a contributor to this and well placed to profit. Since the millennium and Betfair's arrival, gambling has tapped into an era of unprecedented disposable income – although this has been tempered by the recession from 2008. Betfair was brilliant marketed, so what is, after all, a simple concept, took a significant and growing slice of the cake; moreover it can claim credit for increasing the size of the cake, itself. Betfair also utterly prevailed over betting exchange market rivals. The most established, Flutter – which just predated Betfair but was a blunt instrument by comparison – fought to the end until the inevitable occurred and Betfair bought them out, absorbing them into the Betfair fold. In a market where there should have been room for any number of companies, one stands alone, at the top, without a serious threat to market supremacy in sight.

In Britain, the collaboration of Black and Wray has been widely acclaimed. In 2008, a second Queen's Award for Enterprise followed the first in 2003. Further afield, between the two gongs, Betfair secured a foothold in Australia with a view to cornering a slice of the market for gambling in Asia where the passion for betting exceeds that in Europe many times over. Considering the Australian nation's rich reputation for 'have a go' culture that has spawned some of the world's most powerful entrepreneurs this proved more of a struggle than you might expect. Resistance to Betfair setting up in Australia proved even more vitriolic than back at the mother country where established bookmakers like William Hill, Ladbrokes, and Coral challenged Betfair's legality and integrity. In the end Betfair prevailed in Australia thanks to the strength of the company's business model and the same arguments that persuaded British officials, reshaped and refined for use there. In Britain the company has successfully lobbied sometimes unenlightened government departments that Betfair's new way of gambling is a win-win situation of more taxes and jobs, as well as personal profit, and that government should at the very least not hinder progress and development. With the argument for deregulation articulated by well-versed, socially-aware entrepreneurs, official eyes were opened to the wider merit of general liberalisation of domestic betting and gaming restrictions. Most important, the Treasury was convinced of the merit in blessing Betfair.

To the west America remains untapped, offering scope for yet further exponential growth. Gambling on the Internet hit a pothole in the Fall of 2006 when George W. Bush signed legislation banning betting with foreign bodies like Betfair through the web. That said, taming the Internet by government statutes is easier said and signed than done. Blocking access to a website is little more than an inconvenience to the determined gambler with resource to the necessary reroute software. The side door remains ajar. That said, while other Internet operators have ended up facing criminal charges for alleged breaches of the Wire Act, 1961, Black and Wray have approached American interests with offers of investment, collaboration and partnership – along with a warning that if gambling goes underground, governments kiss goodbye to billions of dollars in duty. This is a lesson for likeminded entrepreneurs facing similar statutory obstacles. America may not be able to resist Betfair. When the time comes for America to liberalise online betting coast-to-coast and open up borders, Betfair hopes to have remained an eligible suitor.

The story of Betfair, of Black and Wray, is a story of our cyberspace age. Even after being wedded together for over ten years now, they remain a most unlikely pair. In the same way that the web can unite contrasting strangers many thousands of miles apart, their differences merge behind Betfair's slick, uniform corporate image. The inviting open-plan offices at Hammersmith spread over two floors with riverside views for open-minded thoughts convey a sense of togetherness. Their respective strengths do come together in a way that means the whole greatly exceeds the sum of the parts.

Black is a warm, avuncular family man – four children and counting – albeit with an eccentric side that can leave someone meeting him for the first time feeling unexpectedly detached at any point in a conversation as his thought process departs on an unexpected tangent. As good a companion, especially against a backcloth of live sport, Wray is rather more direct. There is a greater urgency in him to reach the point of a conversation. He has just the two children but might leave them with his in-laws while he travels. (He did on a trip to South Africa in 2007 to attend a wedding and ended up, to his amusement, with Chris Bell, chief executive of Ladbrokes, for company, instead). There is little ceremony with Wray. When they met at that garden party in 1998 it was perhaps only the strength of Black's idea that held them together for long enough that the pair agreed to talk again. Otherwise, there would be no partnership, no corporate identity. Black and Wray would have disappeared back into their own worlds, as if they had simply brushed shoulders amid the bustle of bookmakers on Britain's racecourses, at the casino, or found themselves temporarily facing each other across a poker table. At bridge, with the money down, they might even have been rivals, which could have added an edge to Jeremy Wray's annual summer party. Instead, today they remain a study of contrasts, individuals who still exist apart but bound together, Wray as Betfair's chairman, Black as a board member, with a shared founder's stake.

Of course, both Black and Wray are gamblers by nature. In general, Andrew Black wins. He only ends up in the red when he becomes bored or sentimental. When he loses interest or focus, he also loses his edge, and likewise, his money (which also, incidentally, is as likely to underwrite a horse's supply of Polo Mints as burden the beast with expectations of a weighty bet). Now nearly a decade since he and Wray set out together in business, and although now not involved with day-to-day matters, he remains a totem to Betfair's future. His association with the company – he is still on the board – is comfortably the longest one of his professional life.

Wray's big gamble was to back Black in seeking to introduce technological innovation that brought stock market computer software systems to the worlds of betting on racing and sport, and, along with brilliant marketing, made the pair multimillionaires. Wray gambled with his own time and at a sizeable opportunity cost. He gave up lucrative returns in the City for a tiny office space in Wimbledon, without trappings of his former corporate world. There was no guarantee that he would make a living from his new berth, and if not, be accepted back into the financial comfort of the City. He literally bet on Black.

Black and Wray won handsomely. Those venture capitalists who passed on the chance to invest in Betfair stock have reason to rue their poor judgement in not bankrolling the pair. Thanks to friends and contacts who, along with some of the more enlightened City institutions – in all 170 shareholders – came up with the multimillion pound funding, in seven years Betfair grew from a company with about ten clients to one with a turnover of billions returning a profit of £27 million in the 2006 financial year. Their stakes increased in value over 130-fold. In March of the same year, the 23 per cent stake in Betfair bought by the Japanese Internet group, SoftBank, for £355 million valued the company, overall, at £1.54 billion. This netted Black and Wray, who sold 1 per cent of their stakes, an initial £15 million each, still leaving them with a shared 26 per cent of the business. Others took the opportunity to convert holdings into real money. This is not a story of paper millionaires. The 330-acre farm in Surrey that Black today calls home is proof of the true substance to Betfair's success. In September 2008, customer number two million – a 59-year-old Swedish national, wanting to bet on John McCain in the US presidential race – signed up for Betfair, less than two years after the one million barrier was broken. Others like him generated revenues in the 2007 financial year of £181 million and profits of £19 million, up from £32 million and £7 million, respectively, in 2003.

Both Black and Wray have already registered significant profit from Betfair, namely when 23 per cent of the company was sold, yet still leaving them with the biggest stake. What's more, this initial private sale may be also simply a prelude to a wholesale flotation in the future. Then their return from the company will be worth many times more than what they have already redeemed, to date.

Ultimately, few begrudge Black and Wray their spoils and whatever else they clear when the company does eventually go to market. In particular, few begrudge Black. In his case, money will never compensate him for the double tragedy of his life. Two decades ago, his brother, Kevin, died of a brain tumour. In 1984, Black, at least now blessed with a wonderfully extended family, had dropped out – or been kicked out, depending on whose version you accept – of university and spent the two years nursing his sibling. The decade that followed claimed Black's father, to whom he was particularly close. He contracted MRSA after a routine operation. Black was devastated. He resorted to a life that was simply eating and sleeping. He retreated socially. He felt numb. He stayed indoors watching television, listening to the radio, reading. On reflection he might well have been depressed. At the very least, he went into traumatic shock. Then, he snapped out of his trance. At this stage in his life, Black had already hit on the idea of Betfair. He had been devastated by his brother's death and was also hit hard by his father's passing. In the case of his father, the sadness actually served to galvanise him. He kicked himself up the backside. His refreshed thinking became: if I do nothing Betfair will end up just another idea, and when my own time approaches, nagging away would be the thought that perhaps the greatest opportunity of my life passed me by. His brother and father would have expected more of him, he thought. Then he met Wray.

That so much has ultimately stemmed from the initial meeting between Black and Wray – to them and to the world in which they live – cannot be underestimated and is perhaps hard to comprehend. It may be easier to understand by considering that had Black and Wray not been behind Betfair they would have both been clients. Both fit a modern-day profile of a new type of gambler that is a growing constituency of well-informed, technologically

proficient, affluent risk takers. Betting is as much an investment hobby as speculation to them. Most important for
Black and Wray was that the timing proved to be perfect.
Betfair both coincided with, and helped to create, an
upheaval in betting, the way we bet and the way we see
betting, the way government perceives betting, and how
betting engages with world sport. This book will encourage you to consider how much of this was the serendipity, foresight, and planning of two free thinkers meeting
at a garden party at the right time, with the world ripe for
change and hungry for innovations, and how much was
what everyone who gambles needs: luck.

Walk into the second-floor reception of Betfair's Hammersmith offices and, as well as chairs that look suspiciously
like they have been removed from the *Big Brother* diary
room, there is a window into an office space. Above this
window are the words 'Global Network Operations
Centre'. Through the window you can see a wall of
screens, clocks telling you the time in London, New York,
Johannesburg, Hong Kong, and Sydney. Central is a television screen showing whatever sport at the time happens
to be the most significant in the world, from a betting
perspective.

Behind two long desks which cover nearly the width
of the room and face the screens are casually dressed staff
who seem the essence of calm. That is despite their principal job being to monitor the smooth running of the
systems and online status of accounts held by clients who
in Betfair's years of business have emerged as the biggest
fish in Betfair's sea. When the screens show green, all is
well. When they become coloured in orange, there is a

problem, which the team methodically resolves seemingly without breaking sweat.

Going back to 2003, the scene in London's Old Whitbread Brewery, off Chiswell Street, was, in contrast, altogether more testosterone-fuelled and thick with perspiration. Up to this point, I had only a vague awareness of Betfair. Having accepted a commission from *Esquire* magazine to write about the growing popularity of betting exchanges, I also accepted, along with around eighty others similarly uninitiated, an invitation from Betfair to road-test the concept.

That night, a fag-end Champions' League group game between Chelsea – already certain to qualify for that season's knockout stages – and Sparta Prague was transformed into an epic encounter taking those present on an experience which will have changed many of their gambling habits, if not their whole social lives, permanently. What's more the game was 0–0. Still, there was an intensity in the room. It was then illegal to trade or bet in real money at such a gathering. Instead, each table had an imaginary stake to invest and computers set up for gambling at high speed. Halfway through an otherwise drab goal-less draw in front of a largely lifeless, under-capacity crowd, you might have thought someone would actually be walking out with a real pot of gold, such was the intensity of trading and feeling contained in the room. An IT engineer on hand to fix any screens mid-match received an ear-bashing from one guest for the rate at which his computer was rebooting. From this reaction, you might have imagined that life-changing money rather than a Monopoly version was on the table.

Something was obviously afoot. And yet, some of betting's shrewdest thinkers – Stuart Wheeler, who set up and ultimately floated the spread betting firm, IG Index; John Brown, who worked up from the shop floor to the chief executive's desk and chairman's office at William Hill; and the Tote chairman, Peter Jones – considered betting exchanges to be short-term, or with a minimal future ahead. The consensus at the start of the millennium? Betting exchanges generally were considered no more than niche potential. Betfair was underestimated on two fronts; as an example of a new concept in an industry full of potential for innovation, and as the company that would become the completely dominant market force in what quickly became substantively more than simply a 'niche'.

Hindsight is, of course, a wonderful thing. No one who bets needs to be told that. Nonetheless, there was enough evidence in the many theories of why we bet, or are drawn to gambling, to suggest that person-to-person betting might indeed catch on with those already entrenched in the habit-forming world of gambling. Then there are those with a predisposition for what Betfair was offering – of a certain age and affluence, comfortable with technology and in circumstances that meant speculation was harmless. They may have begun the new millennium with little interest in high street outlets offering a product that had changed little, if at all, in forty years since betting shops were legalised. Yet, when offered the chance to try their luck through a different medium, drawn to something new and contemporary, they joined die-hard gamblers to ensure the success of Betfair.

The numbers tell the basic story. For the newly-born Betfair, revenue in 2001 was £480,000, profitability in the negative to the tune of almost £2 million. The first part of this book explains how technology that drew on the IT system of New York's Stock Exchange and brilliant marketing – on relative shoestring budgets – established a company that was robust enough to absorb these early losses and Flutter, seemingly the only genuine rival in this newly-created market. In the space of under three years Betfair registered revenue figures topping £32 million and a profit of £1.76 million, carrying the company into the black where it has firmly remained. Then in part two of this book, we consider the reach of Betfair beyond its own dedicated world. How the company has been both part of the growth in betting and the revolution that gambling – from basic bookmaking to high-ranking casinos – has undergone, and the reason for changes in what was for decades a business which showed little or no appetite for change. Also considered is how Betfair has changed government thinking on betting, how Betfair has been cause for sport to reassess its 'at arm's length' relationship with betting and how Betfair has proved an inspiration to other start-ups and the potential that exists for growth both domestically and internationally.

How did this all come to pass? Spread betting, the innovation in gambling of the 1990s, never managed to establish a foothold the like of which Betfair can boast today or induce wholesale changes to the betting and gambling industries both in Britain and beyond. How then did the world of sport, historically suspicious of betting, end up working together with a betting company? What compelled the International Olympic Committee to set up a network in Beijing for the 2008 Games with a brief to monitor betting on events over the two weeks of sport? For the answers to that and the rest, first, we have to go back to the start of the new millennium.

Chapter ONE

MILLENNIUM

Imagine a world without widespread broadband. Where your greatest immediate concern relates to whether a millennium bug will ravage your hard disc at the stroke of midnight on 31 December 1999. Having survived that, on top of the shortcomings of your browser and the painfully slow speed at which your computer downloads anything of volume, a similarly substantial source of frustration is the growing number of automated call responses you encounter. These defy every effort actually to speak with someone, rather than to a machine, which seeks to engage you or, worse still, steer you in the direction of an extended earful of elevator music. Alternatively, the bane of your life is the increasingly prevalent call centre. Sure, you can reach someone. But a person actually capable of helping with your problem? That's another matter entirely.

Back in 2000, betting in Britain did at least retain the personal touch. A punt on sports such as horseracing and football was predominately through the 8,000-plus licensed high street betting shops. The means? Good, old-fashioned cash. If you preferred to use the phone, then, once your credit account details had been confirmed, the voice at the end of the line would, by and large, endeavour to accommodate your wishes. The warmest welcome was reserved for your debit card. In any business, cash up front is always preferred to the extension of credit.

In the likes of Australia, the Far East – Japan, Hong Kong, Singapore, Malaysia – and continental Europe, gambling, over and above the established casino world, was largely with state-owned and state-run – or licensed – totalisator 'pool betting' monopoly systems, which often rate customers as a lesser priority behind government revenues. Or, of course, as a consequence of this type of operation taking a hefty share out the winning pool to cover tax and allow for profit, with illegal bookmakers, not least in Asia. Needless to say, with no duty to pay the odds offered were much better. Meanwhile, online betting on sports such as racing and football struggled with technology that made it debatable whether logging on and placing a bet took less time than strolling along to a local bookmaker if one was reasonably adjacent, or in France or Australia respectively, your nearest parimutuel café or TAB-licensed bar. Online casinos and poker sites, commonplace today and popular enough to sustain multi-million pound stock market flotations in the new millennium – in 2005 Partygaming hit the Stock Exchange peaking that year at a market capitalisation of £6 billion – were relatively modest operations at the turn of the century. They struggled to generate enough business to boast of 'banks' – the liquidity necessary to enable serious, high-stakes players to strike substantial bets – that made signing up for them of interest to the more seriously-minded speculator.

As for sport, administrators' overall relationship with betting was being sorely tested by a spate of scandals that suggested the two didn't really mix. In 1999, a plot to disable floodlights at The Valley, home to Charlton Athletic who were playing Liverpool in a Premier League match, was thwarted by police. The conspirators behind this, who sought to profit from the suspension of betting in Asia on the match – in such circumstances bets could be settled on the score when the plug was pulled – were eventually traced to Malaysia. There had been two previous instances of floodlight failure in the previous fifteen months. Plots to halt a further eight games were also uncovered, which, according to estimates, could have netted the conspirators £30 million.

Cricket, certainly perceived as a gentlemanly game – whose players have for years often taken a keen interest in horseracing to kill time waiting to bat or during rain delays – faced an even greater violation. In the early months of 2000, the game became embroiled in the biggest corruption scandal in the sport's history when Hansie Cronje confessed to a string of payments received in return for attempted match fixing.

At the same time in Britain, horseracing's administrators struggled to establish relationships with the betting industry's main operators that would constitute a substantial united partnership against corruption. The two parties were engaged in an elaborate dance. Against a backdrop of apparently cordial and cooperative relations, requests for information – when wrongdoing was suspected – were largely rejected by bookmakers on the grounds of client privilege. Leave it to us, the Jockey Club would perennially be told. At least there was widespread acceptance that there might actually be an issue.

Sport in America had its own troubles with rumours of organised and extensive illegal betting on college sports. Much of this was deep underground. The authorities largely turned a blind eye, concerned more with preserving the reputation of academic institutions and national pastimes. Attitudes mirrored national sentiment about steroid use in baseball. At seemingly any cost, the game's reputation had to be maintained.

By the start of 2000, ahead of Betfair's launch, some rudimentary betting exchanges were already in existence – Betmart and Betswap. Indeed, Coral, the third biggest British bookmaker, was developing a site under its Eurobet banner called play2match.com. These enterprises represented an effort to formalise what had up to this point been informal person-to-person betting – individuals would fax through to small groups details of any bets that there was an interest in making and taking.

Joe Saumarez-Smith, a specialist online gaming consultant whose London offices are next to a vinyl record shop illustrating that some products can survive the most dramatic of innovations, recalls an operation based out of Luxembourg. 'You would ring in the morning with what you were prepared to trade then later on that day before lunch the fax machine would kick in with details of what was available to trade,' Saumarez-Smith recalls. The minimum bet was £1,000, minimum stake to lay was double that. The market was professional punter versus professional punter, in Saumarez-Smith's view. 'There was 3pBob, so called because he took a 3 per cent commission.

Quite often you would see an Indian illegal bookmaker wanting to have, say, £100,000 on the draw in a cricket Test match. There were sometimes bets worth having on cricket, also on European football. Basically the operation served as a clearing house and was of particular interest to those betting in Britain. There was domestic tax – 8 per cent at the start of the Nineties, trimmed to 7.75 per cent in 1992, then a further point four years later – at the time. That said, not many had time to read the faxes.'

With the Internet emerging, operations like Blue Square struggled with the World Wide Web's limitations to present themselves as an alternative to traditional gambling markets. They traded despite the Internet's shortcomings. In the meantime, fixed odds and pool betting through what had become traditional outlets – betting shops, cafes, pubs, and clubs – dominated. As for markets most favoured by gamblers, in Britain, despite some slippage in market share, horseracing was the punters' choice. Football's World Cup of 1998 is often cited as being when betting on sport came of age. But back then the event nevertheless still paled into insignificance alongside the giants of the Cheltenham Festival, Grand National, and Epsom Derby, along with showcase handicaps designed for the very purpose of a wager.

In Britain, there was what at least could have been interpreted as a preface to significant change in gambling. Government discussions over changes to the regulation of the industry were underway. By this stage, the National Lottery, launched in 1994, was six years old. It had already showed how lucrative betting might be – 1,000 millionaires created, tax revenues of around 12p from every pound staked – as well as how relatively harmless a flutter seemingly was to the nation's spiritual and moral wellbeing.

At the start of the millennium, plans for the transfer of responsibility for gambling regulation to the three-year-old Department of Culture, Media, and Sport (DCMS) were taking shape, which would bring to an end any involvement with the Home Office. This most powerful of government bodies, which took on responsibility for the licensing of betting in 1970, had historically wrestled with the Treasury, the latter acutely aware of the potential revenue streams from a more liberal approach to betting. The Home Office generally prevailed in ensuring the continued treatment of gambling as a potential social evil. But when DCMS took over gambling in 2001, the Treasury had a much less weighty adversary in creating major obstacles to the adoption of a more enlightened, contemporary approach to having a punt. The gambling industry could be groomed for development to maximise the benefits to government.

That said, traditional bookmakers in Britain offering fixed-odds betting on high streets, nationwide, had recent form to hand that suggested grounds against being anxious about any upheaval, legislative or otherwise. During the 1990s they had negotiated comfortably the arrival of spread betting – a way of gambling where you speculate on whether the outcome will be greater or less than the market, itself, predicts. For example, Kevin Pietersen walks into bat for England at cricket. Spread betting bookmakers offer his expected runs at 75 to 78. You can either sell, meaning that you win your stake times a multiple of the number of runs KP falls below the target of 75, or buy if you believe he will score more than 78, again winning the number of runs over this mark multiplied by your stake.

Having initially thought that this form of betting might pose some threat to business and profit, there was now a consensus among traditional bookmakers that it would never be anything more than a niche. Indeed, spread betting, itself, feared rather than welcomed the Internet (rightly so it proved). If the Internet did catch on, the spread betting market leaders' technological requirements to service the complexities of what they offered clients were a great deal more daunting than for say, Ladbrokes. For Ladbrokes, for decades the biggest private betting operator in the world, and the other giants of betting, they had to contemplate the much simpler task of merely establishing an Internet presence offering the simplest form of betting, namely fixed odds.

Peter Jones, formerly chairman of the Tote, which enjoys a monopoly of pool betting in Britain, sits back in the most comfortable of easy chairs in his London flat off the King's Road. The area's local William Hill is well known for servicing an affluent community with a keen eye on horseracing. Nearby is Ziani's, an Italian restaurant with a deserved reputation for hosting central figures in the sport often celebrating a success down the M4 at Ascot or off the A3 at Sandown Park and Epsom Downs.

'Spread betting?' Jones, Tote chairman for ten years before stepping down in 2007, recalls. 'That probably had little impact on the established betting shop world. Any major impact it had was on telephone betting. Otherwise, up to 2000 there had been some changes to gambling in Britain but nothing of great substance since the legalisation of betting shops in the early Sixties. Live pictures in betting shops, the National Lottery, fruit machines in betting shops; these had all come in but without being the cause of a massive shake up or revolutionary change.'

So what about Betfair? Or, ahead of its launch, other betting exchanges? Jones screws up his face trying to remember when Betfair assumed any sort of relevance to him, both personally and as chairman of the Tote. A life-long punter, who made a killing supplying data on horseracing to the great and the good before taking up one of racing's great offices of state, he did not even open a betting account with Betfair until 2003.

A book, *For the Good of Racing: the first 75 years of the Tote*, published in 2004 to mark the anniversary of the pool betting operation, makes no reference to Betfair anywhere. There is nothing between the covers to infer that the next quarter-century would be an altogether different experience as a result of the idea that Andrew Black and Ed Wray were refining. Indeed, Jones cannot remember when Betfair was first mentioned at a Tote board meeting that he chaired. 'When it was it would have been in a general discussion, in a dispassionate context rather than as a threat to Tote business or turnover.' At the time, Tote's annual turnover was cruising towards £2.8 billion, the figure exceeded in 2008.

'The arrival of Betfair – and other betting exchanges; there were about two or three – was at a very low level at first,' Jones recalls. 'At the time, the Internet was growing. But there was no broadband at this stage. A substitute for traditional forms of betting? Back then, I didn't think so. How could I? Bookmakers, generally, were certainly not particularly fearful of betting exchanges or Betfair. There was not going to be a takeover. Low liquidity levels at the beginning because of the number of businesses meant they made no real impact on the overall market.' What's more, he adds, Betfair's software was not, to his mind, particularly good.

Jones shrugs: 'The lack of broadband was very important. The sort of trading that would come to Betfair – churning of turnover, which is so important – was very difficult with dial-up. Not easy at all to trade. At the Tote, consensus was that with the old technology, Internet betting wasn't going to take off. I think – and we were in no rush – we did a first deal involving broadband in, if memory serves me right, 1999 with Totalbet.'

Sitting comfortably now, having relinquished one of horseracing's most demanding posts, publicly scrutinised to a depth disproportionate to the importance of its stake in the betting industry, Jones notes how newspapers can sometimes over react to developments. In this case, he notes that press coverage of spread betting reflected that journalists were largely excited about what ultimately never made a substantial dent in the overall betting market. Jones laughs: 'Newspapers? In general they always like something new.'

Looking back, in 2000 Compton Hellyer had every reason to be at least satisfied at his own efforts to break into the otherwise closed market of betting. In 1992, he established the spread betting firm, Sporting Index. Ahead of the millennium, the operation was a business heading towards profits approaching £10 million, albeit marginal compared to established bookmaking. In other words, a solid foothold for a start-up company less than a decade old. With his experience, Hellyer had more reason than most to doubt that Betfair could ultimately grow to the size to which the company amounts today. Modesty to one side, why would Betfair find it any easier to break into the market than his company had?

Hellyer would cash in his holdings in Sporting Index by 2003. 'In 2000, the view we had was that Betfair and betting exchanges would never create the liquidity – enough money in play so that the market could accommodate those who wanted to bet or lay big – they needed. That was the situation for betting exchanges, collectively, but also Betfair specifically, ahead of what became its own path of sustained growth. Betfair did at least seem likely to stick around. Others gave the impression that they might have come to the market but they would as soon go. The volume of betting needed to sustain them didn't seem to be there.'

At least Hellyer can claim to have had some sense of what Betfair would encounter. From his own experiences, he could confidently predict if the company took any sort of hold in the market, there would be a full assault from traditional bookmakers once initial complacency about fresh competition had been replaced by paranoia that the new blood was a threat to future livelihood. He concedes that Betfair did seem to be able to drain the liquidity from others. Yet even with the credit due for correctly identifying the eventual market leader, he acknowledges that he, along with everyone, missed a trick. 'We underestimated them and the threat to us,' he shrugs. 'The way it turned out – with Betfair dominant – made it worse. In truth, six or seven betting exchanges would have been less of a threat to our business. But one horse, namely Betfair, left the rest for dead.'

Relative outsiders to the business sector in which Betfair trades, do have the advantage of distance that usually affords some enhanced perspective. Still, betting exchanges like Betfair – years from such high ground as flotation – were also not exactly resonating with the wider world of commerce and venture capital, either. Andrew P. Lee is Dresdner Kleinwort's (DK) senior analyst of trends in the world of betting. His time spent analysing this sector of the economy coincides almost exactly with the launch of Betfair in 2000. Yet, it was not until 2002, when Lee was advising potential investors on the William Hill flotation, that he recalls making any reference to Betfair and betting exchanges. By then, exchanges – or Betfair – must have had some significance as Lee was responding via the DK quarterly assessment of the leisure market to the suggestion that Betfair would cannibalise William Hill customers. He recalls predicting 'steady growth from steady products', overall, in betting. 'Some were negative about the William Hill flotation on the basis that all punters are price-discriminatory and would be drawn to betting exchanges' odds which were better because of lower overheads,' Lee remembers. His own view then, and now; 'Absolute nonsense.'

In 2000, no one knew how big online betting would one day be. Lee's London offices are in Gresham Street, near St Paul's, named after Sir Thomas Gresham who rescued the royal household's finances in 1551. Even he might have struggled to predict the exponential growth in gaming since the millennium and Betfair's part in this. On the pavement, Lee joins colleagues in the only space available for some calming tobacco amid jittery markets. 'The first online casino?' Lee, drawing on his cigarette, struggles for the date. 'I think that was 1995. The first significant sports betting on the web followed two years later along with Paradise Poker. But without broadband none of them were making any money and poker sites had not got their heads around the jackpot tournaments on which they have built their markets. It wasn't until 2003 that Party Poker launched the first of them that was worth seven figures.'

By virtue of his starting point in overseeing the gambling sector for clients in 2000, Lee is in synch with the timeline of Betfair's extraordinary growth. The inevitably conservative corporate culture of the City meant possibilities for the new venture were downplayed. Unlike newspapers, as Peter Jones noted, the Square Mile is much more taken by the established order than innovation. Much more significant than a new company to Lee, in the year that Betfair was launched, was the increasingly power-ful lobby for abolishing betting duty – at the time, 6.75 per cent of either stake or winnings – in Britain. 'Book-makers in Britain had gone through limited periods of growth. There had not been much regulatory changes to ease the market. Real hopes lay in the potential change from betting duty based on turnover to tax based on gross profits,' Lee recalls.

When fiscal reform came, this was, Lee recalls, ulti-mately considered a 'pretty exciting change to the indus-try' following a relatively low stimulus – regulatory and fiscal – to betting in Britain. 'Gambling will always under perform in growth against GDP (Gross Domestic Prod-uct) and PDI (Personal Disposable Income) if there are no regulatory changes,' he explains. For all the excitement that a newly-born should bring, prospects of a tax review generated a much greater sense of anticipation. (Indeed, whatever Betfair's impact, that has remained the same.)

At the forefront of the advocates for a change in the way that betting operations were taxed, with profits not

turnover in the frame, was John Brown. Now a resident
of Florida during Britain's harshest months, Brown is
today usually far from such concerns save for anxieties
that any stocks and shares he retains in the gambling world
are adversely affected by fiscal reforms. Back in 2000, he
was chairman and chief executive of William Hill so very
central to proceedings pressing the Treasury and Customs
for a fiscal reassessment. Though charming company, his
style of operating in this role was abrasive. Maybe, with
the uncompromising nature of the Treasury in mind, this
was Brown's true calling. Certainly, he ensured that his
case was heard.

The possibility in 2000 that the Treasury would agree
to ditching tax on betting turnover – leaving more money
in customers' pockets to bet with again – and replace it
with a duty on gross profits was a delight to bookmakers.
Compared to the significance of betting tax reform, Brown
recalls no meaningful concern about betting exchanges
generally and Betfair, specifically. The relevance of the
Internet to Brown, who has had his success as a racehorse
owner and a gambler, in parallel with his corporate achievements, was in the impact that it could ultimately have on
the domestic market through operations like Victor Chandler. Victor Chandler, whose company carries his own
name, is known as something of a gentleman's bookmaker
and was once famously described as the industry's 'Indi-
ana Jones'. Well ahead of the millennium, Chandler, whose
grandfather established the family firm, had led a move
offshore to territories beyond the reach of the domestic
exchequer. In 2000, betting in Britain with bookmakers was estimated at £7 billion. What the Internet – in
conjunction with the telephone – meant was a growing

proportion of that trade would be offshore and therefore tax-free, with operators consequently able to undercut domestic betting with odds unencumbered with tax. 'Victor had spotted the potential,' Brown recalls. 'The law then meant that he couldn't advertise without a British arm so he kept a presence in the UK – a Mayfair betting shop – to ensure that he could maintain his profile through marketing. Then [he] shipped out to Gibraltar where he paid no tax on bets that could be taken over the telephone and the Internet.'

Ahead of the change in taxation, Ladbrokes had already followed Chandler to Gibraltar, notes Brown, testily. William Hill then followed in turn, to Ireland. 'We at William Hill had the biggest telephone operation of them all. Never mind the Internet, we required 200-plus staff on-site just to handle calls. I had a look at Gibraltar. We also considered Madeira. Instead we set up in Southern Ireland. I had the idea one day after ringing British Airways. The person I was talking to was speaking from Kilkenny. I thought, why not us there, too? Our lawyers believed that we would not be liable for tax there – on the basis that call centres simply relayed information and there was no actual transaction. In the end, we ended up with our computers in Antigua, our administration in the Isle of Man, and our call centre manned by girls flying out from London, which cost £15 a head. In three months, we transformed what was pretty much just a cow shed.'

The decision-making was based exclusively on fiscal considerations. Brown confirms: 'We were not concerned about betting exchanges. We were concerned with losing potentially all our telephone betting – historically about 10 per cent of the business – to competitors offering tax-

free betting. It wasn't going to affect our betting shops.
Those customers, they go in their lunch hour, or between
shifts. But odds-on betting by big punters – where a
substantial stake is risked for a relatively small reward at
a marginal rate of return that is, because it is marginal,
significantly worsened by any tax take – would have to
go with tax-free bookmakers. The rate of return ensured
that.'

Efforts in 2000 concentrated on correcting this market
anomaly yielded a result in 2001. In meetings between
bookmakers and Barbara Roche (Financial Secretary to
the Treasury, then a Home Office Minister of State),
Brown explained the business significance – a threat to
jobs and tax revenues – of the exodus offshore as tax-free
betting was irresistible to the high rollers. In the March
budget of 2001, the then Chancellor of the Exchequer,
Gordon Brown, abolished existing duty to take effect on
the following 1 January, and replaced the old system with
a tax on gross profits.

At Ladbrokes, historically and by any measure Britain's
most significant bookmakers, the change in tax arrangements were as welcome as at William Hill. Domestic betting
turnover increases of 70 per cent exceeded government's
expectation, a conservative 33 per cent to 50 per cent. It
also exceeded William Hill's projections, creating 1,000
extra jobs there. At Ladbrokes, John O'Reilly, today
managing director of remote betting and gaming, spent
little time pondering betting exchanges in principle, or
Betfair, as a prospective challenger to his employer's
commanding position as the world's biggest bookmakers.
Why would you when, thanks to the Treasury's fiscal
reform of betting taxation, happy days were confidently

predicted to be ahead? What's more, that view was despite the company being perhaps more aware than William Hill of the Internet's potential and altogether more prepared for it to become a growing proportion of total business in time. O'Reilly's sense had been, before 2000, that Ladbrokes certainly had to develop an Internet arm and he had told his fellow board members as much. After procrastinating with the notion – to be fair, O'Reilly had been told to concentrate solely on Ladbrokes' takeover and subsequent sale of Coral after referral to the Monopolies and Mergers Commission – he, as Ladbrokes' then managing director of the international arm of the company, was saddled with establishing Ladbrokes.com.

Ladbrokes launched Ladbrokes.com in the same year that Betfair was launched. 'Betfair was not the first betting exchange,' O'Reilly recalls. This echoes common observations among those who today seek to explain as much to themselves as anyone else why they didn't pick Betfair from the pack. O'Reilly continues: 'There was Flutter, which seemed to be chasing the smaller punter; the one who wanted to bet on how many times a particular word, like "The", appeared on the front page of the *Daily Telegraph*. What they overlooked was that someone then had to count them! At the start, a few people also thought they could be online bookmakers, taking bets.' O'Reilly suggests that they did their money pretty quickly. He further recalls that in 1999, Ladbrokes' domestic turnover was 85 per cent in betting shops and 15 per cent over the telephone. A decade on, he chuckles at the suggestion that Ladbrokes' figures might be very different today if the company had set up its own betting exchange like Betfair with retail outlets in the minority compared to the web.

'Lots since have tried and failed,' O'Reilly points out. 'Which doesn't mean that Ladbrokes could not have tried, or try, and succeed. Of course, we look at everything that affects the market.'

Perhaps a sign that John Brown belatedly grasped that the world he had known for a whole life (he joined William Hill as a teenager at the shop floor in 1950s working as a tea boy) had changed is that he reputedly considered an involvement with Betdaq after leaving William Hill. This was the betting exchange set up in 2000 by the Irish financier and friend of John Magnier and J.P. McManus, Dermot Desmond, which began trading the following year. Brown was rumoured to be in line for the chairmanship, something that he has since denied.

Certainly, what has since the arrival of betting exchanges become known as 'traditional betting' – essentially gambling at fixed odds – had been given due warning that those who sought to develop an alternative means of gambling over the web would face few legislative or governmental obstacles. Today, government has an appetite for the positives that gambling can bring. A visit by Richard Caborn in 2006 to Gibraltar to see how The Rock had become the foundation for a thriving Internet gambling outpost and how participants could be encouraged to return home, reflected what had been at the start of the millennium beginnings of a sea change. Not long after the launch of Betfair a leaked government memo to Betfair, reported in newspapers, further underscored that Britain was 'open for business'.

Back in 2000, Tony Blair set the tone. In a speech on 11 September following the publication a year earlier of the government's strategy for making the UK the best environment in the world to do e-commerce, the then prime minister launched a 'UK online' campaign. The intention behind a raft of initiatives and investment was to get people, business, indeed the government itself, online. 'There is a revolution going on in our economy,' Blair maintained. 'A fundamental change, not a dot.com fad, but a real transformation towards a knowledge economy.'

The government's intention was for Britain to become the best place in the world for e-commerce, with universal access to the Internet and all government services on the net. If you were launching an Internet endeavour that year it was reassuring to know what lay ahead. Namely, the first 600 UK online centres in some of Britain's poorest communities offering training in how to use the Internet – but without perhaps the intention of introducing the nation's offline constituency to the thrills of gambling's web.

Blair, of course, did not specifically mean Betfair when he said: 'We cannot afford to slow down. Although the UK has surged forward and is leading in some key areas, we still lag in others.' Indeed, Betfair was underestimated from the very top down, including those running the country, according to those who follow whispers in Westminster. To begin with, Peter Oborne, the respected political commentator and documentary maker, estimates that to the Treasury and other government departments, Betfair will have seemed like 'just another small start up that wasn't really going to make any difference'.

Still, inadvertently, the path had been cleared for something more substantial. If Blair's general encouragement to Internet companies was welcome, specific changes to the government machine were even more so. The pending transfer of responsibility for gambling to DCMS did ensure that past obstacles to rival betting operators taking a stake of the established market would not be so insurmountable. For largely historical reasons, the Home Office had controlled matters, to the dismay of the Treasury. 'There, gambling faced institutional hostility,' Oborne argues. The Rothschild Report of 1978, with the brief of assessing the business as a whole, set the tone. 'Feckless, connections with organised crime, among other negative observations,' Oborne recalls.

In contrast, the Treasury had long seen gambling as little more than a revenue stream if not by generating tax through betting then via new jobs that a burgeoning industry would create. And a potential transfer of responsibility for gambling to the DCMS, created in 1997, was the Treasury's chance to assume effective control of the industry. This was finalised within a year of Betfair's launch. 'It was very important for the Home Office to be out the way,' insists Oborne.

The new political framework planned for gambling – and a greater tolerance of the activity – meant Betfair could expect to be nurtured by the state, not over-regulated. With the Treasury's assumption of effective control – as a new government department, DCMS was no match for perhaps the most formidable of power bases within any administration – gambling in Britain completed its journey to legitimacy that had started in earnest with the creation in 1994 of the National Lottery. What was once frowned upon for the temptation to individuals it represented would be considered foremost as a business.

Oborne adds that bookmakers missed a trick back then. 'Bookmakers have always had huge political influence,' he confides. 'At party political conferences they are always there, wining and dining MPs. You would have expected bookmakers to crush Betfair at the start, but, like everyone else, they underestimated the threat they would pose.'

By 2000, Andrew Black and Ed Wray had spent more than a year developing Betfair. Finally, launch was upon them. Still, perhaps only Black had any real confidence of exactly what heights the pair might hope to reach.

Wray's most rewarding bet had been in 1998 when an own goal by Scotland in the opening game of the World Cup in France gifted him a 'few thousand'. Wray's own assessment of the state of the betting market two years later in 2000 was far from comprehensive and actually largely inward looking. 'I didn't do a huge amount of technical analysis,' he confides. 'I did it from the perspective of creating a viable business. I tried to work out what I thought people would bet with Betfair, potentially, on average and how many we would need to make the company work. Sure, I did realise that the potential market was big. In the UK alone, there were 8,000 betting shops. And during the football World Cup of 1998 betting online had certainly begun to establish itself. Spread firms also did pretty well. So certainly the market as a whole was something interesting. But I still worked on the basis that I didn't need to know the size of the market as a whole. I wasn't preoccupied with market share over and above achieving that which was big enough for us to mean that if we did a half decent job we would be alright.'

Did spending an extended amount of time with Andrew Black not shape Wray's thinking? 'I massively underestimated the betting market's scale and size,' Wray admits, with a heavy sigh. He finishes this with a resigned chuckle. 'I remember telling Bert my views on what we might need to trade and the potential for this. He laughed. "Look at me and what I bet", he said.'

Black, having been a professional punter, knew the scale of bets that his new venture could tap. In 1992, he collected £25,500 from a win-double betting on High Low to win the Lincoln Handicap at 40–1 and Party Politics to follow up a month later in April's Grand National at odds of 25–1. Yet, Black was also, to a large extent, thinking purely within his own world rather than about the prospect of taking a share of the betting market as a whole. Wray recalls his partner's mindset at the time. 'Bert simply thought, I am a punter, the bookmakers offer a shocking service,' he laughs.

Black admits that there was an academic, almost purely intellectual side to his effort in establishing Betfair. The project as a whole, like his assessment of the betting industry as a whole, was also coloured by personal considerations. Perhaps more than garnering a better deal for punters, he had something of an eye on establishing his 'legacy'. He recalls: 'I decided I wanted to come up with something for myself that would have an impact. I had worked on some fairly creative stuff in my time, the most creative of all for the government and Ministry of Defence using fairly heavy mathematical simulations. I wanted to come up with something that was special. Probably Internet-based.'

Press Black on exactly what he did for the MoD and he is a little vague, either because he cannot say, or does not want to say. Whichever, he is tantalisingly remote (as only he can be). Overall, Black – seemingly on ground which allows him more freedom to engage with the public about his endeavours – considered the betting market in 2000 to be 'dull', with the bookmakers' take on the Internet 'predictable'. To Black's mind, they simply wanted to transfer their existing business to the web. In other words, the Internet would become just a very small corner of their overall retail business. 'They knew they had to go online but the way they did it showed their lack of imagination', he maintains.

Black had begun by relaying to a select few that Betfair 'was a nice idea'. When no one seemed interested, he raised the stakes, in response to meeting such indifference. 'Then I took to saying, this is going to be a big Internet idea. The more time went on, the more outspoken I became.' Even then, Black ultimately fell short of gauging the full impact of his baby. Moreover, even those who felt sufficiently enthralled to join Black and Wray at Betfair had limited ambition.

Would you have quit a handsomely paid, prestigious, relatively secure job to work with Black and Wray? In the spirit of person-to-person betting, what would the odds in your favour need to be? Mark Davies, a colleague of Wray's at J.P. Morgan joined the company – at the time, ostensibly Black and Wray along with Sean Patterson, finance director – a few weeks ahead of launch as Head of Business Development. He would eventually rise to take the post of Managing Director (corporate affairs) and today, in that role, remains immersed in the operation.

Davies, whose father is the acclaimed sports commentator, Barry, was drawn to Betfair because of the concept's simplicity more than anything. 'Before we launched I guess I knew betting was a slightly murky world,' Davies laughs.

'I was an occasional punter. Looking back, it is surprising how few of the founder team were mad keen punters. Most days, I would wander past my local William Hill shop. I'd actually go in on Grand National day so that made me no more than a classic National punter. I don't think I had bet on a horse at all other than that race.'

Along with Black and Wray, Davies – who does boast of having won money on Manchester United winning the Champions' League in 1999 – cannot claim a concise analysis of the betting market compelled him to take a chance. 'It was the trading side for me. I was trading for a living at J.P. Morgan. This was also trading. I understood that. I looked at the prototype for Betfair and thought, my god, that is such a simple idea, so well executed. If one in ten, or even one in 100 react the way that I am reacting to it then it is a viable business. The overall betting market? I didn't really think about it. It was the simplicity of the idea that captured your mind.'

So Davies was betting on best odds of 10–1. Would anything from between 1 and 10 per cent of the market therefore be a success? Ed Wray was eyeing just a similarly small corner of the betting market for Betfair. It was enough for him, like Davies, to turn his back on what had been previously most gainful employment. Black, meanwhile, was the more intimately involved with both the concept – as the creator – and the world of betting, itself. Today, he laughs. On one hand, he maintains he had a vision. On the other hand, he sees himself as a bit of a buffoon.

Not the sort of person, Black shrugs, who is going to come up with the next brilliant idea that would make millions over and over, year after year.

Chapter TWO

SPREAD THIN

Bookmaking is sometimes referred to as the world's second
oldest profession, just on the heels of prostitution. For
years in Britain, both taking bets and what is generally
accepted as a vocation with even more years against its
name than turf accountancy remained tied up in preventative law and restrictive practices. Likewise, worldwide,
with varying degrees of tolerance. Certainly, these were
not trades for the high street. Then in May 1961, when the
Betting and Gaming Act took effect, betting shops were,
at least, granted above-board status in Britain. Though
there were restrictions on what these new establishments
could offer customers and how they might operate, premises that could accommodate anyone over a certain age
wanting a bet were soon widespread. Within twelve
months more than 10,000 opened for business, nationwide. With this, gambling went mainstream and Britain
became a country more densely populated with places to
bet than anywhere else in the world.

And after that breakthrough? Now, looking back over nearly half a century of history, the conclusion is unavoidable; largely no change or significant innovation in the betting industry at all over the thirty years that followed legalisation. Between 1961 and 1991, interiors of betting shops enjoyed a modest splash of paint and the addition of some contemporary fixtures and fittings (if that adequately describes television sets and actual seats, initially outlawed). But externally, windows still had to be blocked out to avoid potential customers being drawn in against their better judgement (also, betting shop regulars noted, maintaining privacy for anyone who didn't want to be seen). Drinks of any sort were only allowed after enabling legislation became law in 1986 and then only the likes of coffee and tea from a machine. As for alcohol, though a pub would most likely be close by – the majority of betting shops in Britain had and have today urban locations – a beer, or, as betting often requires, something stronger, remained beyond the threshold of betting shops throughout the UK. As it does today. Back in the 1980s, bookmakers' doorways would sometimes be graced with lame, thin, plastic coloured drapes that might otherwise have been made up into hula-hula skirts. They merely raised expectations that there might be something colourful through them. Instead, for most of the first three decades following the formal creation of the licensed betting shop, drab spaces accommodated die-hard, regular gamblers. These punters were denied a full range of refreshments for fear that anything too homely might be cause for the weak minded to extend their stay.

Much of this was out of bookmakers' hands. They couldn't just break the law (could they now?). Some restrictions did eventually pass into history. The arrival of television coverage, along with tea and coffee, in 1986 ahead of the thirty-year anniversary of legislation that brought betting shops into being also proved, with hindsight, a relatively major watershed. Not only did it bring to an end the frustration of listening to radio commentary and not even hearing so much as a mention of the horse carrying your money, betting shops became places of extended stays, and correspondingly better furnished.

In 1995, following legislation that brought in, among other changes, Sunday opening, windows were allowed to be clear. What's more, today there is more on offer. In addition to the staples of horseracing and greyhounds, sport is now a huge feature. Furthermore, betting shops are now home to one-armed bandits – known in the trade as Fixed Odds Betting Terminals, or FOBTs. There is also virtual racing, computer-generated events at cyber racecourses such as Lucksin Downs, Sprint Valley, or Steepledowns. Something for everyone and any weather, then. Nonetheless, the central premise holds true. Betting has largely been a trade comfortable with the status quo.

In the end it was thirty-one years after the birth of betting shops before a shake up. If 1961 was a milestone and 1986 another legislative landmark of sorts ahead of 1995, then 1992 should be added to the timeline in bold. That year, Compton Hellyer attempted to take a grip of the profession that had up to then largely remained in a state of paralysis for the previous three decades.

Hellyer, an effervescent presence with the qualities of a rebounding rubber ball that have served him well through the many business cycles that he has experienced, championed a concept called spread betting. This was well established as a means for gambling on the fluctuations of the money markets. Hellyer attempted to adapt this into an alternative to traditional, fixed-odds betting.

Hellyer's company was called Sporting Index. His main objective, in partnership with Lindsay McNeile, who took Ed Wray's role to Compton's own interpretation of an Andrew Black-style figure, was to form spread betting markets primarily on sport. Ultimately, he went after horseracing, too, simply unable to ignore the demand. The operation continues today – indeed thrives, from a solid basis established in the Nineties. Soon after launching, with Hellyer to the fore in a public relations operation that was a masterclass to any corporation seeking profile wildly in excess of market share, you might have expected it to be the principal form of bookmaking into the millennium and beyond. In 1992, spread betting was, or at least seemed to be seen by some, as the future.

As Hellyer readily concedes, Sporting Index's business was an offshoot of an established spread betting market, which was, itself, a derivative of the financial world's futures trading. In the futures' market, traders buy and sell options on shares, commodities, and foreign exchange, in the process speculating on price fluctuations. The goods, themselves, need not change hands. Deals are struck with settlement at some agreed point in the future. Depending on the path of the price of the share, the goods, or the currency, traders either end up in profit or out of pocket and settle accordingly.

Financial spread betting was also speculation on market fluctuations. Similarly, shares, commodities, and foreign currency of sorts didn't change hands. Wagers were settled on prices rising and falling around upper and lower parameters, known as 'the spread'. You just had to guess in which direction the market would move.

Sporting Index's version of spread betting involved taking events, such as the Open Golf Championship and offering spreads – high and low marks – on what, in the case of golf, individual players would score. For example, Tiger Woods to take between 268 to 272 shots. Gamblers would then be free either to buy or sell – with those buying of the belief that Woods would take more strokes than predicted and those selling of the view that he would out perform expectations. With sports like horseracing there would be a points system – for example, seventy-five points for a win, fifty points for finishing second – and the spread would be on the basis of expectations of points won by a particular horse, or indeed jockey or trainer. For example, Red Rum to win the Grand National, a spread of 18–20 points. If he wins, you collect fifty-five (the seventy-five points for a win minus twenty, the top of the spread) times your stake. If he fails to finish even second, losses are eighteen (the bottom of the spread, eighteen, minus zero, the points you have won) times your stake.

For sports like cricket, American football, and baseball, markets would be made for number of runs or wickets, points and touchdowns, and home runs respectively. The most innovative spread betting bookmakers would offer the widest range of spread bets including, for example, the time, during a ninety-minute game of football of the first corner, or throw in. In due course, the arrival of new fads in sport such as football squad numbers – beyond the traditional one to eleven on the back of shirts – inspired the creation of further markets. In this case, betting was, and flourishes today, on the sum of goalscorers' shirt numbers in a match.

At the time of Sporting Index's emergence, John Brown was on his way to assuming the chief executive's chair and chairman's office at William Hill. Ultimately, his company took the threat to market share of Britain's second biggest fixed-odds bookmakers (behind only Ladbrokes) sufficiently to launch William Hill's own spread betting service. Looking back, Brown, who can be both charming and menacing in the same sentence, rarely referencing the benefits of hindsight, maintains that William Hill Index – not the most imaginative of names – was an initiative simply to take some of the 'easy money' the new market offered. His success in rising from the shop floor at William Hill all the way to the boardroom means that today he can ponder the past from a most comfortable Florida outpost. Spread betting's potential? 'A real niche market,' Brown insists. 'I always felt that, right from the start. With spread betting you had to be live and on the market all the time. In other words, it was for only a sophisticated type of punter. Not the regulars at the betting shop.'

So, small, but nonetheless welcome, relatively straight-forward pickings? In fact, William Hill's own spread betting efforts were a huge flop. The money was far from easy and Hellyer maintains that traditional bookmakers cut corners in not paying market makers to reflect their specialist gifts, failing to recruit from the most obvious source; traders from the City's Life Floor wanting a change. Brown prefers to blame William Hill's late entry into the sports spread betting market fray – 1995 – for the subsequent failure of the company. 'When you are late in you don't get in', maintains Brown, repeating a well-worn business mantra. (Ladbrokes, which set up the following year, also ultimately floundered, having failed at financial spreads, too, the previous decade). William Hill, Brown adds, never got a critical mass of turnover, which is essential for an operation to thrive within a spread betting market, or pretty much all gambling endeavours (as Betfair knew, too, well ahead of its own launch). Like Peter Jones, the former chairman of the Tote, Brown places some of the blame on journalists for the seriousness with which spread betting – at its peak, according to Jones, perhaps no more than 10 per cent of domestic telephone betting, itself just a slice of total take through 8,000-plus betting shops – was taken. The Media's fault again, then.

Be all that as it may, what is the significance of spread betting to the emergence of Betfair? When Brown, one of Betfair's greatest adversaries, looks back to recall spread betting's early days he could as easily be speaking about the first few months of betting exchanges and Betfair's ascent to market domination. Indeed, in conversation about Betfair, you can end up asking yourself whether he actually means predecessors like Sporting Index. He confides today in response to a question on these related subjects: 'I didn't think they would take off.' Spread betting or betting exchanges? In this case he is talking about the former, namely firms such as Sporting Index, and not in fact Betfair. Many of Brown's observations about spread betting could be transposed, almost verbatim, to be included in his overall views of betting exchanges; back in 2000, with Sporting Index the grand old age of eight, he at least at first didn't expect the exchanges to take off.

An established industry figure rubbishing newcomers in an effort to preserve market share? What is new about that? Indeed, it is almost as old as bookmaking. The precise importance to Betfair of spread betting's struggle with fixed-odds bookmakers was that this gave Black and Wray a clear and relevant case history of what its main adversary's reaction would be when a newcomer emerged. Even with their respective years in business, both benefited from insight over and above what one might expect from applying a basic understanding of market behaviour.

Andrew Black refers to the 'three Cs' when considering the arc of bookmaker reaction to the emergence of betting exchanges in general and Betfair in particular. That is: 'Contempt, Confrontation, and Capitulation'. The history of spread betting features all three appearing to varying degrees. The path of spread betting in the 1990s – which rose to a peak that decade, after which point the concept largely hit a plateau – proved most educational to Betfair for when at the end of the 1990s Black and Wray unveiled their own concept to the world.

Bookmakers' initial complacency towards Betfair was, Black suggests, perhaps as a result of having survived – ultimately with ease – the emergence of fresh competition in the previous decade. Then, as you would anticipate from a group such as bookmakers with four decades of market domination, once it was understood that the new force had been underestimated and market share was under threat, steps soon began to be taken to preserve what was considered almost a birthright of profit. This would be the period of confrontation, then? Looking back, Black, eagerly anticipating capitulation, chuckles: 'We knew exactly what to expect. I am sure spread betting shaped their thinking. With spread betting, they thought, "Oh my goodness, they are challenging us with this completely new way of thinking." After that, they panicked for a while, tried to copy it, then failed, before ultimately everyone said, "don't worry, it is just a niche", in other words nothing to worry about after all. Then we came along. With their relatively recent experiences, they thought, "just another niche". Except that we were more than that.'

Since selling up his stake in Sporting Index in 2003 as part of a £55 million deal, Compton Hellyer has taken an interest in a host of projects and companies. Mainly these have involved pastimes and pursuits synonymous with the interests of rake-like males of a certain wealth and age (and also, like the 62-year-old Hellyer, those senior to them still young at heart). There is the chairmanship of a golf tours company, as well as an involvement with a web endeavour that seeks to analyse football data to generate predictive statistics. (Hellyer supports Hull City who gained a place in the Premier League, which needed some explaining). Never easy is distinguishing between what is work for Hellyer, small in stature but not in his appetite for fun, and what is play.

If there has been a perfect blend for him in his business career, which began in the altogether more sombre world of the City, it was probably Sporting Index. Sport is an ongoing passion. A gamble also remains central to his life, as you would expect from someone who took a social punt and used the size of a woman's chest to illustrate the nature of spread betting to the lady who subsequently became his second wife; the spread might, he suggested, be 32–34, or maybe 34–36, with Hellyer, ever the optimist, a buyer. Incidentally, the other example in Hellyer's repertoire to illustrate to the uninitiated the scope for spread betting on anything, including sport, was the number of lovers a gentleman or lady might have taken over a period of time. During dinner parties, he went round the table making markets for individual guests – ten to twelve for the prettiest or most handsome, five to six for the more seemingly conservative-minded – by and large to general amusement with the occasional controversial reaction, hopefully, to keep things lively.

Hellyer admits that in starting a business specialising in spread betting on sport, he was just adapting something that was long established with a pedigree of more than two decades. In fact, another company, City Index, founded in 1983 to trade on financial markets, had just beaten him to the sports spread betting market, albeit without Hellyer's all singing and dancing style which affords him the place in history as the *de facto* founder of the application beyond financial markets. Indeed, this and Sporting Index's more inclusive name helped the company quickly assume the dominant market position in its sphere. 'The best business decision I made was to use the word "sporting" in the name,' Hellyer reflects. 'It differentiated Sporting Index. We were something new.'

Exactly what Hellyer adapted for sport was spread betting on financial futures. The origins of that date back at least to the 1970s. In 1974, Stuart Wheeler, a new breed of speculator for the Square Mile who came to wider prominence when donating £5 million in 2001 to a Conservative Party led by William Hague, set up IG Index. This allowed for speculation on the price of gold. If you believed that the price of gold would rise above a given price over a set period of time you would 'buy' gold. If you had faith the opposite would happen, you 'sold'. Again, no gold actually changed hands. All that did ultimately was money. For example, a £1 bet for every cent that the American price of gold changed meant that if gold went up 50c, and you had bought, you took home £50. And, of course, vice versa if the market went against you. Along the way, not a single bar of gold bullion changed hands. Within two years of setting up, Wheeler extended betting to cover all commodities traded in London. In 1979, IG expanded further to take bets on movements in US markets with betting on the FTSE and Dow Jones indices following two years later.

Hellyer fully acknowledges that he was only formally presenting as new and innovative what was already thriving, informally. Long before the creation of City Index – even IG, which, incidentally, went into sport in 1993 – spread betting had an established and illustrious history, albeit underground. 'Sports spread betting was taking place on the floor of the Stock Exchange before us all,' admits Hellyer. 'Traders on the life floor would make a market on say, the number of points in a rugby match at the weekend. Then, depending on the results, they would settle up on Monday.'

Hellyer maintains that it was the people in the City of London financial market who understood market fluctuations, currency market, and the price of gold. 'There was already a natural base for us. It had been tested. They traded for a living. And also with spread betting you have to be prepared to lose a sizeable sum of money. You won't get away with just losing a tenner.' This meant spread betting lent itself to people who received bonuses – in other words, those who work in the City of London again – which could act as a spread betting bank for those bad days. The logic was, according to Hellyer, 'salary goes on the mortgage and to my wife and children but the bonus is mine.'

A loyal and local following was enough for Sporting Index to thrive. 'The Nineties was a wonderful time for the City but, equally, the size of bonus being paid was not nationwide,' recalls Hellyer. 'We belatedly concluded, after efforts to take spread betting north of Birmingham, the best way to get a new client was to have an existing client recommend someone.'

Publicity for Sporting Index was key to the business thriving. In this there was good fortune from launch. This was in the spring of 1992. A summer of sport was ahead and exploiting this was, understandably, the plan. But before then there was a general election. Indeed, campaigning was in full swing at the time of Sporting Index's birth. Very soon, the merit of making markets on this, as much as sport became clear. 'We didn't realise it,' Hellyer admits now. 'But, leaving aside sport at the time, interest in betting on the outcome of the election was great, generally, for spread betting. In this election, betting on the winner with the bookmakers at fixed odds was pretty dead. The outcome was not sufficiently compelling – two potential winners, with Neil Kinnock favoured at the start of the campaign to beat John Major – to engage the general public to have a bet. But spread betting on the overall majority? What the final make up of parliament would be was far from clear. That lent itself to what we were doing. We received huge press coverage on the election, which was a fluke. We originally wanted our launch to be around a football match. But, thanks to the election, we got a flyer.'

Once up and running, and after a month of publicity in a volume that shouldn't even be imagined for a start-up company, press coverage continued. Hellyer, along with his public relations sidekick, Wally Pyrah (his impact was comparable to that which Eric Cantona had on Manchester United, according to Hellyer), reached platforms for self-promotion previously beyond the reach of mere bookmakers. Critically, broadcasters showed a huge appetite for spread betting related stories. This included outlets such as *Test Match Special*. Appearances at the luncheon interval on BBC Radio 4's TMS broadcasts became commonplace. 'We got out and about,' Hellyer shrugs; a rare understatement on what was an orchestrated campaign of hype. 'There I was next to Henry Blofeld on air, part of TMS, and he is asking me what we were betting on runs England might make in their innings.' Such a conversation fell easily into the narrative of a broadcast at moments such as lunch or even between overs.

The advent of Sky's extended coverage of all sports, live, was also key. 'It was obvious very quickly that when an event was live, we would get many more bets,' Hellyer recalls. 'At first we would spend time making markets for the biggest events. Then we realised that, if an event was on television, it was effectively a big event. Manchester United v Arsenal, or Chelsea, or Liverpool was less of a deal to us than Sheffield United v Watford on television if the Watford game was the only one screened. People like to see where their money goes.'

As a rule, human nature sustained Sporting Index in the early days. 'We won money because punters were optimists,' Hellyer admits. 'Our clients always went high. For example, if we worked out statistically that Graham Gooch would make 270 runs in a series against New Zealand, we would make the spread 289–290, to factor in human nature.

People want a good game and for players like Gooch –
England, generally – to do well so they would take us up
and buy at 290. We always wanted to finish short, with
the punters long. And even if the punters won, they came
back.'

A niche was established. 'Let's say, after ten years we
had opened 30,000 accounts of which 25 per cent were
active,' ponders Hellyer. 'When you analysed it about 250
accounts really mattered. Small accounts created liquidity
but what mattered was beating our big punters, that they
lost tens of thousands a year, rather than just the hundreds
that small players might lose.'

Hellyer has a theory about Betfair. The running water of
the nearby Thames creates good karma, he jokes. To match
Betfair's running water the thought of nightingales in
Berkeley Square ensures a degree of serenity and calm for
Stuart Wheeler, who lives nearby on Davies Street,
London. Mayfair's landmark Cipriani restaurant is so close
as to be tantamount to Wheeler's local trattoria. On the
side of the block which is home to his two-floor, high-
rise, penthouse-style apartment is engraved: 'Les mots
juste et injuste sont entendus par toutes les consciences' –
rights and wrongs are heard by all conscience – and 'where
man obeys without being presumed good there is neither
liberty nor a native land'. These are implicit testimony to
Wheeler's reputation for deep thinking that was behind
him coming up with IG in 1974.

His personal thinking ultimately yielded £64 million,
following IG's flotation in 2000, a quarter century on from
when he founded the company. Even after bankrolling
William Hague, he still had enough to buy a castle in Kent.

Since childhood, he had always dreamt of living in such a place and funded refurbishment – as a political animal, an example, you would imagine, of fixing the roof during the good times – by selling in 2003 the last slice of IG he held.

To Wheeler's mind, bookmakers need not have worried to the extent they did about spread betting. Looking back, he cannot recall a year when IG's sports spread betting generated more than 15 per cent of the company's total profits (for the year ending May 2008, £98.5 million, pre-tax, to give a ball park). In other words, relatively unimportant amounts. Those who were commensurate with financial markets naturally bought and sold around the spreads with ease. They were in the business of trading. But beyond them? Spread betting, Wheeler admits, was a surprising struggle for those with simply a passion for sport. 'Some very intelligent friends of mine cannot understand spread betting,' he laments. 'They have been brought up on fixed-odds betting. If they had been raised on spread betting this might be different. The form of betting would be a natural one for them.'

Spread betting's other great weakness was the potential for unlimited losses. Wheeler smiles ruefully in telling the tale of a client who learned the hardest of ways that spread betting was not for the faint hearted. This hopeful client bought at £100 a run in a spread bet on the total runs the England cricket team would manage during a tour of the West Indies over Christmas 1997. The first Test was abandoned without a ball being bowled and England's final total was, as a consequence (coupled with some poor batting), well under the spread set for the tour. With each run below expectations costing the client £100, the tab was finally into tens of thousands, which in all cost him his job and wife. 'You never know for sure what you are going to lose,' Wheeler accepts.

Bookmakers, themselves, did their utmost to put limits on spread betting. Wheeler reckons that, definitively, it was tax that placed a lid on spread betting. 'That was the way they got to us in the end,' Wheeler shrugs. 'We ended up paying two or three times as much as we had been paying. Bookmakers argued with the Treasury that betting duty at the time – in 1995, with spread betting thriving this stood at 7.75 per cent – was crippling them and we were getting away with paying less. They were not wrong. Certainly, they did have a case.'

He continues: 'The main point about tax is that, if you speculate in the normal way on stock indices or shares or commodities, you pay capital gains tax on any prof-its. My recollection, though I am not quite certain about this, was that for some time it was income tax. Anyway the point is that in Britain there is no tax on betting prof-its. So if a transaction which enables you to speculate on, say, stock indices or shares or many other financial instru-ments, can be in the form of a bet, that is very attractive to a client. Curiously enough it is also quite attractive to the Chancellor of the Exchequer! This is because, due to the expenses of dealing, there are in the end likely to be more losers with us than winners. Those losers could, if they had done the transaction in a more normal way instead of with us by way of a bet, have set those losses against capital gains tax but, because they did do the transaction by way of a bet, they cannot do that. Quite apart from that the Chancellor gets normal corporation tax, betting duty, and PAYE from the spread betting company.'

Wheeler gives credit where credit is due. Fixed-odds bookmakers actually moved first on the development of spread betting, he concedes. Before even IG, Joe Coral founded Coral Index, which was the predecessor to Ladbroke Index, renamed when Bass Charrington bought Coral. Struggling with the concept, Bass offloaded the index onto Ladbrokes. He recognises the irony in admitting that it was an experiment by traditional bookmaking that inspired him to create IG. 'Coral Index registered on my personal radar a very long time ago,' Wheeler recalls. 'It offered clients the ability to bet on what was then the FT30 Share Index and on the Dow Jones Index and I certainly remember taking advantage of its facilities, to my own loss, in the Sixties. I thought that what it had to offer was very attractive and so, after I had been sacked from one job and made redundant from another, I approached Cyril Stein, the head of Ladbrokes, suggesting that he should set up a competing company. The implication was, of course, that I would run it. He never said, no, but he never said, yes. So I approached William Hill with much the same result. As you may know, the Coral Group was taken over by Bass Charrington and they did not want to know about this very small subsidiary, Coral Index. So Ladbrokes bought it and renamed it Ladbroke Index.'

Nearly a decade after this, Wheeler recalls asking Ladbrokes – again – to form a partnership in sports spread betting, which was also rejected. He puts traditional bookmakers' failure to profit from spread betting as down to the simple fact that whenever a bookmaker loses his or her market ascendancy by entering a field where they have limited expertise they are no more successful than your average punter. Bookmakers, who were used to being in the know and dealing with clients who were less connected than them with the goings-on in racing stables around the country, found this advantage eroded or even eliminated on unfamiliar turf. 'By adopting sports spread betting bookmakers found that, to match the specialists like us who took bets on a much wider range of events, they had over 300 markets to assess,' says Wheeler. 'Experienced spread bettors with dedicated spread operations would be very good at spotting the one market in which the new boys had under or overestimated matters.' That was true of whichever company it was, IG, or otherwise.

From a personal point of view, Wheeler did ultimately have the satisfaction of buying the shells of both companies' efforts to develop the spread betting market. In Ladbrokes' case this was twice. The acquisition of Ladbrokes Sporting Spreads in 1998 followed his purchase twelve years previously of Ladbroke Index. In 2001, he concluded business by buying William Hill Index.

The embarrassment that William Hill felt about the company's failure in the spread betting market and ultimate sale of William Hill Index to IG is encapsulated in the conditions of sale. Wheeler recalls that, under the terms of the agreement reached, he was unable to discuss the price he paid, or indeed any reason for William Hill having sold out. Indeed, that remains the case today (as if that prevents anyone drawing his or her own conclusions).

Recalling his spread betting days, Wheeler now laughs at some of the misconceptions and misunderstandings. He bears a striking resemblance to the former Conservative Party Home and Foreign Secretary, Douglas Hurd, and has a highly analytical mind. In addition to being delighted by three cover-girl daughters, he seems greatly amused by the absurd.

Back in his IG days in the Nineties, an area of concern for a short while was the markets that spread betting firms offered on winning distances in horse races; it became an issue in relation to the sport's integrity. This presented a dilemma for the authorities. You could manipulate margins of victory against the spirit of the sport without the result – namely who finished first, second and third – being affected. In other words exploit a betting market without jeopardising, in the case of a jockey or trainer, professional livelihoods. Wheeler recalls a particular trainer who took an occasional interest in this sort of wager and was believed to be working an advantage without drawing much attention from the authorities who were satisfied that his horses were, as the rules dictated, seeking to gain 'the best possible placing' as required. 'It is funny how analytical evidence differs from anecdotal evidence,' Wheeler laughs. 'Our guys on the sports desk were at one time alarmed at this. But when they looked at the market for winning distances they found it to be one of our most profitable.'

As far as Betfair, which would encounter its own problems in relation to the corruption of sport, is concerned, Wheeler is one of many to have been invited to become a founding investor. He is not alone is turning them down. Maybe the arrival of Betfair and the betting exchange's trade on sport limited spread betting further, he muses. 'They came to see me. Maybe I didn't understand the concept [which is hard to imagine]. Decent people,' he notes. 'I just didn't think they would succeed. I realised relatively soon after they started to trade that they would'.

Wheeler remembers that Sporting Index also wanted a partnership, which he turned down, too. 'Wrong again,' he jokes.

The architect of that venture, Hellyer, laughs at the times back then. He admits he also missed a trick at Betfair's beginning and took betting exchanges perhaps too lightly. Maybe it was the name? With Sporting Index, that had truly been a masterful choice, not least in raising money to establish the company. 'I've raised money before and since for other enterprises with much more difficulty,' Hellyer reflects. 'My usual line when seeking to persuade people to invest in my latest idea is to say have you got a few thousand you can afford to lose – which is by and large always met with the response, possibly, why, what's the latest idea? In this case, when I said, it was something to do with sport and gambling, the majority would say, almost straightaway, I'm in.'

After launching, returns soon flowed. 'We were in profit very quickly, wonderful, bloody good years, six or seven of them in a row,' Hellyer recalls. In the year ending May 2002, Sporting Index recorded a return of £5.1 million. Bad debts were, according to Hellyer, less than 1 per cent, as spread betting trade had been deemed as involving Contracts For Difference (CDF), with, as a result, debts recoverable through the Courts. Happy was the 'merry band of forty friends' who supplied the seven figures Sporting Index needed to launch, joined subsequently by the respected venture capitalists, Electra Investment Trust, to underwrite the plan for world domination. 'So small you won't even notice', was how Hellyer remembers selling the idea of a £2 million investment to the then Electra chairman, Michael Stoddart.

Profits, without much risk of cannibalisation ultimately proved too much of a draw for Ladbrokes and William Hill. Markets otherwise dead for bookmakers could come alive. For example, rugby league, never a high-roller game for bookmakers, was live every Friday evening during the season. Hellyer rubs his hand at the memory of many a sporting weekend getting off to a flyer. He could reminisce all day.

Raising money, promotions and publicity, reminiscing; Hellyer undoubtedly has gifts. Yet, he cannot quite pinpoint why he was relatively cool about Betfair. 'If you are going to attempt a betting coup one piece of information you need is how much you might lose. On Betfair, you know that. You don't on spread betting so that is at least one reason why people prefer the former. I used to think that we were the most exciting thing that ever happened to betting. Not because of the success of Sporting Index, which was relatively tiny and unimportant in the grand scheme of things but because of the impact it had on the general betting market. Certainly we made traditional bookmakers more outward looking.'

He tails off. Bookmakers may have been compelled to innovate a little. Sporting Index certainly gave the lion's tail a good tug. Then came Betfair. 'We were stopped in our tracks by Betfair,' Hellyer shrugs. 'If Betfair hadn't come up who knows where Sporting Index would be now? You ring Betfair and the operators are so nice. "Good luck", they say. Not like other bookmakers. Betfair take a percentage, they are not part of the wager. Why would bookmakers wish you well?' he laughs.

Chapter THREE

ILLUSIONS OF CONTROL

Why do we bet? To a gambler, this is not so much a question as an invitation. Ask, and in no time odds against well-worn theories would be chalked up somewhere, including the basis for gambling is a desire to lose everything in order to test the unconditional love of a father. It would be odds-on that a good few of them would also feature something about maternal relations, too.

Sigmund Freud on betting would not be anywhere near favourite these days. To summarise his theory, gambling is a form of masturbation would be an extremely simplified précis. Even in full, academics dwell little on these notions today. In a book published in 1995 and titled *Adolescent Gambling*, by Mark Griffiths, professor of gambling at Trent University, he outlined a host of more contemporary explanations behind the subconscious desire to bet. These largely focus on the part of the population – between 0.2 per cent and 1 per cent, according to experts – that are reckoned to be pathological gamblers.

Griffiths, himself, has a taste for casinos. This is leisure time, he reasons, which, along with other distractions, he 'buys' by exposing himself potentially to financial losses. In other words, time and money spent at the tables incurring inevitable losses is no different to that spent watching Nottingham Forest, his other passion, having splashed out comparable amounts of cash on a match ticket. Professionally speaking, Griffiths is not short of subject matter in the shape of the world's many gamblers to analyse in addition to the pathologically challenged who are the focus of much specialist work. National surveys of betting habits almost universally conclude that in the Western world there are more gamblers than non-gamblers. Estimates of the proportion of Britain that bets in some form or other vary from 80 per cent to 94 per cent of the adult population, with up to 68 per cent of Americans and as many as 92 per cent of Australians sharing in the habit. In the UK, recent estimates suggest that, on average, citizens each bet £800 a year with a quarter of all turnover staked on the Internet. All this before even considering Asia.

That a majority in most countries bet, fits in with a conclusion to some of the research undertaken by Emmanuel Moran, published in 1970, one of a number of scholars referred to by Griffiths in his compelling book. He found that gambling flourishes because of the pressures on those to bet, who find themselves among other risk takers. In other words, peer pressure is a big factor in gambling. Other factors unearthed in what compels us, overall, to have a bet include the desire to release stress and tension. This may puzzle those who find a bet achieves the exact opposite. Each to his own.

According to Griffiths, Owen Wolkowitz, Alec Roy, and Allen Doran published work in 1985 that supported the theory that most gambling habits have their roots in adolescence. These desires are then kick-started by an adult shock such as a death or birth. A year earlier, Henry Lesieur and Robert Custer identified phases in escalation of gambling habits; the winning phase, the losing phase, and the desperation phase for those who develop a full-blown addiction. Various views exist on what each of these phases involve. Suffice to say that one school of thought claims to have unearthed a fourth relevant period; the hopeless phase. Reputedly, this is gambling for gambling's sake. The research behind this touched on 'laboratory animals with electrodes planted in their pleasure centres, they gamble to the point of exhaustion'. A word of warning, there, if ever there was one.

Back to Freud: we should note that his theorising on gambling was based primarily on one patient's experiences, whom the good doctor is reputed never actually to have met. (Edmund Bergler, whose idea that gambling is simply guilt relief in losing is rated more credible today, did at least have 200 cases to consider in his research in the 1950s.) So Freud's analogies between betting and masturbation – impulses, promises to stop often broken, guilt on completion – probably deserve, along with plenty of other Freud musings, to end up discarded. Certainly they are currently discredited along with much of Freud's other work. Back in 1920 Georg Simmel gave them more credence than they might expect today, equating a bet with foreplay and winning with orgasm. Losing akin to ejaculation? Apparently. Well, I never.

In Bergler's day, Griffiths maintains, behavioural theories began to take a hold of the debate as to why people bet. The argument here was that if you won at the first time of asking or early on in your gambling experiences, you would bet again. After that – as most gamblers who start off winning do eventually lose – the simple thrill of having a bet in the hope that you might win is what shapes the behavioural pattern. Indeed, some argue that the more you lose, the more an eventual win – and a return back to that elated state of mind that came with early successes when all things seemed possible – is cherished and desired. Gamblers can be a nostalgic bunch, it would seem.

Modern-day arousal theories of betting – the desire to experience again the thrill of success – to some extent take us back to Freud, though there is a distinction made between sexual arousal and other forms of heightened human states that gambling theories mean by 'arousal'. Cognitive therapists, something of a fad in the present day for those who prefer not to handle questions on maternal relations when on the couch, perhaps represent the opposite view. Some of these emphasise that gamblers suffer, not from heightened states but from the illusion of control. Research in the 1980s unearthed within gamblers the state of mind in which they were happy to claim that winning was as a result of skill while maintaining that losing was a consequence of bad luck. If you are a gambler, ask yourself this: do you think you are in general better than everyone else? If the answer is a deluded yes, these theories urge you to bet carefully. Things may yet spiral.

Consider for a moment a more sophisticated form of gambling. In the financial markets, they prefer to call the process speculation. The selection of top traders featured in Jack D. Schwager's American bestseller, *Market Wizards*, can claim tangibly to have enjoyed a considerable edge. In other words, they believe themselves to be better than the market on the grounds of annual dividends from their betting. The book is one to which Andrew Black often refers when considering the mindset of those who speculate or – call it what you will – gamble. Titles of chapters, each featuring the gambling philosophy of a respected, successful trader in stock, currencies, and commodities range from 'Respecting Risk' to 'The Art of Selection', 'One Lot Triumphs', and 'Everybody Gets What they Want'. The final chapter is, tellingly, 'Understanding The Basics'.

In *Market Wizards* – it is hard not to note that the author's name is Sch-Wager but this is no invention – there are seventeen individual traders featured all of whom expand on highly contrasting approaches to investment. What does this say to us? Perhaps instead of looking for one theory that fits all, best to consider some further words from Griffiths, on why we bet. In *Adolescent Gambling*, he writes: 'Gambling is a complex, multidimensional activity that is unlikely to be explained by any single theory.'

Simon Cawkwell is seated in front of a bank of computer screens, looking out onto an affluent Chelsea street rich in BMWs, Porsches, and Aston Martins with, naturally enough, personalised number plates. His contributions to academic speculation by the likes of Griffiths on the reasons for gambling are modest. Cawkwell is a most helpful and accommodating sort of cove. But he offers no deep insight into the subconscious reasons for him betting. Simply, he does it to make a living so that he can continue to call home an expansive ground floor flat that is in an area with such horsepower alongside a liberally sprinkling of the area's renowned Four-by-Four 'Chelsea tractors'.

The screens in front of Cawkwell in his study room looking out on to the well-heeled neighbourhood show listings of stock market prices and fluctuations in currency rates. To the right of the electronic information wall is a television showing a live feed of the afternoon's horserac-ing. To the left is a small library of tax manuals, and some back issues of *Investors' Chronicle*. Rather than a psycho-logical digression offering insight into what drives him to speculate huge sums on a daily basis at great risk, this is all Cawkwell needs to conduct his business – in addition to tea at regular intervals brought in by his wife. A little Buddha figure on the mantelpiece watches over proceed-ings, serenely, alongside photographs of adoring daugh-ters. This is not the office of a troubled soul. Sure, he analyses his trading back to days in short trousers but this hardly qualifies as the sort of case study that occupies the likes of Professor Griffiths.

On the matter of betting, Cawkwell, a large man both figuratively and philosophically, is quick to become nostal-gic. 'Gambling at Rugby school was such an exciting world,' he recalls. 'Captain Heath's tips in the *Daily Mail*, I was fascinated. I was always interested in statistics. Though I'm no statistician, this awareness of the maths did help me back a few winners. In those days, the extra money was handy. Then I read *Memories of a Fox Hunt-ing Man* by Siegfried Sassoon – Edwardian England; another world to try and understand – and *Memories of an Infantry Officer* by the same author. In these books, a hunting acquaintance has a horse laid out for one of the

Flat season's big handicaps. I was fascinated. Something like Flying Banana and £10 each way! I really cannot remember. Was it the Cambridgeshire Handicap at Newmarket? Whatever the details, I was gripped by the thought.'

Cawkwell wanted to sample more of what was behind this, himself. 'This was in the 1960s. We would catch the train to Sandown. I could well be wrong but I recall that a gin and tonic en route was 2 shillings and six pence with admission to the track at 30 shillings. I remember one afternoon in particular. There was practically no wind so the air was thick with cigar smoke. I looked down the bookmakers' rails, where they all stood. I could see only a blue haze. The way the bookmakers used their voices to shape the market was fascinating. It was like trading on the Stock Exchange in those days and showed me, up close, how this was done. I knew I could learn from this environment as there were some masters in action.'

He sighs, deeply adrift in the past: 'I was earning £600 a year working at Cooper Brothers, the accountants. More interesting to me was the Druid's Lodge, with private gallops on the Wiltshire Downs. They knew exactly how good their horses were but no one else did. What a marvellous state of affairs.'

Cawkwell is also known, among fellow professionals, as Evil Knievel, a billing he made up for himself when, preferring to remain anonymous, he circulated a critique flagging up the vagaries of the late Robert Maxwell's financial set-up well ahead of its ultimate collapse. Being the first to rumble that Maxwell's empire was far from financially sound is perhaps his most substantive claim to fame, so far. In this particular case, by 'short stocking' he made a fortune playing the markets. (Short stocking is leasing shares, then selling them at a price in the expectation that the price will fall. Then buying them back at a reduced and profitable price, ahead of returning them to their original owner.) There have been other great days. At the same time, from the day he opened his first bookmakers' account with D. Upex of Argyll Street, the premier turf accountants of the day (evolving ultimately into Heathorns before being swallowed up by Jennings-Bet in 2007), he has won – and lost – millions betting.

As Griffiths had warned, rooting out why people bet is complex. Rather than considering the general question, why do we bet, let us narrow our inquiry to asking, instead, why do the likes of Cawkwell choose Betfair above other bookmakers when betting? Analysing beyond why Betfair is his choice of outlet for bets today could prove as difficult to fathom as the multitude of digits and colour codes on his screens.

Even with access to someone who is by reputation something of a professional gambler as a point of departure, offering potential insight to the mindset of those who bet, there is a more fundamental obstacle to finding an answer to the question: why do people in growing numbers trade on Betfair? Any analysis of the Internet behaviour is hampered by the pursuit under scrutiny having little more than a decade of evidence to consider. Gambling reputedly goes all the way back to when Thoth, the Egyptian god of gambling among other perhaps more worthwhile pursuits, won a bet with the moon to add five days to the lunar calendar, making possible – so legend has it – the creation of the human race. Yet, the most recent innovation of Internet wagering, significant only since

2000, remains virtually untouched substantially by research.

To the end of 2008, the only truly significant study of Internet betting behaviour drawing on a representative sample was a paper published the previous year. Titled *Assessing the Playing Field: A Prospective Longitudinal Study of Internet Sports Gambling Behavior*, Richard A. LaBrie, Debi A. LaPlante, Sara E. Nelson, Anja Schumann and Howard J. Shapper put together research that ultimately appeared in the *Harvard Medical Journal*.

The five researchers cannot be accused, like Freud, of drawing on a limited sample. Over 40,000 account holders with the Austrian-based web sports betting operation, bwin, were quizzed on the assumption that, unlike with other surveys, those questioned with the absolute guarantee of anonymity, actually answered truthfully. Overall, splitting behaviour into that related to fixed odds and betting-in-running, they concluded, among other revelations, that the latter lost less (18 per cent of stake) than those who took fixed odds, who were 29 per cent down, and that women bet for shorter periods than men. Also concluded was that 'big gamblers' don't all fit into one category; some bet big and infrequently, some bet almost compulsively yet for relatively small stakes, and some – of course – bet big and often. Overall, the work of LaBrie, LaPlante, Nelson, Schumann, and Shapper is, like Cawkwell, at least a point of departure. As for other insights, pending new research we are reduced to considering the case of Bryan Benjafield. Benjafield, a bookkeeper, was sentenced in August 2008 to five years in prison for stealing over £1 million to bet on the web. 'When one sits at home alone in a room, the figures become meaningless,' the court heard. Bearing in mind, with the Internet it is possible to place a bet of many thousands simply by pressing a button, relevant also might be the idea that some gamblers suffer from the equivalent of Attention Deficit Disorder (ADD) with primary symptoms of inattention and impulsivity critical when your finger hovers of the keyboard.

Mark Griffiths' view of betting exchanges and Betfair is that they have revolutionised betting. 'Phenomenally successful, with people having thirty to forty bets a day,' he maintains. 'Why? There are three reasons why people are drawn to them. First and foremost, they represent tremendous value. Compared with betting shops and casinos, where the house has an in-built edge, Betfair takes 3 per cent to 5 per cent of your winnings, which means that if you are in the know, or you have skill, you can actually win.'

He continues: 'Betfair is also betting with real people. The site makes money by charging commission but what it does essentially is introduce gambler to gambler. Furthermore, trade on Betfair is also based on skill. Gamblers like that idea [the illusion of control, perhaps?]. If money is a way of keeping score, Betfair – and other Internet gambling outlets – offers you a pure way to assess your success.' Those who gamble on Betfair are probably gamblers to begin with who have telephone accounts, then, via the Internet, gravitate to Betfair, he adds.

Gamblers like Harry Findlay and Dave Nevison are clearly taken by the first of Griffiths' reasons for Betfair's success. Findlay is the owner of Denman, winner of the 2008 Cheltenham Gold Cup. If you don't know that already it is not for want of him trying to tell you.

Likewise, the success he has had gambling on Denman. Findlay is open, up-front, and relatively candid (which is not always the case with gamblers).

Nevison is a self-styled professional punter who wrote his autobiography, *A Bloody Good Winner*, in 2007, following up with the diary, *No Easy Money*, in 2008. His other claim to fame is a high-fives session with Michael Atherton, the former England cricket captain, who happened to be round his house when Nevison landed a £4,000 bet from a stake of £22. The odds ranged from 180–1 to 80–1.

Nevison and Findlay – universally known as Harry the Dog for his love of greyhound racing – display a devotion to Betfair that verges on religious. Nevison believes, 'Betfair has changed everything', while Findlay maintains that there is a 'moral' justification for favouring Betfair. His argument is that you can check at all times what you are losing – and winning. It stops the lies, Findlay argues.

Press Cawkwell hard on why he has converted to Betfair, and he recalls a feast – 'gargantuan; on and on'. Shortly into the millennium and not that long after the launch of the exchange, he noted discrepancies in the odds between the low-margin odds shown on Betfair and high mark-up prices offered by traditional bookmakers. Accordingly, he accepted the arbitrage, gladly. Like Findlay, Evil Knievel cannot today resist the value Betfair offers comparatively. Placing the highest premium on this may be the first lesson for anyone planning to teach themselves the dark arts.

Cawkwell, himself, claims to be self-taught. 'I am', he insists. He has little time for those who will not, similarly, put in the hours or adapt to embrace new concepts that bring an advantage. 'It is sick and thick to say you don't like the technology you need to use to bet with Betfair,' Cawkwell insists. 'My father learnt when he was nearly 90. To him [it is relevant to note, here, a university don], it was simple enough. I have a friend from my days at Rugby, a punter, who doesn't use Betfair. Doesn't like betting with a computer. How stupid. All it is, is an attitude of mind.'

By talking about his betting in general Cawkwell does begin to offer up reasons why punters were drawn, and continue to be drawn, to Betfair from elsewhere. Arguably, leaving to one side that simply the odds are better, the most fundamental aspect of all emerges (what's more, this takes us back into Griffiths' world). Cawkwell's biggest issue with traditional bookmakers is that he is unable to place bets that represent the full extent of his belief in an outcome. In other words, if he wants to wager £25,000 that a horse will win at Royal Ascot – incidentally, where he pulled off his greatest coup, once leaving the racecourse £135,000 to the good – he can on Betfair which, with liquidity, simply matches him with those who oppose his view. Fixed-odds bookmakers would not take the bet, he argues. Most would be alerted by a well-known name seeking a wager. Consequently, only a portion of the bet would be accommodated, if any, before the odds started to tumble. In other words, their card marked, they would not allow him to express fully his view of the certainty of an outcome and for the stakes to reflect that.

Maybe here we are back to the illusion of control that drives some gamblers. Perhaps, more important, with present-day society in mind Betfair's success is because it is a market for betting and also an outlet for expressions –

usually strongly held – of opinions in tune with a modern age that encourages all to have views and to hold – and air – them stridently? Despite the perceived erosions to personal liberty that there have been – often through necessity – during the Internet age, freedom of expression is in fact one tenet that the World Wide Web has helped promote and spread. Just think of the number of blogs currently in circulation. It follows, certainly, that in the modern age service industries such as bookmaking have to be accommodating in this respect. At the same time, bookmakers haggle over how much a serious punter can wager and at what odds when the prices are there for everyone to see. By kicking back bets, bookmakers are hardly entering into a partnership. 'Is it too much to be able to enjoy expressing fully your opinion,' Cawkwell asks? 'With Betfair you can do that. Not with the bookmakers.'

Simon Champ, like Cawkwell, is both a speculator and a gambler. It is hard to be sure at which he is best. His career in the City of London has generated wealth enough for him to own property in some of the capital's most sought after real estate pockets. There was also enough for him to bankroll a sausage and mash outlet – Banger Brothers (Bros) – fulfilling a commonly held fantasy among men in abstract trades, many of whom dream of owning, if not working in, their own restaurant. Today, after success with the stockbrokers, Cazenove, he runs his own brokerage. Even in a downturn, he has prospects. 'We won't make serious money for now, but we will soon enough,' he insists.

Betfair has worked both ways for him. As a gambler, he made, reputedly – he won't say, exactly – more than

£100,000 trading the exchange on Greece winning the 2004 European Championships. At the start of the tournament, Champ spotted that Betfair odds on Greece to win were, at around 120/1, nearly double traditional bookmakers' best odds of 66/1. By the final, which Greece won 1–0, beating Portugal, the odds had tumbled. At the quarter final stage, Champ, who rejected hedging on the basis that this sort of story needs a decent punch line, win or lose, committed to taking a group of fellow gambling friends to Paris for the weekend if Greece held their form and won the tournament. He estimates that Greece's ultimate success cost him £25,000 in the French capital while there is some suggestion that the rest went on a weekend in Las Vegas. Again, he is a little coy. 'I have been a few times,' Champ admits.

A generous client did pay for Champ's trip to Portugal and a match ticket to watch the final there. Generosity on an altogether different level will be possible if Champ ever sells his personal holding in Betfair. In March of 2000, he invested £25,000 in the company. Based on conservative valuations, that is now worth north of £3 million.

'I was living with two mates in Kensington,' Champ recalls without, it should be noted, too broad a grin. 'I went to a presentation about the company. There were about twenty-five people in the bar, and three screens. I cannot remember the name of the place. Mark Davies did a lot of the talking, and was good. Plus there was Ed Wray. We knew that he had had proper jobs in the City. That did help give the project credibility. Bert was there, too. Not much else you would say. On the way home, I do recall thinking that the whole evening hadn't been terribly impressive. I had my doubts about the concept. I was also aware of Flutter. At the time, I had no kids, no wife, the two guys who lived with me paid rent, which covered the mortgage. I'd been approached between learning what my bonus was going to be and the cheque arriving. I wasn't completely convinced. But I got home and thought, why not? Then I ran it past my flatmates and we decided between us to put up £50,000. I was single, no dependents, and could easily manage £17,500.'

Ultimately, his stake rose as one of the two flatmates pulled out on the day the trio were due to deposit their cheques. 'An expensive decision,' Champ reflects. Some compensation was that the person who had cold feet at the last minute was subsequently best man at Champ's wedding. The speech was at least a chance to erode some of the groom's capital gains.

Champ has no inhibitions talking generally about his betting. 'I've always been a punter, intrigued from an early age by what was behind the windows of the old, seedy, sweaty betting shop,' he admits. 'My mother bet on the Grand National every year which was my first exposure. I backed West Tip to win that race in 1986. Then there was a £1 six-horse accumulator at the Cheltenham Festival which would have cleared £23,000 if Raise An Argument hadn't been pulled up.'

He pauses briefly to ponder the inevitable mixed fortunes that all gamblers must endure, then continues, recalling darker times than even Raise An Argument's Cheltenham. 'I had a William Hill account and did some spread betting, until I lost nine grand on a game of football betting on the number of corners that there would be between Leeds and Roma.'

The switch to Betfair, save for reasons of boosting his own stock holding, concur with the reasons for Nevison and Findlay choosing the exchange over traditional fixed-odds betting. The prices had an edge, Champ confides.

Go a bit deeper with Champ and there is a more substantial reason. Like Cawkwell, the basis for preferring Betfair is that he has the chance to pit his wits against other people to the full extent of his beliefs. 'I like to bet on lower league and conference football,' Champ confesses. 'I am a fanatical Mansfield Town supporter. I can get odds and a bet on Betfair, which I would never manage with fixed-odds bookmakers.'

In 2003, the American sports weekly magazine, *Sports Illustrated* highlighted gamblers' general dislike for being kicked back about a bet. Noted was the preference in Las Vegas, Nevada, where betting on sport is legal in the US, for 'dumb money, the kind that comes in small increments from yahoos tipping Coors beer for breakfast.' An investigation in the *Racing Post* newspaper in September 2008 highlighted the gripes of gamblers – including Findlay, who maintained: 'No one is allowed to win.'

Champ concurs. 'Bookmakers don't take a bet like my money on Mansfield Town which they would not be able to hedge [lay off with other bookmakers by striking bets, themselves]. The market with Betfair has liquidity of over £500,000. That means I can have my bets – £100, £200 staked. I am pitting myself against other people. We are able to oppose each other to the full. Then the game decides who is right.'

The ability to have the bet you actually want to have certainly gives the impression of at least a level playing field to begin with. Furthermore, it helps maintain the illusion of control and self-determination. For some, this illusion may be at the heart of their subconscious preference for Betfair, or indeed why they belatedly began to gamble through Betfair when previously unmoved by what fixed-odds bookmakers offered. For others, it may just be a simple desire to gamble unencumbered and to voice opinions through the process of having a bet and then see them tested. In other words, to have an answer to the question, are you really better than everyone else?

To these reasons for betting with Betfair, we should add a degree of camaraderie that an involvement provides. Professor Mark Griffiths could be guilty of overstating that Internet betting largely eliminates social aspects of gambling on which casinos stand to profit handsomely (be warned, casinos strive to make things feel friendly and welcoming as the longer you are there, the more the house will make from you). Understandably, the Internet largely by its nature is an invention of solitude. Betfair confounds that. The company's Internet Forum serves as a network that transcends betting shop culture where, over and above between regulars, and no matter bookmakers' claims about the fraternal nature of their premises, few words are exchanged in the spirit of togetherness. The Betfair Forum is complementary to the betting markets themselves, in providing an outlet for opinions, aggregating those who take a special interest in areas otherwise of no interest to the wider population in general. Indeed, in August 2008, the *Guardian* newspaper described Betfair's Forum as 'surely the largest aggregation of punters anywhere on the web'.

Betfair's Internet Forum is inadvertently a study of human interaction, with thick skin an advantage. Most traits are on show including humour, (though you will have to be able to take as well as make a joke). This is not only evident in the names that people choose for their postings such as Andy Murray's Barber (AMB) in the exchange that follows. Little asides – for example, a remark about AMB's cutting technique (geddit?!) – begin to explain why people stay within the Forum for hours at a time. The language and vernacular may at first seem excluding to new comers. For instance, 'LoL'? That is easy, laugh out loud. But 'head to head' as H2H and 'scoreboard' reduced to SB take a little longer to fathom. That said, once the community's syntax is clear you are in. You have become a signed up member of a club that never closes, with free membership potentially for life.

There is never a shortage of content. Sometimes – though not, by any means, always – the subject is as tame as how mid-ranking women's tennis detracts from the high standards of competitors like the Williams sisters. Take what follows about the clash in Bali's Commonwealth Bank Tennis Classic between journeywomen Jill Craybas and Marta Domachowska, an otherwise nondescript contest featuring two players who wouldn't usually register unless they happened to be playing at Wimbledon in the later stages of the women's singles. In the Forum, much ground is covered while, at the same time, those online look to close out betting positions that they have taken on the match. The group that forms for this could be around a table, chatting while playing cards.

gulfstreams the dream: 10 Sep 07:02. Quite tempted to go big on Craybas here, even though the H2H is 0–4. Anyone else with similar views?

Dovotr: 10 Sep 07:21. Last two matches have gone to three sets. I've backed craybas but hope to get out early

Kellypavlik: 10 Sep 08:14. craybas always involved a serious amount of breaks of serve

Basacasa: 10 Sep 08:14. Just started with one break each

Spaniard: 10 Sep 08:16. does any1 know why the scoreboard is soo f_cked up, points going bananas?

Spaniard: 10 Sep 08:21. break-a-thon here, i think domachowska will be 2 strong in this match

Agassi 77: 10 Sep 08:22. ridiculous match so far

Thepunter: 10 Sep 08:34. 1 hold by Doma so far ... lol

andy murray's barber: 10 Sep 08:37. what a useless pair of tw@ts these two are

Rommel: 10 Sep 08:39. hope you dont talk like that when ure snipping

Spaniard: 10 Sep 08:39. what a joke how most womens serves are so easily broken. Some1 needs to teach them to serve

urryup'arry: 10 Sep 08:40. They might as well just knock it up over the net like they do in the warm up

Spaniard: 10 Sep 08:41. wow a couple of holds lol

Rommel: 10 Sep 08:43. score?

Swedsil: 10 Sep 08:45. Craybas *3–5 40–BP. That mean
    SP Marta

Leefee: 10 Sep 08:45. (in response to 'urryup'arry)
    They might as well just knock it up over the net like
    they do in the warm up? errrrr … thats exactly what
    most of them do!!!!!!

Swedsil: 10 Sep 08:46. Marta 6–3 *0–0

andy murray's barber: 10 Sep 08:47. they are more
    interested in a week's break in bali i think

Spaniard: 10 Sep 08:49. who ever is controlling this
    scoreboard should be shot, how hard can it be, it
    constantly f_cks around

Agassi 77: 10 Sep 08:52. SB miles behind

Spaniard: 10 Sep 08:52. lol

Thepunter: 10 Sep 08:55. % chances for craybas to hold
    here ? 5% ?

Spaniard: 10 Sep 08:56. 1% u mean

andy murray's barber: 10 Sep 08:59. 11 games, 8
    breaks – quality lol

Agassi 77: 10 Sep 09:00. pathetic match

Swedsil: 10 Sep 09:01.Craybas 3–6 *2–1

Agassi 77: 10 Sep 09:02. Craybas will hold now

Swedsil: 10 Sep 09:03. Marta 76% chance to win from here …? (6–3 1–2*) 1.31 backers must SEETHINGS or just having a bad day

Agassi 77: 10 Sep 09:07 all red, i'm tired of this ****

The final posting by 'Agassi 77' is a reference to his trading position. All red? That is universally understandable, and hardly a unique conclusion. Nonetheless, for such a poor match, quite a debate, a party even, has taken place. Most remarkable is the service provided throughout this by the Forum member, Swedsil. He dutifully and happily serves as the conveyer of the match score after Rommel, alongside in the Forum, asks for an update. Only at the end of the conversation does Swedsil begin to reveal the true reasons for a presence in the Forum with a calculation of the percentage chance of Marta to win after the first set. He is there to bet. Indeed, that is why everyone is in the Forum.

For those who believe Betfair to be in the one-dimensional business of betting, the range of topics and issues covered by the Forum is striking. The list of categories – from horseracing and a host of sports to politics – which have dedicated pages at Betfair.com is consistently over thirty-five and within those categories those who post comments cover an extraordinary range of topics. Take an exchange on 9 September 2008 about the US presidential elections, just after the addition of Sarah Palin to the ultimately unsuccessful McCain ticket. This is illustrative of how broad-ranging discussions in the Betfair Forum can be. In discussing the presidential election, the pseudonyms – Canadian Scotch, Dr J, The Priest – serve to hide only identities of posters rather than their ignorance. At the same time as the dialogue, a bet possibly between those involved could happen at any moment. If you have a special interest, you will find likeminded folk easily enough on Betfair in no time and dialogue can extend to over 1,000 comments covering ten Betfair web pages. Underscoring the discussions is always the possibility of a bet based on an opinion held or information gathered. Over and above that, the dialogue is educated, often witty (as well as, inevitably on occasion in bad taste), and conveying a degree of togetherness. Punters stand alongside one another, albeit in cyberspace. In a betting shop, where punters gather to take on the 'auld enemy' this is harder to generate. For all the remoteness, the bonds between Betfair players seem stronger, itself reflecting the strength of markets. Want a bet to substantiate your view? You will be accommodated.

Betfair is also home to the highest caste of gambler. Go to a casino with a mathematician who has a system designed to win at the tables and, in the event that you do, wait for the tap on the shoulder, followed by the offer, first of a drink, then a taxi home. Betfair accommodates such gamblers, including the self-deprecating one who bills himself as The One That Got Away.

The One That Got Away: 17 Aug 20:58. Right, i have a bank of £300 where i shall have 2 attempts to reach £1000. Each bank will consist of £150 and i will be playing the correct score market either prior to Kick Off or In Play. I got this idea from the Football Forum and believe that over a month it is easily achievable. Lets see if i can make the easily achievable the actual reality!!! Bank One Bet 1-Lay Marseille 1–1 Auxerre (currently 1–0 at HT) @ 8.8 £18.27 possible profit Bank Two Bet 1-Lay Valencia 0–1 Reakl Madrid (prior to KO) @ 10.5 £15.00 POSSIBLE PROFIT

Betfair's Forum is not the only Internet space that offers an insight into the appeal of Betfair as a means of betting on your own terms. GamCare is an organisation set up in 1997 to support problem gamblers whose addiction has begun to undermine the rest of their lives. In 2007, the organisation set up a Net Line, to complement the telephone help line at the end of which are expert counsellors to help talk down those who find themselves perilously placed because of betting.

Net Line was an Internet route to advice. With the growth in online gambling this was a natural move for GamCare. In addition, as part of the service, a forum was established in the belief that those with degrees of addiction to gambling could offer support to one another, over and above expert counsel that GamCare could provide.

Many of these gamblers are what would be described as pathological, whose like have featured in much of the research into the reasons behind gambling. What some of their postings reveal is how Betfair is believed to offer gamblers a chance to shape their betting to suit themselves.

To some, traditional bookmakers draw them into bets, which they would rather not have rather than stick to subjects where they have strong personal opinions based on knowledge. Betfair, in contrast, gives you 'the office', a sense of being in charge of affairs. In other words, the illusion of control.

Posting on the GamCare forum, one problem gambler called Indebted, maintained: 'One of the things I am is open minded. I can appreciate that exploring solutions which might involve gambling in some form would make many people uncomfortable. I still stand by my opinion that money can be made on betting exchanges.' He continued: 'It is a different type of gambling, and it really stuck in my mind when some people said they quit it despite being well ahead money-wise!'

In the same forum, but part of the site that allows addicts to keep an online diary of their attempts to control their betting, is a post from JD. He covers his decision to give up gambling until the start of 2008, and his belief that betting on football only with Betfair – in other words, on his terms – would enable him to control his losses. 'I will be honest with people as I feel like a bit of a fraud on here as I have no intentions of stopping gambling altogether as the diary title (*From Here Until The New Year*) says,' JD confides. 'This is because after keeping records of all my bets for the last two years I actually make a consistent profit on football betting. My problem is whatever I win on football I've blown on the horses and much more as I know very little about them and as there are races every ten minutes of each other it's too easy to chase after a loss. My plan is to stop altogether until the New Year then stick to football betting only as win or lose. I don't chase and honestly think I can make money from doing this. I may be naive. I don't know.'

Once again, we are back to an extent with the illusion of control that academics suggest is a root cause behind the adoption of gambling. More prosaic, GamCare listings like those on Net Line, which have a confessional honesty and integrity, do suggest that at least one of the reasons why Betfair thrives is because the company meets the desires of gamblers everywhere to be independent. Of course, GamCare is committed to helping those for whom paternal supervision is required. Be that as it may, the insight of those subscribing to the organisation's web services reinforces the notion that the ability to express opinions through money staked without any moderation by bookmakers is perhaps Betfair's Unique Selling Point.

Back at Simon Cawkwell's London flat, he offers a candid admission. 'I am a steady loser with Betfair,' he confides. Cawkwell's efforts to profit from short stocking are certainly not with a view to bankrolling the gains into supporting lifestyles of other Betfair players keen to pick off the ill-informed and profit, themselves, accordingly. It is more so that his losses are the price he pays for the ability to stake bets as he pleases. In other words, the need Cawkwell has to express his opinion.

At the turn of the millennium society was brimming with similarly opinionated, moneyed potential Betfair customers. At the website, they found the chance to share their views in the sharpest of environments.

'I spread bet for a bit,' says Cawkwell, a little sheepishly. 'Then I experienced a drowning, which I have never forgotten. England were playing the West Indies. The West

Indies were eighty-something for four with Brian Lara at the crease. I went short on the innings total at £100 a run. In the end, Lara made a huge score.' Likewise, the West Indies, as a whole, as others chipped in along with Lara.

That was that, admits Cawkwell. 'For me Betfair came of age in 2002. J.P. McManus [the well known Irish race-horse owner and gambler] had a runner at Cheltenham called Like A Butterfly. At the time, Betfair markets were offering to match bets of over £100,000 at odds of 9–4. The lot went in less than a minute. I remember thinking, Betfair has come of age. Any bet I wanted, I was sure that I could get on.'

Cawkwell interrupts his recollection to take a phone call. His screens, which while we have been speaking went into sleep mode displaying nothing distracting, have flashed back into action. Down the line, there is some discussion about Tesco. The sense is that the issue here is the share price of the supermarket chain rather than a problem with grocery deliveries.

Cawkwell puts down the phone: 'When I was a young man, someone owed me £50 so I chased down the gambling debt. They wrote to my father, a university don who specialised in logic, about some menacing letters I had written in an effort to get paid. You shouldn't have anything to do with people like that, he warned me.'

More comfortable would Cawkwell be trading with the likes of Simon Champ. At work in the City of London, he reckons that it is now almost redundant to mention that you have been betting on Betfair when discussing gambling. 'It is a given,' he maintains. 'Mention odds and it is understood that you are talking about markets formed on Betfair. Maybe some over forty, fifty years old might have issues about using the Internet and technology. But generations below that want to express their opinions by having a decent bet. That is what we can do on Betfair.'

When Champ was looking for a name for his new company, Liberum fitted the bill. The name derives from the Latin word for Independence.

Chapter FOUR

YES, NO, AND YES

From Wimbledon to Hammersmith, via Parsons Green, Putney, and Russell Square. To take in all these destinations, the journey would mean crossing the Thames before heading north to Bloomsbury then passing back through some of London's best postal codes to finish up at a pretty good spot for watching the Oxford v Cambridge boat race. For Andrew Black and Ed Wray the locations plot their path, as Betfair, to the £1.54 billion-plus company that today employs 1,350 staff predominately in Britain, Malta, and Australia with headquarters occupying two floors of prime office real estate overlooking the Thames across the water from the iconic Harrods depository.

Along the way, offices, starting in Wimbledon, en route to Hammersmith, have been progressively more and more grandiose, reflecting the company's growth. In February 2002, Betfair recorded its first £1 million market. That October, Black and Wray were heralded as Ernst & Young Emerging Entrepreneurs of the Year, ahead of the following April when Betfair was awarded a Queen's Award for Enterprise in the Innovation Category. In 2005, by now well set in Hammersmith, Betfair claimed to have matched – as in brought together a layer and a backer – one billion bets, and walked away with a second Company of the Year gong at the Confederation of British Industry's Growing Business Awards. In 2006, Betfair boasted one million customers. In less than two years, the company had doubled that. A second Queen's Award also arrived in 2008, this time for International Trade.

Today Betfair maintains that the website handles an average of five million transactions daily, more than the total number of deals over the same time on all Europe's stock exchanges, combined. Over 99 per cent of trades are reputedly completed in under a second. In one average – if that is the right word bearing in mind the scale of things – week, page impressions are 4.7 billion, Betfair claims. *Silicon Valley Insider* declared Betfair in September 2008 to be the third most valuable private-owned digital start-up venture, behind only Wikipedia and Facebook (which, incidentally, carries adverts inviting members to play Betfair poker and casino games). Britain's Advertising Standards Authority signed off Betfair's boast of being the nation's biggest online betting company, and the world's biggest online betting community.

Praise for the site is virtually universal and as widespread as praise has long been for the original idea and thinking of Black. Recurring among those touched by Betfair is the notion of envy (without too much bitterness) that such a simple concept escaped them and was in turn so brilliantly executed. A good few in the same market kick themselves for not competing earlier, too. There is also a sense of the collective about Betfair (at least in those who hark back to the company's formative years). Absent is the 'them and us' culture that has traditionally under-scored betting, with 'them' being anything from book-makers, legal or otherwise, to casinos. Maybe talk of family is overstating it. Remember also that 'them and us' market-ing, emphasising the battle between punter and 'auld enemy', has proved good for bookmaking business. Many bets have their roots in this conflict. The polarity has been cultivated. That said, those who have spent towards a decade now with Betfair are very much at home there.

How exactly did this come to pass? At the time of the launch of Betfair, in June 2000, the company was far from having the 95 per cent-plus grip on the global betting exchange market – part of an online betting industry esti-mated in 2008 to be worth over $20 billion – that it enjoys today. Indeed, Flutter.com, considered back then to be the giant in the market – certainly, with over $40 million behind the project, in terms of funding – would have been favourite ultimately to assume the commanding position that, instead, Betfair holds today. Betdaq – the name is a play on the Nasdaq exchange – was another market rival unveiled in 2000, just after Betfair, then launched the following year. This was backed by the billionaire Irish entrepreneur, Dermot Desmond, the majority shareholder in Celtic Football Club among other investments, world-wide. Up against Betfair were some deep pockets.

Central to understanding Betfair's success in business is the concept of liquidity, key to any exchange's ability to thrive. Liquidity is the amount of money circulating in the market of a betting exchange. Without liquidity, those

who want to trade can find they simply cannot be accommodated. An insufficient amount of money is in the market
to meet the stakes potential newcomers may wish to play.
Without liquidity they must pass, or look elsewhere. The
first trader on a market begins the process of creating
liquidity. Others drawn to what is being traded hopefully
follow, building up the liquidity, which increases the
strength of the market, which in turn encourages more
to come to the market. This in turn makes the market
stronger still. Growth ultimately fuels growth, which fuels
growth. And so on.

Clearly, in liquidity there are notions of chickens and
eggs. Whichever of these ultimately came first – it is still
even money – Betfair has in less than a decade established
liquidity in abundance. In September 2008 Betdaq had
liquidity manageable by a payroll just one tenth of
Betfair's. At the same point, WBX, a newcomer to the
market in 2006, needed a staff of only thirty-two after a
year of trading compared to Betfair's army, and generated
turnover of, in instances, less than 1 per cent of business
in comparable Betfair markets. From this, and the head
count then, there is no doubt about the dominant party.
In fact, Betfair drains other markets of liquidity. The
vibrancy of the Betfair market has long sustained the
fiercest competition for trades, and consequently generated the best prices coupled with a high likelihood that
wagers can be accommodated. In betting, money chases
money.

In exchange markets, one company usually breaks free
from the pack. That is the market's nature and is what,
in under two years, Betfair did. By 2002, the company
reached the stage where if you wanted to bet with an

exchange there was little or no reason to go anywhere else. Then, because of the nature of liquidity, and because the number of individual markets for betting was kept tight and focused, concentrating liquidity, Betfair's overall market advantage grew and grew. The company accounts of 2007 show customer numbers between 2003 and 2007 increased almost ten fold. Then in little more than another twelve months they practically doubled again. Profits have also kept pace; in 2003 £7.52 million, in 2004 £10.52 million, in 2005 £17.12 million, in 2006 £27.01 million, then £19.39 million in 2007 after a year of heavy internal investment. The fruits of that were profits of £29.77 million in 2008.

So liquidity is the key, the engine that has driven Betfair to such commanding heights. But, of course, the arc of Betfair – its success in establishing this liquidity that meant by mid-2002 the world of exchanges was, pretty much, Betfair's – still needs some explaining. Let us try and be as simple as possible here. A single sentence? If the growth of a company from nothing into a multi billion dollar entity can be reduced to this it would be that Betfair is a concept brilliantly adapted to the Internet, then – crucially – marketed to the public to the same standard of the tech-nological wizardry behind the site. In other words, Betfair's supremacy of liquidity was no accident. Thanks to slick marketing, money was drawn, sucked in, to Betfair, creating the necessary liquidity. This was then processed swiftly and largely efficiently, further encouraging trad-ing.

In addition to this combination, there were other factors. Timing was key. In 2000, broadband was poised to spread, vastly improving Internet usage. Andrew Black is both a technician as well as creative. 'With broadband, the more complex parts of the site sold better to people,' he admits. 'We had a version that was low-weight for those with relatively poor low-band service. But it was a pretty horrible facility compared to the all-singing and dancing version available. When broadband became more standard we started serving a much more sophisticated version with much functionality built in. For sure, broadband was extremely helpful. With the full service, we were a sophisticated site.'

Betfair also established good links with government that ensured that the baby wasn't snuffed out at birth when regulatory issues were raised by mainstream rivals. 'Utterly paranoid' was the state to which traditional bookmakers were reduced, according to Ed Wray. They wanted Betfair banned. Nonetheless, Betfair represented a clean and acceptable face of gambling – even the chaotic Andrew Black scrubbed up well as required – which lawmakers needed little encouragement to embrace. The bookmakers' parliamentary lobby, historically powerful and well funded, failed to deliver the usual services rendered for the clients, in this case elimination of the competition on regulatory grounds. The speed at which Betfair established credibility was important and impressive. To John Healey, a Labour MP and key figure at the Treasury during Betfair's visits early in the millennium, the company achieved this immediately. From the first visit, he maintains.

Underscoring all this was good corporate governance. Mark Davies, one of the first to join, recalls a number of decisions that illustrate sound judgement from the early days onwards. For example, the rejection of Freeserve as a preferred partner. 'In our first year we were offered the chance of a partnership for around £600,000,' Davies recalls. 'Freeserve was, at the time the dominant Internet Service Provider [ISP] in the UK. I was keen. At the time, Freeserve *was* the Internet in the UK. They were everywhere. I feared that if we lost out on this deal – and also with our lack of resources at the time – that would have been that.' Ultimately collective governance arrived at a different consensus. As a consequence, Betfair declined the offer. Subsequent arrangements with MSN, Yahoo, and Virgin have shown preferred partner deals are less than decisive in achieving market domination.

Of course, the merger with Flutter stands out as, aside from launch, the major landmark in the company's history. With this, Betfair was elevated beyond the reach of any rivals. The coming together of the two companies produced synergies that even Andrew Black did not anticipate. 'We had customers who were extremely valuable to the business, they had a lot of customers, just not the big ones that we had,' he explains. 'The key Flutter accounts? Let us just say, for the sake of argument, that they were betting £100 a week. By bringing them into the Betfair fold – as some might not even have known that we were an option – the extra liquidity meant their trade could increase significantly. Leave to one side the software. What always matters is liquidity. Flutter customers came to Betfair and started betting more simply because they could.' Liquidity brings liquidity.

The Flutter deal further reflects that Betfair was a well-run operation which made the right decisions – when they really mattered, that is – at the right times. In 2000, Betfair was certainly concerned about Flutter, due to launch a month earlier. 'Ed was terrified,' Andrew Black recalls ('Flutter scared the life out of me,' to be precise, according to Wray). Black continues: 'Ed thought they were the same as us except with thirty times the financial backing. He was convinced that they would launch with a product identical to ours with more money for marketing than us. We would be dead in the water.'

Ultimately Wray was pacified. 'When I saw what they had done, I thought, this could be quite good for us, in fact they might inadvertently help,' he reflects. 'We were a proper exchange. Take Flutter and, for example, a £100 bet. This required you to find someone to take the £100 bet. We thought, what about the person who only wants to take a £70 bet? You should be able to do that with others taking the remaining £30 if they want. The use of money, as Bert would put it, was the difference between us. Marketing-wise, they had plans to spend a lot of money. That was good for us. They got people interested in the concept. Then they would realise we were better.'

Since Flutter, there have, as you would expect, been many other significant forks in the road where Betfair has chosen the right path. Also occurrences which could be, retrospectively, identified as significant milestones, consolidating and building upon Betfair's fundamental advantages. For example, the rescue of Sporting Options, a one-time rival exchange, positioned Betfair as a champion of the punter. Sporting Options was founded in 2002 and claimed to be operating in profit after eighty days. When it folded two years later Betfair compensated out-of-pocket clients, in the process of welcoming them into the fold. Historically, the betting industry was not exactly renowned for this sort of customer care.

You might also cite as key Betfair's partnership with Aintree in 2004 to become the Grand National's official betting partner from 2005–2007, and other showcase sponsorships – Channel 4's television coverage of the 2005 Ashes to name one – as pivotal moments that confirmed a company in the ascendancy. The Grand National is Britain's flagship betting day. For three years, the Betfair standard flew high. The signing of Memorandums of Understanding with sporting bodies like the Football Association in Britain, the International Olympic Committee, and FIFA (football's world-governing body) were hugely significant, too. These ensured that, for the first time, a gambling organisation was formally committed to supplying an administrator with commercially sensitive information about trading when there was a potential question mark against the integrity of the sport. These went a long way to address criticisms that bookmakers lodged; namely how betting exchanges, generally, and Betfair in particular, had created new opportunities to cheat through the website enabling the laying of as well as the taking of bets.

There have been other milestones. The weekend before Betfair launched on 9 June 2000, the company was on the front page of the *Sunday Times* Business Section, a prominence very, very few new – indeed established – companies achieve. Subsequently important was the site's translation into German, Dutch, Greek, Italian, Swedish, Norwegian, Finnish, and Chinese – how significant will the last of these ultimately prove to be? – in November 2003, and the launch of sites in Spanish and Turkish two years later. Likewise, a licence to trade in Australia, which was granted in 2006. This allowed the company to have as back-up a sister operation through which business could be channelled in the event of a UK Internet melt down. Australia also meant the door to Asia was ajar. In addition you could point to recognition like the Queen's Award for Enterprise, of which Betfair has two (the first, in 2003, for innovation, most importantly gave Betfair significant corporate credibility). Or the point at which Betfair raised a (in corporate terms) meagre £1 million to launch – two rounds of funding followed ahead of the Flutter deal – that established a culture of prudent housekeeping mirroring that the vast majority of investments were less than £50,000. That has always served Betfair well, ultimately enabling the company to rebound from the collapse of a deal with a 'leading global financial services company' – which cannot be named for legal reasons – to inject, at the time ahead of the Flutter deal, much needed capital.

According to Andrew Lee, senior business analyst at Dresdner Kleinwort, Betfair's ultimate supremacy was, with hindsight, a 'no brainer' once the deal with Flutter was signed. Lee points out that putting Company A and Company B together does not mean the new entity, Company A&B, automatically dominates. He recalls that in January 2002 at the time of the Flutter deal, Betfair 'wasn't exactly thriving'. Indeed, Betfair systems struggled under a lack of investment while merger talks were ongoing. Be that as it may, as a markets man Lee, with the benefit of hindsight, emphasises the importance of liquidity in the world of betting exchanges. 'It was obvious very early on in the betting exchange market that there was going to be only one winner,' he maintains. 'Once Betfair, which really took off after merging with Flutter in 2002, had markets with liquidity, they were able to leave everyone else streets behind. In other markets this is not the case. For example, with Internet poker it is different. With that, every site will always still be able to offer the chance to play and should attract some customers. But when Betdaq, launched in 2001, offered zero commission, which should have been a big draw, Betfair, with a liquidity advantage, was still posting better prices in the company's own markets.'

Lee, who now opts for Betfair when enjoying a punt usually on cricket and rugby, adds that bookmakers will try to hide the fact that they wish they had thought of the idea themselves. Except if they had thought of the idea first any attempt to set up an exchange would only have served to undermine established business. Betting exchanges have a nasty habit, without the weight of overheads, of shaving profit margins in traditional betting markets as a result of extra competition, which favours customers.

Of course, when handing out the plaudits in the world of dot.com business, it is important to distinguish between real money and the on-paper variety, at the time of Betfair's launch abundant in the imaginary pockets of many in Silicon Valley. Certainly, the valuation of Internet start-ups around the millennium resulted in companies from that dot.com sector acquiring a bad name for inflating real worth. Corporate credibility of the soundly based operations like Betfair suffered as paper tigers claimed asset holdings worth preposterous sums without anything concrete on which amounts could be based, and in particular without significant monies flowing through the respective business models. In acclaiming Betfair as a success, there is, in addition to the bricks and mortar of

Riverside Walk, Hammersmith, and the growing awareness of the brand, a substance to valuing the company as
a ten-figure concern. In a deal that was concluded in 2006,
SoftBank, a Japanese Internet group, paid £355 million for
a 23 per cent stake in Betfair. Extrapolate from that and
Betfair's worth, in the summer of 2006 at prevailing
exchange rates, hit $3 billion.

That figure in 2006 was based on real money changing
hands for a significant stake. In all likelihood, fluctuations
in the rate of exchange not withstanding, the value of
Betfair has risen since 2006. As for the onset in 2008 of a
financial crisis, bear in mind that historically betting thrives
during economic downturns.

If the substance of Betfair remains in doubt, a visit to
Andrew Black's present family home should put matters
to rest. Thanks to Betfair, he lives on a 330-acre estate in
Surrey. Ultimately, he seeks to establish there a bloodstock
nursery. With wealth now into nine figures – a tidy portion
of that in cash after the SoftBank deal – he has the assets
to fuel a passion for racing well beyond the means of simple
devotees. Equally, he has an obsessive drive when the imagination catches fire, and is well known for his extremes of
appetite – literally. Compton Hellyer recalls him opting
for a lunch of two main courses rather than a traditional
opening starter portion. Black is also mindful of Robert
Sangster's wisdom that warned of how racing could eat
away at your net worth. A hugely successful bloodstock
entrepreneur, who died in 2004, Sangster started with
Vernons' Pool as an inheritance to underwrite his own
quest for the great races of the Turf. After years of success,
Sangster, self-deprecating about his racing despite huge

accomplishments as an owner was asked, how do you make £1 million? Echoing the sentiment often expressed by those in the aviation business, alluding to the cost of running airlines, he would advise: 'Easy. Start with £2 million and invest in horses.'

In one of Black's bathrooms at home there is a copy of *Rough Guide to the Internet*, alongside *Gentleman's Guide to Calculating Winning Bets*. A large – even by Black's standards – dog patrols the gateway to this unofficial library. He represents just one of the obstacles – saliva enough to drown a grown man – to those seeking secrets into how to turn an Internet start-up into an entity worth a multiple of at least 100 of the original investment staked.

Black's grandfather was Sir Cyril Black, a Member of Parliament for Britain's Conservative Party and, as a Baptist, a most outspoken opponent of legalising betting shops. To his grandson, who clearly didn't inherit Sir Cyril's anti-betting gene, the logic to starting up Betfair was very simple. 'I looked at the betting market before 2000,' he recalls. 'My main take was that it was addressed in a dull and predictable manner. Regarding the Internet, bookmakers in Britain knew that they had to incorporate this new outlet. But when they did they showed their over-all lack of imagination. They just transferred their established business model for retail betting to the Internet. I decided I wanted to come up with something, myself, that would have an impact.'

Black sums up bookmakers' approach with a nod to the logic behind turkeys not voting for Christmas. Book-makers had a business model featuring retail outlets, nationwide. Internet operations were sustainable with-out incurring the cost of such a network of shops. But for

bookmakers to create markets that offer something reflecting those different lower costs – in other words, better odds
on an exchange – more attractive to customers on the Internet, over and above what they were offering in their shops,
they would have to accept that the web would damage their
main business. 'The reality was that they couldn't go down
a different road because that would interfere with the overall business plan,' Black reasons. 'Instead they stuck to the
original model, which was suboptimal.'

Back before the millennium, and ahead of talking with
Ed Wray in the summer of 1998, Black was partially occupied with an Internet idea he had that involved football; a
predictive programme that would assess the odds on a
football match taking in all manner of variables and ultimately giving you a price that could be compared to the
bookmakers' best offer. His logic was that football was a
growing market.

He laughs. 'I couldn't find a buyer and probably also
didn't do a very good job selling. I didn't know how. I
tried Ladbrokes. I had a few conversations there until they
walked away. William Hill? I didn't even get through the
door there. I went to the *Racing Post*. They showed some
interest but no more than that. Frustrating. I wanted to
produce the definitive football model and could see exactly
how to do it. I could visualise it and I understood the maths
completely.'

At least the *Racing Post* proved an early opportunity
to road-test thinking behind the Betfair concept. 'At the
time of working on the football model, I was thinking
through the betting exchange,' Black recalls. 'After I had
discussed my football model with the *Racing Post*, I had
another long conversation about exchanges. I told them

how my exchange would work. I had already produced a model of it. I cannot remember if I showed anyone this. Certainly I did explain that in the future we would not be talking about horses being 3–1, 7–2 or 4–1, that we would be saying 3.4, or 3.7, and also that we would say "buy and sell" instead of "bet and lay", and that the whole market would fluctuate on the Internet. One day someone is going to make this happen, I said. The people at the *Racing Post*, they just smiled.'

Black, himself, now beams. He continued around the houses. 'I began to tell everybody about this idea. I wasn't secretive at all. I went to see more and more people. At the start, I began by saying, "I've this nice little idea." Still no one was interested. Over time I began to say, "this is going to be big, huge; this is not going to make a little bit of money but hundreds of millions." As time went on the more outspoken I became. I visited a friend who was also setting up an Internet-based company. I said to him, "sure you might make a bit of money. But me? I am going to make many, many times more what you think you might make. And it will happen," I added. All completely outspoken and over the top.'

Black was banging his own drum, loudly and repeatedly. Nobody seemed to pay him the slightest bit of attention, he recalls.

At the same time, Black was working on a range of web projects for clients. He was paid for all that work, luckily. 'With the betting exchange idea on my own I was just very naive in putting together a business, actually "monetising" the idea,' he shrugs. 'But I wasn't naive in terms of building the model. I had created one – a good one. I just never managed to sell it.'

Prospects did improve at Jeremy Wray's summer party in 1998 at the Young Chelsea Bridge Club. Black spoke to his cards partner's brother, Ed. 'What I needed was a partner who could compensate for my weaknesses,' Black confides. 'If Ed had not come along, the whole thing would have been a complete disaster. As a schoolboy, I had got to know Jeremy. We had become mates very quickly. [He was] a route to a different set of mates to the ones I had grown up with in Wimbledon, so quite exciting. In fact, I told Jeremy about the idea. "Interesting," he said. But he was doing his own thing. He did, however, mention it to Ed.'

Black believes it helped that Ed Wray only knew him largely through bridge. He pauses, before seeking to put himself into perspective. 'I had a vision. I outlined it to mates of mine. They would think to themselves, this is a good idea, why hasn't anyone else thought of it. Then friends would look at me and think, it is Andrew [or Bert if close], this is just not going to happen. He is just not cut out for business. Too much of an idiot. People in business? They were different to me, was the logic. I wasn't that type. I was just some crazy, day-dreaming fool.' On his own, Black shrugs, his friends were probably right.

The conversation at Jeremy Wray's summer party was combative. Black recalls Ed Wray quickly assumed the devil's advocate role. '"I hear you have some idea," was how Ed began,' Black remembers. 'I talked him through it. I had created a version, which I still have, of the exchange, which meant I was able to put prices in and see how it would work. I said to Ed, the world is not going to be the same at all in the future, that with the Internet we would be talking about odds of 3.4 and not

the traditional fractions, 3–1, 4–1. I gave him the spiel I
gave to the *Racing Post*. He was quick to push back at
me but I had answers. He obviously realised quite
quickly, "heh, you have thought about this a bit". In some
ways he asked the same questions as others but he was
much more methodical. Maybe because he knew me as
a bridge player, first and foremost, there was less of
"Black, the buffoon" in his mind. Bridge is an intellectual game and I am a good player and deserving of the
corresponding respect. Sure, Ed probably thought that
I was a bit crazy. Most people did. But he wasn't so familiar with the downsides to me that others knew.'

It would be another ten months before Ed Wray signed
up. That was the time it took for him to embark on a
sabbatical from matters at J.P. Morgan and decide that
Black was worth a punt. 'He obviously didn't think that
I had the world at my feet [sufficiently to] give up his job
straightaway,' Black concludes.

As bankers might consider, the opportunity cost of
Wray fully terminating his lucrative employment in the
City of London at J.P. Morgan to take up the challenge of
turning Black's idea into a reality was substantial. For one,
his salary would drop, pretty much to zero. Indeed, this
does not include the losses his decision to sign up meant
for the world of cooking. Wray, in Black's eyes at something of a crossroads in his life – hence the possibility of
a sabbatical – was on a cookery course. He disputes the
notion, commonly held, that the main reason for taking
up cooking was to meet girls.

Wray's take on Black's idea (which Black, himself,
confirms) was that he thought the potential was a lot
smaller. 'I didn't do a lot of technical analysis of this by

looking through market assessments to see the scale of what we were embracing. I did it another way and worked out what people, on average, might bet, and how many of them would we need to make the company work. As an industry, betting was ripe for innovation then. Fundamentally, things were the same as in the Sixties. Things were perfect for change. The punters were ready.'

Ultimately, the degree to which the market was ready took Wray by surprise. 'Bert, himself, was a punter. He would say that the service he received was shocking. Still, I thought things would turn out to be a lot smaller. Of course, I massively underestimated how much people gamble. Bert would laugh when I suggested what we might manage. "Ed, look at me," he would say. I actually realised two months after launching how much I had underestimated things.'

Wray insists: 'I always believed that there was an opportunity in sport. I was a reasonably enthusiastic punter, a few spread bets on cricket, bets with bookmakers on horses. I would buy the *Racing Post* when I went racing just to make sure no one was in any doubt that I knew what I was talking about. Spread betting, itself, was way too complicated. I worked on the trading floor at J.P. Morgan. I understood because of that. But other intelligent people were baffled by spread betting. With Betfair, I did think there might be an issue with how many people would understand how to lay bets. In fact, once we were launched and the website up, most people took to that very quickly. The immediately healthy trading element of the site surprised me. Very quickly, we saw people back a horse at the equivalent odds of 5–1 then lay off at 3–1, and back a bit more at 7–2.'

Wray now looks back even further for confirmation of why he was drawn to Betfair and sensed that the business plan had real foundations. 'Even when I was at J.P. Morgan it used to drive me mad how under utilised sports was. A huge industry; you would see millions of people going to watch football at the weekend. I would always think, how little focus there was to what they were watching and their experience. As for betting, the market was completely one-sided. Normally, if you thought something was too cheap you could buy it and if it was too expensive you could sell it. In betting that was not the case. Even on the Internet. Established bookmakers were taking their models online on the basis that if something worked to one format it would work in every format. The football World Cup in France, 1998, was when online sports betting started really to establish itself. But it was no different to what was offered before.'

Sitting in his Betfair chairman's office adjacent to the boardroom and with a pool of Personal Assistants outside, Wray pauses to look out over the Thames. Some clear, blue thinking is coming, most likely incisive, something of a personal trait. He is less likely to stray in conversation than Black. He stays on track, and, when veering off-course, is quick to correct himself, giving the impression that time should not be wasted (no bad things in his world which can change rapidly). What he is about to recall would have saved the wasted time – and money – of a thousand Internet start-ups, on behalf of all their investors. At the time of Betfair's own birth, Wray remembers some of the best advice he has ever received. 'It was a fellow from Goldman Sachs,' Wray confides. 'He made me really believe that Bert and I were on to something. He said, "ask yourself three questions: does the business model appeal intrinsically? Would it have worked twenty years ago? Could it work now, thanks to the Internet? If the answers to these three questions are yes, no, yes, then you have a chance." I asked myself the questions. The answers were yes, no, and yes.'

Ed Wray's office at Betfair's headquarters does offer wonderful views of the Thames. On the walls are pictures of iconic sportsmen, among them Muhammad Ali and Roger Federer. They are showed in action, in their working clothes; boxer's trunks and tennis whites. Often, Wray's corporate fatigues are some distance from classic, City of London style. He is out of J.P. Morgan now, and in general there is a relaxed policy to dress at Betfair's offices. Consequently, Wray is frequently without a tie. Actually, cuff links with the crest of Worcester College, Oxford, where he studied engineering, economics, and management, are a better indication of Wray's personal attitude to business wardrobe etiquette. For all the days he arrives in an open-neck shirt, he is more formal, than informally disposed. You suspect there is a tie or two in the desk drawers.

He is formal by nature, perhaps shy, withdrawn even. Mark Davies confesses that sometimes he is left bewildered by Wray's inability to express that something is beyond him or temporarily confounding ahead of a proper analysis of the issue (and most likely a solution). You send a question to him relating to an issue for some feedback or initial thoughts which, for one reason or another, he cannot answer, Davies laments. Then nothing, no email, no phone call, no message. Just silence, he shrugs ...

Andrew Black – who, after all, knows him well – confirms that Wray can be a bit remote. 'Some find him easily threatened,' he suggests. 'Push him too hard and he can just cut himself off. Ed rarely trusts someone the first time he meets them.' Wray is equally cautious about money, Black confides. 'Sean Patterson was our finance director. He is incredibly posh – related to Princess Di, I think – with a huge tongue that doesn't seem to fit in his mouth. He would say, we have no money. Ed would panic. I'd say, if we haven't enough, let's raise some more.' With emphasis, Black maintains that Wray is highly, highly intelligent. To him their relationship during Betfair's early days was akin to being at sea. 'Two people, almost brothers, stuck on a ship adrift with neither able to escape the other,' he explains.

From what is in essence the bridge of Betfair, Wray smiles while returning to the past and less comfortable moments. Of course, in the matter of getting Betfair off the ground, funding was far from simply an amusing distraction. In this, Black and Wray quickly found that the market offered fewer rich pickings than the strength of their idea – and Black's conviction – perhaps warranted.

The primary difficulty was that Flutter had been before them. When Betfair went to the market with a business plan, most of the institutions which might have been predisposed to backing a business of Betfair's type had indeed coughed up investment for someone else.

Flutter was an American-backed company professing to have a claim on exactly the concept that Betfair was rolling out. Slick, inclusive sales pitches to big business and venture capitalists speaking the same language had been well received at a time when, thanks to the dot.com boom, it was a sellers' market.

Wray grimaces at the memory: 'We got our business plan out before the Christmas of 1999,' he recalls. 'We had a few meetings and failed miserably to get any interest, except from our lawyers who said they would work for us in return for a stake in the business. I had raised money for companies through the public bond market, sometimes £500 million at a time. But this was different. Raising five million, four million, one million? Altogether different.'

It was a stressful time. After failure to generate any interest up to the end of 1999, for the New Year, the pair had changed tack. Institutions had shown almost contempt, other than those that had invested already in potential rivals and were keen to check out the competition. Investors predisposed to gambling like Stuart Wheeler had said, no. Using their shared knowledge of the City, Black and Wray drew up a list of former colleagues and associates from the City who would – they knew – in the spring be receiving notification of what bonuses they were due to be paid. Letters inviting them to speculate on Betfair arrived after they learnt what rich pickings they were due but – crucially – before bank accounts were credited.

Black and Wray, along with Davies, ended up courting the likes of Simon Champ, stockbroker and sometime hugely successful Betfair punter. Probably as important as the £25,000 that he invested (a friend kicked in the same to make £50,000 in total) was the government Enterprise Investment Scheme, which ensured tax breaks for those who came aboard. In addition to the fruits of timely correspondence, very welcome indeed, Wray reflects.

At this stage, other figures – key to Betfair's success – began to emerge. Two of particular consequences were

Dwayne Williams, a New Zealander, and JoJo Primrose. The former was Black's wingman in IT terms. In four months – bloody quick considering its size, notes Black – the pair created a website with gismos and flash movies aplenty, along with, to Black's mind, superb artwork. 'We nailed it,' he claims. In her own way, Primrose, recruited to oversee marketing, did, too. As well as the front of the *Sunday Times* Business Section the weekend before launch, Betfair made national radio *Five Live* the weekend that followed. Ed Wray featured in a discussion on the then Charlie Whelan Show.

In earnest, Andrew Black began work on Betfair's website in February 2000. Overall, for all the site's complexities it was the simplicity of Betfair.com that was its strength. Indeed, this remains the case today. Designed by a serious punter, namely Black, the site accommodated the needs of that constituency.

Black remembers the competition. 'Back then, there was Betmart, Betswap, a few others; they all went live at around the same time,' he recalls, with a smile. 'Then Flutter, and after us, Betdaq. Betmart, Betswap, Flutter, they had all gone down the same road, whereas we had taken a completely different one. Most of the sites were created in the image of eBay. Most had also raised money on that basis. At the time, that was the market: what is going to be the new eBay, how will an eBay for betting work?'

Critically, Betfair's site had the capacity at high speed to aggregate bets. Indeed, that was what made it an exchange in the financial sense of the word, rather than a market like eBay that brought buyer and seller together. If one person wanted to lay a bet of £100, then one, two, three, however many players could take part in the bet. Again, the best use of money.

Black saw Betfair as akin more to the New York Stock Exchange (the model that he had in mind when creating the site). As well as aggregation shortcomings, the limits to the majority of market rivals at the time, including Flutter, was their sites' inability to behave like a bookmaker. On Betfair, thanks to an exposure algorithm, you could lay a horse to win for say £10 at odds of 10–1, and stand to lose £100, and in the same race take another bet on a different horse for £100 to win at odds of even money. Both events could not occur so you would not be exposed to losses of more than £100 and Black programmed, accordingly, in a way that others struggled to match. Betfair was a true exchange and not just simply a gamblers' dating agency with bets unable to sit together in parallel.

The role of honour for the site begins with Dwayne Williams, according to Black. As principal wingman, he was paid £42 an hour for three months, then a princely £50 after some renegotiations. Black might want a flash movie down the side of the page, or a new scroll bar. It was Black's tune and Williams danced.

Williams, now back home and working for SRG Group, recalls arriving ahead of Betfair's launch from the Southern Hemisphere with his wife for some sightseeing. Ultimately, their intention was in getting work to sustain excursions to mainland Europe and around the UK. He laughs. 'It was pure luck that I ended up at Betfair. I had no betting experience and had been in London for only two weeks. I sent my CV to an agency, got a call back within fifteen minutes about an interview. In the end it was down to just me and one other guy [who, incidentally, joined Williams at Betfair later]. There was some negotiation over my rate of pay but I wanted the job.'

Office hours were, routinely, 8am to 10pm. Having been interviewed by both Black and Wray, Williams remembers a phone call from the former advising him to forget the suit when he started. 'There were other sites to look at, including Flutter,' reflects Williams, also recalling that socks and sandals met the dress code. 'Actually, we didn't really look at any other sites. With Flutter [which launched just ahead of Betfair], we discussed it, sure, and looked to check it out. But from a technical point of view I felt that we had the edge, at least initially. Andrew would talk to me, sometimes on a very technical level. He sat on my shoulder and conveyed to me what he wanted. Clearly, he understood betting systems. Altogether, we kept it clean and simple to use. Of course, we also made the site as fast as possible. In IT, you are always aware of speed. In this, the matching process was central, a core area. Also the responsiveness of the site. Those were areas on which we concentrated. To be honest, much of the concept went over my head at first. I am not a gambler. It did take me quite a while to get my head round what exactly Andrew had in mind. He had a prototype, I was working to his specifications. Then further down the track the magic of the matching began to grab me.'

Williams was first in, along with Anuraag Jain, an Indian specialist in databases. 'A man called Vikram left after about a month,' Williams remembers. 'A couple of months after that, Mick Whiffin joined to help out with Project Management and work on the Admin tool. Actually, he was the one who originally went for the web developer job at Betfair. He was with us for about six months or so. Shortly after launch Martin Baines, a South African, and Greg Solomon, like me from New Zealand, took up the numbers. We were never more than seven, the initial core development team.'

The area of development that caused greatest concern was the database. The server could be boosted but, as Williams explains, the database was a single box of fixed size. Increasing that to cope with growth of the site, once up and running, was the greatest challenge. Substance to Black's claim that he and the team 'nailed it' is that today, there are still plenty of the original concept in the site. 'Of course, it is so much more polished,' Williams concedes. 'I also had no idea how big it would become. Seeing people use the site – for the first time when we went live in June [2000] – has always been the biggest thing for me.'

Back in late March, the website had been nearly two months in development. The recruitment of JoJo Primrose at this time ahead of a proposed launch in June gave her less than twelve weeks to devise and execute a publicity campaign that would propel Betfair to the head of what seemed to be an increasingly competitive market.

The main concern within Betfair about launching the company, which Primrose (formerly at Bloomberg as well as News International), shared with Black, Wray, and Williams was that the concept would be intelligible to the layman, not least journalists, and that the website was easy to use. Black had largely taken care of the latter. To meet the former challenge, Primrose, without any grasp of betting prior to joining Betfair, established a 'sales spiel' from listening to the likes of Black talk about the site and its capabilities. 'Simply a stock market for betting was the line,' she recalls.

A further concern that emerged for Primrose, who after three months travelling after leaving *The Times* passed up employment at a new web wine 'exchange' to work for Betfair, was the difficulty of finding a public relations and marketing agency to take Betfair's money. Agencies were at the time increasingly sensitive to situations where there was an element of doubt as to whether the client was good for the bill – Lastminute.com had just crashed adding to a sense of distrust. Primrose was used to agency 'beauty pageants' when looking for someone to share in *The Times'* seven-figure budgets, so Betfair's quandary was a culture shock. She recalls the depth of gratitude she felt towards a company called Circus when the team there agreed to take on Betfair's cause.

On reflection, altogether more straightforward was the marketing strategy, itself. Micro management by Primrose of her £120,000 budget to the satisfaction of proudly prudent Ed Wray was easily achieved. She just didn't tell him that the plan was to spend £20,000 on a launch party. Primrose laughs that Wray could never grasp why such events were so expensive. Needed for such a launch event was an accompanying buzz to register with those who would be Betfair's early client base. 'We knew that at first this wasn't going to be mass market so we had two initial targets, those in the City of London and the readers of the *Racing Post* whom we saw as dedicated gamblers,' Primrose explains.

'Circus came up with the idea of a New Orleans-style funeral procession with a coffin through the City. The idea was that Betfair was the death of the bookmaker. At the launch party – which we held in a Sports Café – we also had people impersonating bookmakers who were picketing the site protesting against their demise. Bert loved the idea. Ed was not so sure. He felt we shouldn't antagonise bookmakers in that we were entering that market, ourselves.'

The notion resonated at least with the *Sunday Times* Business Section picture desk. Primrose still bristles with pride at grabbing for Betfair what represents hallowed space in corporate minds. 'Their pages are usually so boring that they much prefer someone doing a stunt, preferably in a bikini,' she jokes. 'I was told, "set up the picture of the bookmakers' funeral, we might do the story".' The result was that Black and Wray donned clothes as required to convey the message that the book-makers were on the way out. This hit page one on 4 June, before the following week's launch with Primrose spending the night before gripped with anxiety about how the photo and accompanying text would play.

Primrose remembers that very quickly, the *Racing Post* sensed that readers would have a keen interest in the new venture (and subsequent reviews – largely favourable – of what Betfair had to offer reflected this). Within weeks of launching, Betfair adverts were soon carried along with enthusiastic letters from punters who had used the site – also important, Primrose stresses. The significance of the adverts was that it meant that the betting industry's news-paper considered Betfair to be *bona fide*. With hindsight, Primrose notes the significance and also the overall ben-efits. 'The *Racing Post* gave us a route to the hard-core gambler,' she explains. 'This was a godsend. The paper also gave us credibility. The *Racing Post* cannot just take anyone's adverts inviting readers to bet with them. They have to be sure that whatever organisation is paying them for advertising space is not simply a set-up to take punters' money. The paper came to see us. Those of the team that visited who were gamblers were quickly sold on the concept. Actually, they became our champions within the *Racing Post* office. We would take full-page adverts with a graphic of a horse's head and speech bubbles coming out suggesting what the horse might be thinking.'

Today Primrose lives in a bucolic retreat with a burgeoning brood far away from corporate affairs such as those of Betfair. Williams is on the other side of the world. Thousands of miles from him and a distant memory to Primrose, save the one local to her – few places are cut completely adrift – are bookmakers. Inevitably, they had to come into Betfair's frame of reference at some stage following launch.

For Primrose, the easiest marketing tag was 'come and be a bookie'. Guided by Mark Davies, Betfair was careful not to repeat claims that bookmakers were now dead and invite clients, accordingly. The difficulty with that was there was potential to make Betfair a regulatory issue. The inference was clear; if you are playing at being a book-maker you should have a licence and would need to pay tax.

Tax itself was a complex matter for Betfair as turnover – in the early stages of trading when duty was levied on that figure – was not the same for a betting exchange as in a betting shop. Betfair secured a tax status from the Treasury, which reflected this.

In the early days, overall, bookmakers' attitudes towards Betfair were verging on the pathological. Wray recalls the depth of animosity in bookmakers at the time.

'At first they dismissed us, then they became utterly paranoid, but we never thought that we would destroy their
markets,' he pleads. 'When I did our business plan I looked
at the demographics in Britain of the betting shop trade.
We genuinely thought that we would actually grow that
market a little bit for them, with only a little bit of cannibalisation at the margins.'

The problem was that in growing, Betfair was hitting
bookmakers in their pockets. Betfair players – as *de facto*
bookmakers offering other players odds – were unencumbered with the cost of maintaining nationwide retails
outlets. Accordingly, odds on Betfair were often better
than with bookmakers. In Britain, the odds that are paid
out in a betting shop are actually determined by the market
for betting at the races. Trade on Betfair grew sufficiently
to begin to have a depressing effect on the margins at the
track, which in turn hit bookmaker profitability. Indeed,
once allowed, on-course bookmakers added laptops to
their day-to-day equipment for all-weathers at Ascot,
Aintree, Cheltenham and the rest. This meant the Betfair
market further shaped racecourse odds.

According to John Brown, then of William Hill, bookmakers had two grievances related to this. By sanctioning
Betfair's tax position, the Treasury was virtually blessing
Betfair, making it altogether much harder to contest the
concept on regulatory grounds. What's more, Brown
believes that Betfair only survived infancy because of
betting tax's abolition, which at the time was paid by bookmakers on turnover. The abolition of betting tax in 2001
and its replacement by a tax on gross profits was largely
reckoned to be Brown's idea. There can be no doubt that
he didn't aim with this proposal to ensure Betfair avoided

crippling tax based solely on turnover. In Betfair's case, because of the churning nature of the exchange model, the tax burden would have been prohibitively high.

From the company's very outset, Betfair confounded bookmakers with its approach to customers. Betfair's slogan today, '*Betting as it should be*', has a reassuring tone. There is a warmth to it, largely absent from the advertisements and branding of Ladbrokes and other major players. Back in 2000, the company had not yet struck on the beautiful simplicity of the phrase. Nevertheless, punters were, in contrast to bookmakers' customer care, treated differently.

Behind this catchphrase lie some major peculiarities. As well as welcoming customers to their own world, the approach today is to divide punters into categories such as 'serious', 'enthusiastic', 'occasional', and 'big stakes', and then seek to meet their demands and needs, reducing the likelihood that they might spend time away from the site. In this, Betfair retains its individual take on the business of betting, even though it now warrants a place alongside the gambling Establishment. Betfair stays very close to the website's winners, Andrew Black says laughingly. 'We need both winners and losers to work. Sometimes I take one of the former out for golf.'

As with spread betting, bookmakers' attitudes to Betfair changed over time beginning with launch weekend. 'Radio Five was the Sunday after the Derby following our launch the previous day, and I was in a studio at the BBC,' Wray recalls. 'England had a game in the European Football Championship Finals of that summer. One of the bookmakers' PR men was linked to the studio by phone. He said, it is a nice idea, Betfair will be sure to interest people but exchanges won't work out because punters will still favour their own betting shop or regular bookmakers. Except, we were offering odds on England to win Euro 2000 that were much better than the same bookmakers.'

By the following year, relations were deteriorating (or as Black would explain, from the contemptuous to the confrontational). Wray remembers: 'Early in, I think, 2001, Channel 4 television was broadcasting racing from Sandown. It was a midweek day, so not even the week-end. Anyway, in between covering races, the programme featured a piece with Mark [Davies] where he talked about exchanges. One of Ladbrokes, William Hill or Coral rang up to complain. They demanded airtime. They got it and their complaints were taken apart. It was the best thing that could have happened. Mark's interview was fine. I am sure viewers found it interesting. But the majority would have said, OK, whatever. But as soon as a book-maker came on to declare vehement opposition to the idea people thought, hang on a minute'. Share an enemy, make a friend.

Of the solutions available to bookmakers, two stood out. Firstly – and probably most sensible – bookmakers might have set up their own exchange, either individually or collectively. Certainly there are grounds for arguing that Internet and betting shop are two different markets. They could therefore have at least tried, despite the poten-tial problems two different sets of prices might bring. In rejecting this remember that bookmakers also had long enough memories to recall their entry into the world of spread betting, followed by their relatively hasty exist; (incidentally, Black thinks that in this respect, experiences of spread betting were very important).

A second plan would have been to try and buy Betfair, hardly uncommon in similar market situations. Then, equally common, Betfair could have been wound up. This strategy was undermined by Betfair's apparent reluctance to sell at anything less than the high valuation placed on the company by its founders, which had risen considerably in no time from £5 million during funding, to, comfortably, an eight-figure sum. Black recalls, in return for a stake in Betfair, one of Europe's most respected financial services operations making a move before a merger with Flutter removed the need to seek outside funding.

'We were running out of money,' Black shrugs. 'We were actually practically insolvent. But we had delivered a classy website from the prototype I had originally developed. I knew we had a good product. All the statistics were pointing in our favour. That said, the dot.com market was collapsing around us.'

Black relates that the potential investors (confidentiality agreements prevent Black from naming them) had shown an interest in the Internet and had invested in 'some big chunks of other stuff' at the time. 'We decided to negotiate with them. There was a guy from there who was a smart operator. He had seen our site and thought we were going places. "You are going to rule", was how he put it. We discussed an investment based on valuation of the company that was eight figures. We were happy enough with that. At the same time companies around us were halving in value.'

All was set, until just before the deal was due to be signed. 'They came back,' Black, still incredulous, recalls. 'They said that the market was in a bad way, but that they would still like to invest, only at a lower figure valuation.'

A valuation 25 per cent down on the original deal? Not a big issue, Wray maintained. Black disagreed. 'I thought under the terms of the original deal they were getting us on the cheap. "Look at our numbers," I said. "I don't care about the rest of the market.""

Looking back, Black maintains that it was the right call. '[There were] all these companies on the Internet then with their projected revenues with money coming from other Internet companies. We were different, and all on our own. Money has always come direct to us from our customers, totally independent. We were unaffected by the market and didn't have a business plan that was projecting that the company would make money in five years' time.'

Wray was, says Black, horrified at losing the deal. 'I said, "I will not have these guys take the piss." Ed and I argued. We went to see Sean, our finance director. He was depressed. Ed called our prospective partners back and said we were not moving on our valuation. So that was that.'

Black was unmoved. 'I said, "guys, this is a fantastic company. Anyone should feel privileged to invest." Sean argued, "we have no money, we are going to have to shut up shop. No money. Fact."' Black reckoned otherwise. 'I insisted,' he recalls. 'We are going to the moon.'

Lift off with launch on 9 June, when Betfair took over £1,000 on a race, had heartily confirmed in Black's mind that he 'was on to something'. He was right, Wray – on this occasion – wrong and one of Europe's financial giants missed out on owning what would amount to a tidy investment. Growth in Betfair was encouraging. Equally, progress was a source of both great excitement and also, less obviously, frustration. Betfair ultimately became

Britain's biggest sponsor in terms of number of races carrying Betfair support. But in the first two years of the company, advertising would have to be reined in when the site and support systems became unable to cope with additional users signing up. Ed Wray shakes his head. 'I still look back with frustration at the times when we have had to restrain growth. You think, what a lovely problem to have. But when it happens you feel instead that you have reached this position and the system cannot cope, while all along you have been working as hard as you can. OK, you think, buy more servers. Then you are told that will take six weeks.'

He recalls the really early days when inevitably there were some technical problems. 'People were very supportive when the site crashed. Back then, I would sometimes help out with the phones. A customer would call in to complain and I'd answer. "Who are you, exactly?" I'd be asked. Ed Wray, CEO was the answer. The response after that was usually along the lines that the client was just disappointed not to be able to access the site.'

Betfair had established a chat room in which customers would express their feelings – that is when they were able to get back online. An early decision was that there would be an absolute minimum of censorship in this space which became something of a perennial hang-out for, among others, nerdy gamblers, at least according to JoJo Primrose. As well as answering phones every now and then, Wray would join the cyber debate in an effort to address grievances. 'I would steel myself before entering the chat room,' he says laughing.

The broad corporate shoulders of Betfair managed to absorb the worst the public could throw. At the same time, bookmaker attacks on Betfair remained relentless. Black, Wray, and Davies were surprised, not that bookmakers came after them – of course that was going to happen – but by the vitriol of their assault on Betfair's very being from the beginning.

On the other side of the world now, Dwayne Williams, knowing both Black and Wray, laughs at their recollections of the failed deal with a European financial giant hoping to take a stake on the cheap. He still feels a little protective over the baby he helped create. Like Black, Williams takes almost parental pride in the work he completed for Betfair before calling time on his European odyssey. Looking back, he confesses that he did become rather anchored.

Williams had the honour of being given the Number One Account. As Betfair No. 1, and the man responsible, in the eyes of Andrew Black, for crafting a website that has taken Betfair well beyond a scale that even the most optimistic might have imagined, the Kiwi ponders his decision to receive simply an hourly rate rather than equity.

You might laugh. You might cry. Williams opts for the former, and chuckles, dryly, when the matter is raised. 'After three months, I discussed it with Andrew. I knew that if I took shares I could be tied down. At the time, I thought I might well end up working in a few different places.' There is a moment of silence. 'I do wonder,' he adds, though the laugh that follows suggests not for so long.

Black remembers the discussions. 'I used to try and persuade him to take a stake. He came over from New Zealand and wanted to work for three years. He virtually stepped off the plane and came straight to our offices. I suppose he got out of it what he wanted. He left for home with a fair bit of money. He worked like a slave. I would say dance to this tune and he would dance. A very intelligent guy. Everything he did was to the standard I worked.'

Those of the original 170 backers who did keep the faith, though not exactly working like slaves, were handsomely rewarded when the SoftBank deal facilitated the sale of initial stakeholdings for up to 132 times the original investment. Many invested more than once, including those involved in the very first whip round. 'Everyone we rang to ask a second time for money said yes,' recalls Black. 'The reality was that while the dot.com world was collapsing everything we had ever said about Betfair had happened. It was clear that we had delivered in spades. We did not have a begging bowl. We had hit our targets. What we were really asking was, do you want another piece of it because we are going to let you in for more.'

Both Black and Wray recall meeting up with those whom they had invited to invest but had declined. 'They would sometimes complain, why didn't you persuade me more,' Wray smiles. Black, himself, relays that some former friends no longer talk to him having missed out.

Williams seems genuinely incapable of harbouring a grudge, although he does take mock umbrage that he can't even trade using his historic No. 1 account. 'A while back, I received a Betfair "Know Our Customer" email. I was required to supply some ID proving that I was who I said I was.' Williams jokes: 'Naturally, I refused on principle and they shut me down.'

IT can produce surprisingly strong emotions. Periodically, Black becomes almost tearful with nostalgia, whispering his recollections in reliving this period of Betfair. Not least when considering the part played by Williams, whom he decided to hire at the same time that his wife, Jane, was in labour (another reason, perhaps, for Black's deep attachment). 'If we had hired anyone else it would have been a different story,' Black insists. 'He was the superstar. Where we really landed on our feet was IT. I still don't really know how it happened. If I did anything for the company in the early years, in addition that is to having the idea for Betfair in the first place, that was routinely to clear out the IT development team. I would get frustrated. Folk would come in and quickly show that they simply didn't get it. I would say to Ed, "they have to go". Betfair was a difficult site to build. We – a small, elite team – built it really well.'

To Betfair's IT success there is an amusing footnote. The original business plan devised by Ed Wray for Betfair is in his possession. Its password is locked for safe keeping but Wray has forgotten the code. Even Williams cannot apparently help him, other than to suggest he tries 'Betfair'.

As for the history of Betfair, an important detail needs clarification. For some weeks after JoJo Primrose began work as head of marketing, what Andrew Black had created was nameless. Needless to say, Primrose's job was directly – and greatly – affected by this. This was not least because one of the ideas he'd had was PollyParrot.com. Or, worse still, in Primrose's view, Flutter, a word from the 19th century that meant the consequences of a sexual encounter, that more importantly would not resonate with exactly the sort of high rollers who were needed for success.

There is some disagreement as to the origins of the name, Betfair. Universally accepted is that The Sporting

Exchange, the corporate billing under which Black and Wray had set up the company and continue to use today, was never an option. Even though it was, as required by law, to be always on the office door, from Wimbledon up. Simply, the domain name had gone.

Today, Black and Primrose remain on the most friendly of terms. She chuckles. 'Sporting Exchange? It became clear that "sporting" was too obscure a synonym for betting and the exchange technology bit needed to be explained to be understood. Betfair? Yes, that was one of a number of names we considered. We put it to a simple office vote. I cannot remember what the others were. Bert? I seem to recall that he favoured something different. In the end we were pretty near launching. We didn't spend days on it. It was just a quick decision – short, memorable, the double meaning of "a fair" where people come to bet together and "fair odds", compared to the bookmakers. Plus it began with "B" which thus kept its position in alphabetical lists of bookmakers.'

Andrew Black doesn't dispute the logic. Yet with Primrose's recollection of events he has some reservations (as did Mark Davies about the name Betfair, which, he now confesses, he didn't like at all). He also disregards Davies' recollection that Open Market Betting was used ahead of Betfair's christening and that Ed Wray determined the final name. Betfair was his suggestion, he claims.

'One evening, the name came to me,' Black maintains. 'It was a painful process. We were going to be Sportex in order to be more about sport than betting. That had gone and we were not going to enter into an agreement to buy the domain name. I was getting frustrated trying to work out names. I would arrive at the office every morning and throw a few out there. Once I had come up with Betfair, I liked it. It had two sides to it; the fun fair or a fair, antiques, say, where things were bought and sold. And it also suggested that bets through the site were just.'

He recalls the decisive moment, the morning after his epiphany. 'I would come in each morning. Every now and then I had a new idea; Bet Community, Bet Mart – there was one of those, eventually. I would go through the various options. I didn't think it had to have the word bet or betting in the name. But I was still tearing my hair out. Once I had settled on Betfair – I really did like the dual aspect – I turned up at work and said to everyone I was going to write in marker pen all the options for a name I could think of on the board that was on the wall. So I began with Community Bet, then Polly Parrot which people would certainly remember, and in a list of seven, Betfair at the end. Then we went through them and got to the end. At this point, I said, "all the fun of the fair, fair company, only two syllables, and short, easy to remember". Consensus was that the last one was best.'

Chapter FIVE

REVERSE MOP-UP

'*You Bet: The Flutter Story and how two men changed the world of betting*'. This working title of a notional book that will now, most likely, never be written raises a chuckle from Josh Hannah. Vince Monical, who founded Flutter with Hannah and launched the company a month ahead of Betfair, also has cause for a wry smile at the notion of such a tome. To the winners, the spoils.

By the summer of 2001, two principals had emerged in the betting exchange market, Flutter and Betfair. Betfair, we now know. Flutter? An American-backed version, the company was well funded by deep venture-capital pockets, with Hannah and Monical Flutter's version of Ed Wray and Andrew Black, respectively, at least broadly speaking. The pair were, ahead of the millennium, swept up in the search for the next eBay. There had seemingly been a model for every market. Betting would be no different. Monical had the idea, Hannah shared his opinion of its merits. Together, they raised the money – over $40 million – and launched in the spring of 2000.

The following summer the first tentative moves were made to bring both operations together to create one all-powerful, well capitalised – Flutter's finances were still rock solid – exchange in what was largely perceived as a one-winner business. By Christmas time, amid great secrecy, negotiations hardened. On 31 December 2001, the two companies came together in a deal that gave 70 per cent of the new entity to Betfair and 30 per cent to Flutter.

The precise details, in particular Flutter's substantial stake in the new joint venture, were not widespread. Indeed, review the general assessments of the deal back then, or today conduct a straw poll among those in the trade, and you quickly conclude that Betfair took over Flutter, swallowing up a company that needed to find cover from the heat of competition Betfair was generating. As the *Daily Telegraph* reported, 'Online person-to-person bookmaker, Betfair, bought its rival, Flutter.com in a deal that will create a business handling more than £500 million of bets a year.' This interpretation was hardly challenged by confirmation of Ed Wray as the new holding's chief executive, in control of Hannah's baby, nor efforts to spin this. 'I'm as disappointed as hell not to be chief executive,' the *Daily Telegraph*, in the process of confirming the deal, quoted Hannah. 'Ed is one of the luckiest guys in the world.'

The *Guardian* newspaper was in little doubt what had happened. 'A couple of days before Christmas it was announced that Flutter was "merging" with Betfair,' Greg Wood, the *Guardian*'s Racing Correspondent, wrote early in 2002. 'The merger was nothing of the sort. Betfair was taking over and from that point controlled 98 per cent of the exchange market.' Bloomberg, the business news service, subsequently confirmed impressions at the time of the coming together. In 2006, looking at the deal in an article considering the success of Betfair, they concluded that Flutter had been 'outflanked'.

Mark Davies, a central figure in Betfair's communications strategy by the time of the merger, insists that Betfair 'bent over backwards' to convey a sense that the coming together between Flutter and Betfair was exactly that, namely a merger. His office is across the floor from Ed Wray's, at Betfair's Hammersmith seat of power. A copy of his father Barry's autobiography, *Interesting, Very Interesting*, stands on the shelf chronicling his broadcast career achievements. Considering how close we are to the stretch of the Thames upon which they hold the boat race, Davies could be excused for having any testimony to his own part in sporting history taking up wall space. He was in the Cambridge University Blues rowing squad from 1992 for three years, narrowly missing out during the period on a place as coxswain in the full Blues' boat that takes on Oxford annually.

Looking out onto the water where he gave no quarter, Davies ponders the notion that corporate history could have taken a different path. 'At the start of the discussions about a deal, we were seen as having won and they were seen as looking for a way out,' he reasons. 'We were salvation for all those investors who had backed the wrong horse. But if they had pulled out as talks about a merger were beginning in earnest? Maybe it would have been more damaging to us than them.'

Formerly a trader at J.P. Morgan where, ironically, he dealt for a brief time in Ladbrokes bonds, Davies leans forward, elbows on the round table in his office, and looks altogether more serious. 'In 2001, we went through a period when, because we expected to merge and knew Flutter's money would come in, we didn't try and raise money ourselves after the last – and third – round of funding in the spring,' he confides. 'Consequently, we did not invest in the website, which began to fall over, culminating in a 24-hour stoppage in October. Flutter at the time, they had the software.' He adds, candidly: 'By this point Flutter was beginning to make up significant ground.'

At launch, and in the early month of both exchanges' lives, to the lads at Betfair Flutter remained a source of amusement. 'We used to laugh at the Flutter boys a lot,' continues Davies. 'We'd joke that they were management consultants and we were bankers so they were all about presentation and gimmicks whereas we were all about execution without the thrills. We got the job done and the product was infinitely better.'

By the middle of 2001 jokes were at a premium. Flutter had undergone a wholesale revamp in the previous months, which was beginning to make an impression on Betfair's command of market share. 'Our technology was going nowhere,' Davies concedes. 'We were not coping with the volume of business being generated. As I remember it – and maybe with hindsight it wasn't so bad – we were falling over on a daily basis. Volume was too much to handle and we were not investing as we should have been.'

It is a strange scenario to ponder given today's market. Betfair stands astride the domestic and international betting exchange markets, seemingly untouchable. And yet, if Flutter had pulled out of the deal to merge that was key to today's state of affairs? Davies thinks for a moment, about this. He speaks with additional care (remember, he has a decent-sized stake in the company). 'We would have been in trouble,' he accepts, chewing on his occasional choice of confectionery, wine gum Cherry Lips. 'Certainly, we would have had to raise money fast [never a problem, in Andrew Black's opinion]. If the battle had played itself out to the full, would we have won? I do remember a conversation in January after the deal asking questions along those lines – even allowing for the possibility that without talk of merger we might have kept our foot on Flutter's throat.'

In the end it took nearly six months to bring the companies formally together in a split that broadly reflected market shares at the point at which negotiations had begun. At the end of this time, thanks to the success of Flutter's revamp, and the duration of extended talks, market share was heading north of 30 per cent for Flutter and south of 70 per cent for Betfair. Flutter also still had an eight-figure dollar balance in the bank. Andrew Black, who had during this time found himself torn between heralding Flutter's revamp – one artist appreciating another's work – and attacking his market rival for essentially copying the best of his work, remembers Ed Wray saying to him that it was great to have got what Betfair wanted, namely the favourable split. 'I said, yes, on the basis of the final result,' Black admits. 'That said, it could have ended in catastrophe. Ed was right but I still feel we risked our necks. In all, everything took far longer than necessary. We nearly lost it. Ed would say, best deal of all time and he would be right. But it would have been criminal to allow things to fall apart. Both businesses could have died. We could have cut our throats.'

Davies concurs. He leans back in his chair. This is not a moment for sweeties. His personal opinion? He nods: 'We got out of jail.'

Back in 1998 at Bain & Co, based in San Francisco, Josh Hannah, who graduated from Berkeley, and Vince Monical, a Wharton Business School alumni, barely had time between deals to ponder who had done what to whom and how, when business needed to be concluded. The pace of investment in the Internet at the time did not allow such luxuries.

In the Nineties, the two former colleagues remember a business environment very different to the one in 2008 and beyond blighted by a credit crunch with paralysis in banking. The Internet was everything. 'Then, the idea of starting an Internet business was inescapable,' recalls Hannah. 'That was all anyone talked about. John Doerr of Netscape gave a talk a couple of years before the thinking behind Flutter took shape. He said that the Internet was actually being under-hyped, which seemed ludicrous. It made the cover of *Newsweek*. He said, we're moving too slowly, Amazon is just a prototype for the future, the entire knowledge will turn over in eighteen months. Did this resonate with me? I was always a bit nerdy, but I still thought, I don't think so. Then, once I was heavily involved at Bain, the rise of the Internet was inextricable.'

At the same firm, Monical was working, adjacently, with private equity groups and venture capitalists – 'very practical and tactical'. These were hoovering up different players in the Internet person-to-person market with the intention of making them more efficient. Investment in companies such as Autoworks were done on the basis that the database could be built up.

'We – me, Vince, and another colleague, Mark Peters – were working on a number of ideas, ourselves,' Hannah remembers. 'I loved the way that eBay had created this consumer-to-consumer marketplace, compared, say, to Amazon which had simply taken a mail order business online. Before the Internet what eBay did would not have been feasible.'

Hannah was no punter, at least in a pure gambling sense. An avid poker player, he considers sports betting too remote from the action. As far as horseracing is concerned, in his native California he views the pursuit as much more of a minority passion than in Britain. The state's Bay Meadows racetrack closed in 2008 which was of little surprise to Hannah, still detached from his local Golden Gate Hill venue. 'I don't know anyone who goes,' he maintains.

Compared to Black, or even Wray, Monical was only a moderate player. 'Sometimes Vince and I would have a bet between ourselves,' confesses Hannah. 'I was no more than a casual bettor; office pools, a bit on sports when I was in Vegas. The odd $100 with Vince. After graduating, I did bet a bit on American Football. Overall fairly clueless.'

The betting market still came into their range. There was the potential for a great business model. A network of individuals would form likeminded groups. Money actually changed hands, which made the concept much more plausible than sites where, for example, it was just advice that was on offer. 'Vince and I both lived in the same Bay area,' Hannah recalls. 'One day we got the train home and he mentioned an idea that he had had about six months earlier; person-to-person betting. He said that it probably wasn't legal in many places. So that was that. I said, "heh, it is a big world. If it is not legal here in the States, it will be somewhere." I was hooked.'

The thought of applying the concept to betting began to take a deep root. Monical remembers: 'I talked to my brother, who worked at a law firm in Chicago. He established it was illegal in the US, so I sat on things for six months until that train journey. Then we set aside four months of evenings and weekends to develop a plan.' Research unearthed that by far the most plausible locations were Australia and Britain (which at the time Monical had visited for just three days en route to Monte Carlo as part of Bain's in-house training, with Hannah yet to set foot at all). It was now just a matter of time – and funding.

On the strength of a fifteen-page business plan, a venture capitalist – and this hugely reflects the times – wrote a cheque for $5 million and said to the pair, get on a plane to London. If this seems an improbable amount, Hannah reminds you to remember the era. He figures that the initial $5 million was no more than a bet on him and Monical to 'figure something out' and make a market. 'With respect to raising money, our timing was perfect,' Hannah boasts. 'Once we had arrived in the UK, we figured out how to open a bank account, rented flats, hired some people and went about setting up a business. Then we had to find further funding. In fact, the second round of funding wasn't much different to the first. Our site had still to be launched so there was nothing to see. All we had done was to hire a few people. But this is the lesson of liquidity; the first $5 million is more important than the last five. In 1999 when we went back to the market for further capital, the US market was saturated so all the big

US funds were looking to Britain, where there wasn't a tradition of venture capitalism or significant entrepreneurship in the technology sector. The VCs were looking for people like us, either known to them, or recognised.'

A pair of highly qualified American consultants closing in on a market without serious innovation in the previous forty years? Hannah maintains it is no accident that any money that was likely to be looking for an opportunity like Flutter or Betfair went to the former. To the likes of Chase Capital, Benchmark, and Bernard Arnault, chairman of LVMH (Moet Hennessy-Louis Vuitton SA), Hannah and Monical were a lot more polished than Andrew Black and Ed Wray when presenting plans for world betting domination. Flutter closed a second round of funding a further $39 million to the good, having, to Hannah's mind, 'sucked the oxygen out the market'.

Flutter was designed for mass-market participation. 'We could have built a business like eBay or Nasdaq; eBay is, of course, person-to-person,' Hannah reasons. 'On Nasdaq, you buy a share and it never actually occurs to you who sold it. The stock simply comes out of the ether into your ownership. With the benefits of scale Nasdaq could do this, whereas with eBay you had individual transaction. We thought that person-to-person betting was going to be mass market but we also thought that the social element would be key. If you are a [Tottenham] Hotspur fan and I am a Chelsea fan you might send me some taunting emails before a game. Then we would end up having a bet. The business was about this individual connection.'

Flutter's precise direction was based on two considerations; that their market shouldn't become heavy duty and that no single sport, such as horseracing, should dominate.

The first was out of necessity. Many of those who had bankrolled Flutter did not envisage the company's core endeavour to be facilitating individual punters staking huge amounts of money. For example, Arnault probably had Net-a-Porter, the fashion website, in mind as a model, simply bringing together buyers and sellers.

As for avoiding a dominance of one sport, this was strategic. Hannah and Monical simply could not begin to appreciate exactly how much certain individuals were prepared to bet on horseracing. Hannah concedes: 'We had no idea that there were people who gambled the amounts they do today and no idea that they do this on horseracing. We felt sure that Flutter could be mass market. We did a lot of things right but a few core things wrong, one of which was certainly to underestimate the size of the serious gambling market. Did Andrew and Ed know? Andrew did. We had no idea.'

Monical jokes that before he and Hannah could grasp the nature of high street betting shop culture in Britain they first had to understand what was meant by 'the high street'. Monical's logic was straight out of the bay and valley. 'We were building a product to establish a database which we would moneterise [meaning exploit commercially] later so – with the board pushing us away from the heavy bettors' market – our marketing was broadly based. We chased equally the heavy bettors, those crazy for sports, and the sports' enthusiast with the attention diffused across these three groups.'

Sitting comfortably in a London five-star hotel bar, over from America, Hannah is the model of a modern-day entrepreneur. His iPhone keeps him in touch with a young family far to the west. If Andrew Black and Ed Wray are a contrast with traditional betting culture in Britain, Hannah is a further step removed. He refers to 'The Hotspur' when he really means Tottenham or Spurs and expects good service. Hannah left Britain in 2005 some way short of being fully anglicised.

Also far away are the days when Hannah hatched Project Motorhead with the mission statement 'Kill Betfair'. Perhaps only his habit of referring to Betfair as 'them' or 'they' and Flutter as 'we' or 'us' harks back to days of old. Back then, if Project Motorhead failed, there was still Project Colin, with the same goal, specifically to take over Betfair's horseracing markets. This scheme was reputedly named because in the offices of Flutter there was an employee called Colin who – is there any easy way to say this? – looked like a horse.

Hannah sits back in his chair, comfortable in surroundings that are easily affordable to a man whose own stock in a company which he retained at the time of the merger is now worth millions of dollars. Since returning to San Francisco, he has set up the Internet operation, eHow.com that he describes as one of his two greatest business achievements, the other being Flutter. Any irritation he feels about having been portrayed as the defeated party in a corporate scrap is offset against his continued presence on the board of directors, a position he maintains out of a sense of responsibility to his original shareholders, still involved, and his own stock.

Today, he returns to the past and the point at which his journey to the Betfair boardroom began. In a world where being first to market was considered a necessity to prevail ultimately, Flutter launched in May 2000 followed,

potentially a crucial few weeks later, by Betfair. Cheaper
– at commission rate of 2.5 per cent – by 50 per cent, better
funded, and first to the market. By the end of the following year, only Betfair existed.

Hannah happily acknowledges the upside of the
coming together. 'The reason I was willing to deal was the
liquidity,' he maintains. 'There was a chance that we could
run away with the whole market. Under the terms of the
merger a 70/30 corporate split? A bit unfair. I would have
preferred 60/40. But there was so much synergy, our "30"
would grow to become a great deal more than the absolute
that was 40 at the time.'

Hannah's faith in the potential rewards from a merger
was based on a firmly-held belief that the exchange world
was a winner-takes-all market. Ahead of this, he maintains
that in the early months of trading neither company
excelled. 'Equally crappy,' he snorts. Betfair was, he
suggests (and we must remember that the Internet industry is not immune to partisan thoughts), held together with
duct tape. 'Knowing what we know now, on one hand we
cannot complain about how things worked out. But on
the other hand, we might have had a better shot [of ending
up dominant in the market] than I gave us credit for at the
time.'

Neither he nor Ed Wray will confirm who arranged
the drink over which the merger between Flutter and
Betfair was first mentioned, nor who first mooted a future
together. 'The whole objective of such a deal is to have the
other person bring the subject up,' Hannah laughs. 'The
drink? We met about something else. Talking it through
it made sense. Likewise on paper. Could we reach an agreement? We had to value our cash and their expertise.'

Any merger had difficulties attached. Not least that Andrew Black hated Hannah (with a passion, according to Mark Davies). The depth of feeling related to Black's view that the Flutter team had copied Betfair in revamping their website. To Black this was akin to copying a book someone else had written. Black, being Black, opened a Flutter account. Invited during this process to express his likes and dislikes, he nominated Betfair and copycats, respectively.

Even more substantive an obstacle was Wray's refusal to budge on a 70/30 division of the new entity in Betfair's favour, and the recruitment of a team of negotiators that even Black perceived as being unnecessarily hard-nosed.

Wray might have paid the price for extending negotiations. 'When we were in talks with Betfair, we would look at our weekly results,' Hannah reflects. 'We agreed to a 70/30 split, then, as time passed, it was, "heh, wait a minute, maybe we need to renegotiate based on our numbers. We are gaining market share." Away from the relative pleasantries of the negotiating table, where politeness always prevails, face-to-face, this meant an undercurrent of annoyance.'

Hannah laughs: 'Ed also had this fear that the deal could bankrupt his company, despite them having no money and with us having millions in the bank. He was afraid that there might be some huge liability on the books. He could not get over this until we created this vastly convoluted structure that took months of attorney time to establish. In fact, when we merged, Betfair was effectively bankrupt.'

* * *

Vince Monical takes credit for being first to have had a notion for merger. 'I identified this as a possible course of action a long time before talks began and began talking to Josh about the option,' he boasts.

Today, Monical, who like Hannah also returned to America, is director of commerce and analytics at Google. Looking back, he believes that the differences between Betfair and Flutter began the moment he and Black had the first thoughts in the direction of betting exchanges. He reasons: 'Here is how I see it. When I had the idea of person-to-person betting I started by thinking how we would raise some money to fund it. Andrew Black? He started building a prototype. That was the difference.'

Regarding the merger Monical believes that there was a bigger picture to see. 'We had to decide what was the battle and what was the war,' he reasons. 'Bookmakers were beginning to mount a campaign against exchanges. We had to fight the real enemy and the best way we could do that was together.'

Monical accepted his current position at Google in 2005, having joined in 2003 as Head of Vertical Markets. He has sixteen brothers and sisters – Mrs Monical is the world record holder for the most children to graduate from college. As 'Lucky 13', Vince's first entrepreneurial stroke was, aged twelve, to earn enough money to buy an Atari game player which he then offered to the captive market of his siblings at a 15c discount on the arcade price for a go. He notes a lot of other businesses today mirror the circumstances of Betfair and Flutter; namely two online competitors with one or two offline giant rivals. The quality of product improves with depth of market (in other words, liquidity) and there are huge efficiencies of

having only one place to go, starting with advertising, he
argues.

Such analysis of mergers cannot undo the past perception of Flutter's union with Betfair. Certainly, as Betfair
grows, the belief that Betfair simply swallowed up Flutter
becomes more and more set in stone. Who runs Betfair
now?, Hannah asks Chief executive, David Yu, formerly
Chief Technical Officer for Flutter before joining Betfair.
Flutter can't have been so lame, can it? Unfortunately, most
journalists in researching the merger between Flutter and
Betfair today begin their quest for background with a visit
to the information website, Wikipedia. This records the
respective merger split of spoils as 84 to 16. In pondering
newspaper coverage of the deal in Britain, Monical
observes: 'A pair of management consultants from the Bay
area coming to Britain with an eye on the betting industry,' he shrugs. 'That was never going to be a love fest with
Media.' Still, even the interpretation of Bloomberg, which
might have been expected to be less partisan than, for example, the *Daily Telegraph* and *Guardian*, does little for
Hannah and Monical, either.

Perhaps if a friend of theirs had broken the news? Actually, the story of Betfair and Flutter coming together could
have hit the streets earlier than it did in exactly this form.
Everything hadn't been signed but agreements had been
reached. On this basis, Black, Wray, Hannah, and Monical
gathered in Hyde Park, with a couple of horses, for a public
relations picture that would accompany a release to newspapers about the deal. 'We had a bit of paper [a make-
believe contract], the horses, and a horseshoe with the
names of Flutter and Betfair joined together,' Hannah
recalls. (Incidentally, Black and him are now firm friends,

not least because he appreciates stories like Black, on selling a chunk of Betfair stock, reputedly going to the bank with a cheque for £4 million only to be told that, even on making the deposit and despite being well known by tellers, he could not draw so much as a penny there and then.) Hannah laughs: 'Jim Ledbetter, a writer friend of mine, lived in London back then and was a senior editor of *Industry Standard* web magazine as well as a contributor to the *New York Times*. By chance he rides up on his bike, just as we are in the middle of the shoot. "Hi, Jim, how is it going!" This would have been a huge scoop for him. We talked for five or so minutes. Finally, he said, "bye, got to go now." He didn't even notice.'

So it is written: Betfair took over, absorbed, soaked up, scooped, appropriated Flutter, all potential headlines with some scanning better than other, only a shortage of alliterations to rectify. As a former journalist on the *Financial Times*, David Freud's alternative billing for the deal would be something like 'Good All Round'. Bringing together two contrasting operations to trade as a single entity is not groundbreaking. In this case, Freud, author of *Freud in the City, 20 Turbulent Years at the Sharp End of the Global Financial Revolution* and a well known, respected pundit on market moves, admired the potency from a distance. Andrew Black estimates that Betfair's turnover ahead of merger was over £7 million a week with Flutter managing £3 million. As a united force, you might think £10 million, or £9 million discounting for Betfair's more expensive commission rates and any overlapping clients. Thanks to liquidity facilitating maximum stakes for Flutter clients (who were previously denied this because they were betting in weaker markets), Betfair and Flutter together soon topped £20 million a week. The Betfair homepage boasted as such.

While at UBS, Freud brought together Flutter and UBS Capital, a major stakeholder. For the union of Betfair and Flutter he has developed his own phrase. 'A reverse mop-up,' he jokes.

PART TWO
BEYOND BETFAIR

Chapter SIX

SPORT

$$E\{U\} = (1-P)[QU(Y+G)]+(1-P)...$$

On August 17 2002, betting's relationship with football in Britain experienced a quantum shift. Anyone who had until then disputed the possibility that a company directly associated with gambling could form a similarly direct partnership with the game couldn't argue with what was in front of them, literally in black and white. At 3pm that day on to the field of play ran the starting XI representing Fulham Football Club in the Premier League against Bolton Wanderers. Across the chests of their white shirts was the name of Betfair, the club's new corporate partners, boldly in black.

By virtue of his father, Barry, a sport television commentator, Mark Davies has long been well aware of the reach football has. Having worked sporadically in *BBC Sport* and filed occasional cameo cricket reports for the *Daily Telegraph*, he also knows fully the pecking order of football first, other sports, relatively speaking, nowhere. With this in mind, Davies moved quickly when the opportunity arrived to take Betfair to the biggest sports audience of all.

The association with Fulham, a gateway to the Premier League's worldwide television audience, came about after Davies got wind that shirt space was available for as little as £550,000 a season. 'I called Ed Wray,' Davies remembers. 'I asked him, what would he do if we could sponsor a Premier League team for less than 600K. Straightaway, he said, do it.' Davies also oversaw Betfair's sponsorship of Channel 4's 2005 Ashes cricket coverage. Davies maintains that people didn't see Betfair as sponsors of the television broadcasts but the Test matches, themselves. 'Still, for all that brought, the power of the Premier League is undoubted,' he insists.

The deal with Fulham was the first time a betting organisation had been allowed to sponsor a football team in Britain at the highest level. Betfair took the relevant governing bodies through the company's agnostic outlook to results – Betfair had no commercial motivation to fix a match, only to encourage betting on the game from which the usual commission would be redeemed – before receiving the go-ahead. With Fulham and Betfair united, the company sat back to enjoy a boost to general awareness courtesy of sport's most high profile billboard.

For all the impact of this to Betfair – 'The Brand' instantly went global thanks to the worldwide audience for English football – the relationship with Fulham had a much broader significance. The association opened the door for a number of other similar sponsorships to follow. Betfair had argued the case with the regulators – namely that Betfair did not, as a company, stand to gain from one side prevailing over the other, simply from extra business which meant they were as keen as administrators to maintain standards of integrity – and prevailed. Others subsequently won their own debates. Consequently, today, it is not at all uncommon for shirts to bear the names of other betting operations such as bwin, sponsor of AC Milan, Real Madrid, and Bayern Munich, and poker websites like www.32red.com, which backed Aston Villa between 2006 and 2008. In 2009, Boylesports, Mansion.com and SBO.bet.com graced the shirts of Sunderland, Tottenham Hotspur and West Ham United, respectively, in the English Premier League.

The backbone of Betfair's case, which opened the door of football sponsorship to others, was that, over and above the company's neutral status with respect to the result, with an Internet exchange there is transparency of who is betting with whom and for exactly how much. Transactions leave an audit trail. In cases of any suspected wrongdoing, at the end of that audit trail – should an individual have sought to utilise the opportunity to take and make bets pursuing ill-gotten gains – is the person central to events.

Actually, Betfair took this a stage further. The company aimed to exploit to the maximum the notion that betting exchanges, founded, in contrast to cash-centric bookmakers, in a culture of deposit account and electronic bank transfers, are able to oversee betting on sport way beyond traditional bookmakers, for whom cash remains a huge part of trading. Soon after the Flutter deal, Betfair approached a host of governing bodies and sporting authorities on whose sport Betfair made markets and invited them to sign Memorandums of Understanding (MOU). These would mean Betfair handing over information on trading and flow of money to sports administrators if foul play was suspected. If a sport's governing body had reason to believe a fix had taken place or there had been a conspiracy, Betfair, with audit trails, would have an idea of who might be involved in any wrongdoing and would collaborate, accordingly.

By 2008, more than thirty sporting authorities in all had signed memorandums with Betfair. The merits of MOUs are pretty undeniable. Take two examples from tennis, which has had an MOU since 2003, and snooker. In 2007, Alessio di Mauro, at the time ranked 124th in the world, was suspended for nine months and fined $60,000 after being found guilty of making 120 bets on tennis between November 2006 and the following June 2007. On the back of information supplied by Betfair, and to general acclaim for the assistance, Di Mauro became the first player to be sanctioned under Association of Tennis Players anti-corruption rules. The following August, ex-world snooker champion, Peter Ebdon, was beaten 5–0 by Liang Wenbo, ranked No.40 in the world at the time. The game was investigated by the Gambling Commission, which found neither player guilty of any impropriety. Nonetheless, it caused commercial sponsorship to come under threat, according to the World Professional Billiards and Snooker Association. At this, WPBSA signed an MOU.

In no sport has the impact of an MOU with Betfair been felt more than in British horseracing. This was Betfair's first agreement in 2003. It set the sport on a course down which an historically unprecedented number of corruption inquiries produced a string of convictions and suspensions. Gary Carter, Robert Winston, Dean Mc-Keown; these are just a number of jockeys since the launch of Betfair, now into double figures, banned from riding for varying lengths of time on the back of information supplied to the authorities after suspicions were aroused.

Following the success of Betfair's MOUs in providing information to the authorities that formed the basis for a number of findings of wrongdoing, in 2007 the racing authorities went further and rewrote rules. In that year, after a wide-ranging fact-finding mission, new regulations took effect governing the exploitation of inside information for financial gain at the expense of the general betting public. These new restrictions on jockeys and others essentially tipping off members of the public who could use the inside information for their own dealings, were, the old Horseracing Regulatory Authority (HRA) maintained, only possible because, with Betfair's information, there was a perception that you would be caught. Racing was never 100 per cent 'clean' but since the start of 2006 was 'much cleaner than it was', according to the HRA. The authorities could have easily said 2003, thanks to the MOU signed that year, which itself became possible because of what happened in 2000, namely the creation of Betfair.

Historically, racing has little choice in having a close relationship with the betting industry. That is because the potential source of corruption – namely betting – is also horseracing's primary source of income, the world over. For decades now, racing has pretty much universally been funded by a share of the spoils from betting, either through the government or racing authorities themselves running pool betting; or, as in Britain, by a statutory levy on commercial bookmakers collected and distributed by a government-created body. This, among other reasons such as money laundering rooted in betting and associations between betting and organised crime, is why illegal gambling is such a concern.

Racing and betting in Britain have largely reconciled themselves to the need to co-exist. Bookmakers today are the sport's biggest sponsors. That is over and above the statutory levy through which they further fund the sport. Moreover, in the past bookmakers at the racecourse were restricted to limited areas, effectively betting ghettos. Following deregulation, parties now mix relatively freely. Rightly, bookmakers, as well as funding the sport, are seen as providing a service to racegoers and correspondingly they are allowed to offer their goods where their customers might want to shop. Many fewer parts of a racecourse today are free of bookmakers.

Nevertheless there has been a longstanding and ongoing state of friction between the two parties, classic co-dependents with the potential both to destroy each other or contribute to shared success through co-operation. Bookmakers had always balked at providing information about possible fraud on the grounds that self-regulation was their preferred management. Instead of an MOU, leave it to us.

Bookmakers' objections to MOUs – which embarrassed them by showing how a betting organisation could co-operate fully with sports administrators – were that full disclosure sat very uneasily with a general betting culture of nods, winks, and whispers. There were also practical objections to Betfair's claims of the virtues in co-operation, namely inadequacies of the exchange's audit trail. John Brown of William Hill memorably queried Betfair's ability to track dealings when, as he put it, 'someone on Kowloon High Street places a bet of £10 million'.

Brown's view of the relationship between client and book-maker is that it should be akin to that of doctor and patient, bank manager and account holder, lawyer and accused, or perhaps, most apt, priest and confessor. He also argues corruption is fuelled by Betfair, in offering the opportunity to lay bets. In essence this means anyone can be a bookmaker. 'A dereliction of duty' was how Brown summed up the government's willingness to entertain Betfair. Betfair was the problem, he argued, offering a gilt-edged invitation to those seeking to corrupt the game.

This was an argument that Brown lost. In 2005, enshrined in the Gambling Act of that year was a requirement on betting operations to assist fully with the provision of information if wrongdoing was suspected. This measure took effect in 2007 and at a stroke improved book-makers' relationship with British horseracing. Betfair, you might say, had become law.

Betfair disputes the notion that the company has introduced the concept of taking bets on horses to lose. That has been possible – in this they are right – with traditional fixed-odds betting. It is just that the maths is of a complexity beyond mortals without, say, the brain of Andrew Black.

Belittling exchanges for their alleged role in providing an opportunity to corrupt, overlooks what corruption existed before the millennium and Betfair's foundation. Like the matter of liquidity and market domination by a single exchange, namely Betfair, there is an element of chicken and egg to the issue of whether Betfair corrupts or shines a light on corruption. In other words, did the emergence of Betfair as an alternative to the traditional bookmaker offer an opportunity to take as well as make bets, in the process tempting otherwise honest players into corrupt strokes? Or did Betfair's willingness to provide information about suspected wrongdoers enable the authorities to root out existing corruption?

As is usually the case there is some merit in the perspective of both Betfair and bookmakers. Indeed, Brown, during his time at William Hill, received unexpected support in 2004 from the then chairman of the British Horseracing Board, Peter Savill. At odds with the Jockey Club – at the time responsible for the regulation of horseracing ahead of handing over this to the new HRA – Savill described betting exchanges (even then, effectively Betfair) as 'virtually impossible to police'. Savill was also more specific than Brown. He warned of the problems when a paper trail led to 'No. 21 Kowloon High Street'. He stopped short of supplying post or zip code.

Knowing the criminal mind, in order to establish the likelihood of individuals succumbing to temptation and seeking to corrupt sport is usually the stuff of Columbo or Cracker. The many contradictory accounts of scandals such as the Kay, Swan, and Layne affair of 1964, in which footballers from Sheffield Wednesday and Mansfield Town went to prison for match fixing, show that summarising in a single sentence the motivation behind corruption in sport is never easy. More straightforward is the assertion that Betfair's partnership with Fulham Football Club showed that betting and sport from the very top – football – down could co-exist at close quarters. The relationship was for only a single season but still broke the mould. Brought closer was the day when a name embossed across a football jersey will promote not a betting exchange or poker site, but a traditional betting shop giant such as

William Hill or Ladbrokes, leaving the names of Kay, Swan, Layne and others to the historians.

Academics have done their best to define the thought process behind corruption and duplicity. In 1996, Professor Isaac Erlich published a theory of crime, linking perpetrators' acts to economic utility gained. This was then adapted by David Forrest and Robert Simmons to cover sport and the thought process of athletes contemplating a fix. Apparently, an athlete's willingness to be corrupt is based rationally on what he or she stands to gain, in the broadest sense. Or to be more precise, where E {U} is the utility from fixing, $E\{U\} = (1-p)[qU(Y+G)]+(1-p)[(1-q)U(y)]+p[U(Y-F-R)]-U(Y)+U(C)$; current wealth, probability of detection, financial penalty if caught, and possible loss of reputation are all included in the equation, along with any thrill or feelings of guilt.

Unclear from this research is whether four years before Betfair $E\{U\} = (1-p)[qU(Y+G)]+(1-p)[(1-q)U(y)]+p[U(Y-F-R)]-U(Y)+U(C)$ covers the aspects of betting exchanges that John Brown and Peter Savill believe are so dangerous. Perhaps a new study is due. Over to you Forrest and Simmons.

After Di Mauro, tennis couldn't wait for the latest psychological breakthrough. A comprehensive review of the sport's protection against corruption was announced. Like horseracing, rules had to be redrafted or revamped. A commissioned report, 'Environmental Review of Integrity Issues in Professional Tennis (ERIIPT)', outlined in 2008 a host of changes to tighten the sport's defences against corruption, many of which would have been empty without the means, through Betfair, of gathering evidence against those set on seeking ill-gotten

gains. These changes built on the initial Memorandum
of Understanding signed with Betfair in 2003. Thanks to
the MOU with Betfair, in all, some seventy-three matches
between 2002 and 2007 involving suspected betting
patterns were reviewed as part of the ERIIPT inquiry;
forty-five of these matches raised specific concerns from
a betting perspective, which would warrant further
review. Related to them, suspicious patterns in twenty-
seven Betfair betting accounts registered in different
countries raised concerns about players which would
warrant further attention. The report stated: 'Patterns of
suspected betting activity have been noted.' The report
concluded: 'All the indications are that a co-ordinated
and focused Anti-Corruption Programme with an
adequately resourced Integrity Unit is needed to address
the integrity concerns.'

Following the suspension of Alessio di Mauro, Etienne
de Villiers, then president of the Association of Tennis
Professionals (ATP) warned: 'If we do not have a sport
with integrity, we do not have a sport.' Such a statement
was bold, both implying the possibility that corruption
exists and suggesting that the means exist to address it.
Would de Villiers have been in a position to act on his
sentiment without Betfair?

From the very top floor of 151 Shaftesbury Avenue, you
might expect a decent view of London. In fact, the city's
great architecture is largely obscured. From the office here,
high above theatre land, all you really see is an array of
rooftops and television aerials. A few cranes and above
average-sized satellite dishes complete the disappointing
panorama.

Facing such a vista on a daily basis, it is easy to understand why Tom Chignell and Mark Phillips of the British
Horseracing Authority's security department have sought
to liven up their work environment with posters on the
walls. Less comprehensible is the subject matter of two of
the posters: Ian Botham leaving the field at Headingley in
1981 after his heroic century that turned that summer's
Ashes series against Australia, and Geoff Hurst at Wem-
bley in the 1966 World Cup Final. Chignell was only a
few months old for the former. As for Hurst's match-
winning hat trick, that was six years before Phillips was
even born. Neither Chignell nor Phillips can recall who is
responsible for their gallery. Abandoned on their shared
work surface are unwashed coffee and tea mugs alongside
a cereal bowl with the remains of breakfast still evident,
stuck hard and dry to the china. Like the poster selection,
neither party accepts blame.

The sepia image of Botham may have a hidden relevance. A subplot, which emerged long after the game and
series were concluded, was that some of the Australian
players had wagered money on England to win at 500–1
when, ahead of Botham's arrival at the crease, the position
was seemingly hopeless. No impropriety is suggested but
of course, thanks to Botham, the likes of Dennis Lillee and
Rodney Marsh, while tasting defeat, also profited handsomely.

The black and white image of Hurst – not to mention
the crockery – is completely at odds with the modern-day,
technologically-centric duties of the pair. The task set
Chignell and Phillips is to oversee British horseracing to
ensure that wagering stays within the rules and would not
prompt suspicion in the way, inevitably, cricket fans raised

an eyebrow on learning of Australian success with the bookmakers in 1981. The computers they use are of another age, compared to the Sixties and England's World Cup heroics. Indeed, in the Eighties the set up would have been considered the futuristic stuff of Hollywood.

Of course, monitoring the sport for wrongdoing and sharp practice has long been the role of whoever was responsible for racing's integrity from the days more than 200 years ago now when the Jockey Club took up governance of the sport. The goal didn't change when a transitionary body, the Horseracing Regulatory Authority, took charge in 2006 before being absorbed into a new British Horseracing Authority (BHA) in 2007 that had supplanted the British Horseracing Board, itself created in 1993 to take on many of the Jockey Club's functions. The difference today is that because of a Memorandum of Understanding with Betfair, Chignell and Phillips have a state of the art, live, direct feed from Betfair of trading on racing taking place. More detailed information is forthcoming, as required.

At the centre of this partly chaotic work station are three screens, showing live racing and also spreadsheets of wagering on Betfair in real time. 'These show just numbered accounts,' Phillips explains. 'We usually have an "on-watch" list to monitor, totalling at any one time about 150. Of these maybe three dozen are under serious scrutiny.'

The on-watch list is of those accounts in play, which have shown, at a minimum, grounds for extra monitoring. There may be no wrongdoing. But patterns of betting may be cause for concern. 'We used to speak to Betfair every day,' Phillips continues. 'We might say that we have seen something. Now with the new system we do not need even to talk. A new database means we can run searches which are even more sophisticated than before, including [the performance of, in relation to bets struck] jockeys, trainers, and owners.'

The Betfair and BHA logos share the screen when Chignell calls up details of the MOU agreed between the two. Chignell studied at the University of Trent, something of a centre for excellence when it comes to research into betting. Phillips is the son of a bookmaker – 'Dad doesn't talk to me anymore,' he jokes – who previously helped out his father at anywhere from Cheltenham and Ascot to the South West point-to-point circuit. He has also worked for some of the bigger betting operations. 'The pair were hard to find,' admits Paul Scotney, Director of Integrity Services and Licensing who oversees Chignell and Phillips. This is bespoke work.

Scotney, like many over the years who have been tasked with monitoring betting on horseracing, is a former policeman. He chews gum methodically. His office coat stand is in fact weighed down by ties, suggesting a routine that is varied and subject to last-minute changes of venue and consequently dress code. Hopefully it is not a hint of indecision.

'Corruption in sport goes back to the Chicago White Socks and Shoeless Joe in 1919,' Scotney shrugs. 'In Britain, cricket in the previous century was fixed,' he notes. He dates the origins of any corruption in racing back even further to the sport's very beginnings during the reign of Charles II.

Returning to more recent times, Scotney is upbeat. 'In the 1970s I used to go racing and there were some bookmakers who would make me think twice before having a bet with them, or buying a second-hand car from them for that matter,' he suggests. 'I joined what became the BHA security department in 2003. The MOU with Betfair was signed that June. Before that there was already informal co-operation and sharing of information. In the beginning, the stewards would see something suspicious and we would contact them, or we would hear from them. Then we had to jump through a number of hoops to make the case for receiving further information. On occasions, we would have to make the case in writing. It was not guaranteed that we received everything we wanted.'

Today, the system is pretty much automatic. 'Irregular betting patterns?' ponders Scotney. 'There are those every day. What we are looking for are suspicious betting patterns. We look at where the market is irregular and ask, is there anything suspicious? We have an alert system, ranging from ordinary to red. If we are in a red alert situation then the stewards at the racecourse must hold an inquiry into the running of the race.'

Scotney's department actually has the muscle to stop a race even taking place in certain circumstances. This is not a capability that Scotney has had reason to flex to date. Nevertheless, the English philosopher Sir Francis Bacon was the first to suggest that knowledge is power. Knowledge has certainly empowered Scotney and his department.

Christopher Foster is entitled to a smile at the change that has been brought about by the arrival of Betfair. Foster has been a lifelong servant of British racing. Today he holds the rather distinguished title, The Keeper of the Match Book. This dates back to when horseracing in Britain consisted of races between noblemen who were members of the Jockey Club (only two runners for racecourse stewards to keep in view). Yes, there is a book logging when members paired off to test their prides and joy, confirms its keeper. Yes, quite old now, he accepts.

In the past, Foster has held other jobs, including Jockey Club executive director. He is also a director of Wincanton racecourse, a trustee of the National Stud, and governor at Westminster School. One post he didn't exactly apply to fill was fall guy for *Panorama*'s investigation into corruption in racing in 2002. Foster appeared on the programme, a layman's take on a sport packed with customs that went with the turf, but in the main confounded BBC sleuths, to substantiate the Jockey Club's claim that the sport was well regulated and on top of corrupt practices. This would have been easier had he been able to convey that a wider police inquiry was at the same time in progress, compromising exactly how frank he could be when challenged for information about certain high-profile cases. The police probe effectively required the Jockey Club to suspend any pursuit and prosecution of certain people strongly suspected of being in breach of the sport's rules. After all, corruption in racing was relatively small beer compared to the smuggling of industrial quantities of Class-A drugs that those under suspicion were masterminding. Racing's authorities at the time took heed of a bigger picture. *Panorama*, largely ignorant of this, pressed ahead with efforts to dismantle the sport. Foster, probed repeatedly in this area by *Panorama*'s judge and jury style inquest, offered all he was able to; he substantiated the idea that racing was a well-run shop without compromising police work. He took the fall by way of a brief cameo to camera sprinkled with pauses and qualifications, edited down from hours of interviews.

It is not going as far back as the days of match racing, but Foster can still remember how things were before the arrival of Betfair and the signing of an MOU. He sighs. 'Then, a very considerable frustration. Basically, we never got any collateral evidence. There were, of course, plenty of rumours flying around and, from time to time, traditional bookmakers would make helpful noises about providing us with information. But when push came to shove they would hide behind customer and client confidentiality. When we wanted evidence from them they were reluctant to give it.'

Foster adds that the bookmakers were keen enough to involve the Jockey Club when they, rather than administrators, wanted assistance. 'The high point, or should that be low point was a race involving a horse called Man Mood in 1996,' Foster grimaces. 'As bad an example of the lack of co-operation from the bookmakers as there has been, in that we were given sight of useful information, promised access to it for a disciplinary case, only for it to be subsequently withdrawn.' Man Mood, contested a two-horse race and was well clear only to falter suspiciously during the run to the line, ultimately finishing second. In this instance, William Hill was at first keen to co-operate and supply evidence of betting so that charges could be brought against those suspected of a wrongdoing. The bookmakers then pulled out. The suspicion lingers that, their end resolved, their enthusiasm to go further was limited on the grounds that it might be bad for short-term business.

Betfair's arrival prompted Foster to ponder what he describes today as 'an interesting concept'. He recalls, naturally enough, that with betting exchanges generally there were a lot of regulatory matters to resolve, not least around the ability Betfair offered clients to lay horses to lose. A meeting seemed at the very least necessary. From this, initially scribbled on the back of an envelope, came the first MOU between racing and the betting industry.

'We didn't go into great lengths at first,' Foster admits. 'There was no drive to produce a legally watertight document. Instead we put our points down on paper, they added theirs and very soon we had a non-binding agreement that would – and this is the important aspect – work in practice. It took hardly any time at all.'

Foster and the Jockey Club were well aware of the dilemma that Betfair presented the sport's regulators. On one hand, Betfair planned to supply unprecedented degrees of information on who was betting on what and how much. Equally, betting exchanges offered the chance to lay a horse and consequently take advantage of any information you might have about the wellbeing of that horse.

Foster is sure that the net effect is handsomely positive. The MOUs (with Betfair) have produced two effects, insists Foster. Firstly, they prompted bookmakers themselves to draft similar – albeit less tight – agreements, and secondly the regulatory authority for British racing began successfully convicting those suspected of wrongdoing, in the process establishing the most effective deterrent of all; namely that the odds are that you will be caught.

'Three decades ago, because of the lack of hard betting evidence, the chances of you being caught corrupting a race were slim,' Foster maintains. 'The chances today, thanks to the MOUs, are much higher. When Betfair came along we had not had a successful conviction for years, despite there being some anxieties about betting and certain individuals. The MOU with Betfair was a new concept. Inevitably there were tweaks to what we originally agreed. For example, the rules were changed to ban those involved directly with a horse from taking bets on that horse to lose and likewise for those with inside information about a future runner's wellbeing. They should not be able to profit at the expense of others by taking bets on a horse they know not to be up to running at its very best.'

Foster has good reason to feel satisfied. Remember he took the fall for racing in 2002. He struggles a little to suppress a self-congratulatory smile. 'We accepted that in racing, as with any sport or walk of life, there are always some bad apples in the barrel. We had a fair bit of intelligence about them. The calls and warnings we received from Betfair were often alerting us to the same names that we already had on file. Our intelligence was clearly not that bad, we had just been unable to act upon it.'

Bookmakers always seemed to find themselves in legal tangles when in discussion with established operations about MOUs, Foster laments. 'I don't recall any occasion when a bookmaker's evidence has been decisive in a corruption case,' he concludes. This is consistent with Scotney's view. He believes that bookmakers would never have even discussed an MOU without the pressure on them from Betfair's agreements.

As a non-executive director of the BHA with specific responsibility for integrity, Ben Gunn takes great pride in the success British horseracing's administrators – with help from Betfair – have had in seeking convictions against those found to have been in breach of the sport's rules.

Like Scotney, a former policeman (though unlike the former, it is hard to imagine the latter on the beat) Gunn, himself, likes a bet. His concern for the integrity of the game meant that his own habits had to be considered in the context of the temptations of office. First he offered to resign from the Gambling Commission, set up under the terms of the Gambling Act (2005), if his own betting could at all be viewed as undermining the overall thrust of the new body. Ultimately, a system was agreed by which any bets involving sums over £500 must be declared.

Gunn was being very, very hard on himself. His average wager is far short of the limit he approved. What's more, he has barely the time to indulge in his affection for modest flutters. As well as duties at the BHA and with the Gambling Commission, he runs his own consultancy, Campbell Gunn, which specialises in advising on sport regulation and integrity. He also completed the ERIIPT report for the world tennis authority, following the Di Mauro case. This was the culmination of a process that began after the game first became widely tainted with allegations of scandal following a match at the Lyon Grand Prix in 2003 between Yevgeny Kafelnikov and Fernando Vicente. The former was expected to win only to lose amid a deluge of bets on his unfancied opponent ranked well below him in the world standings of the day. (Neither player was found guilty of any wrongdoing.)

Gunn, who wrote his report on tennis with Jeff Rees, a fellow ex-Scotland Yard detective, maintains that just as horseracing has benefited from Betfair, so has – and will – tennis. At very least, reform in tennis once Betfair highlighted the potential for corruption helped generate momentum to address a situation where no less then seven governing bodies – 'like separate silos,' Gunn suggests – sought to take a role in maintaining integrity. This number of different policing bodies inevitably left some areas over covered, and others lacking cover, he suggests. By the 2009 tennis season, the sport's Tennis Integrity Unit addressed Gunn's concerns and is, incidentally, headed up by Rees.

If Scotney has an excessive number of ties on his coat stand, Gunn at least restricts himself to one, albeit occasionally placed jauntily in his jacket breast pocket rather than round his neck. The colour often matches his cuff links or other carefully selected shirt or socks. Rather than an extra in *The Bill*, he could as easily sit on the secretariat of any major, worldwide sport, in addition to his established commitments to tennis and horseracing.

Gunn's assessment of football and cricket is that they are similar to racing. In other words, with a MOU the threat of corruption becomes much more manageable. FIFA, football's world governing body, appears mindful of the need to seek information about betting on matches, ahead of kick off. In 2007, an early warning system – EWS – was formally established with offices in Switzerland, where FIFA is based. Though this has no facility for identifying the account holders perpetrating suspicious betting patterns – a point that Betfair, itself, highlighted – it is at least a potential gauge of the scale of any corruption. According to Gunn, the Olympics is a low-risk event in that there is little betting on athletics. 'The corrupt go for the biggest liquidity because that is what offers the best chance to make money,' he reasons. The MOU that Betfair signed with the International Olympic Committee before Beijing 2008 nevertheless illustrates how readily sporting organisation from the very top down see the merit of having a MOU.

In making the case for MOUs to sporting bodies, Gunn often draws on horseracing. The sport serves as a great yardstick as a leader in this since a review in 2003 on which Gunn, himself, served.

'Before Betfair, for a traditional operation such as an investigation into an individual, inspectors would be more on the ground at the racecourses,' reveals Gunn. 'In 2003 I looked at some of the charts being used by the horseracing authorities to root out corruption. They were huge with pictures and lots of arrows going in all directions. I said, "these are brilliant, but who is the target?" They were compiled from a range of information sent in by intelligence officers. For example, A meets B at Ayr, who meets C at Chepstow. Now the emphasis has moved to an intelligence-backed picture rather than looking for faces. There is still an element of being at the races, checking out faces, and gathering information. But the emphasis is not about walking around seeing who is talking to whom and taking a picture, that old-style method of gathering "intelligence". That wasn't much more than information. You need to develop info into intelligence.'

Translating such info into intelligence is the skill, Gunn explains. 'So is converting intelligence into evidence – which is what you need at the end of the game for enforcement. That is altogether harder work. You can spend a lot of energy on information without converting any into evidence and then being able to use it in enforcement. You have to prioritise. Now racing is beginning to see the sophisticated proceeds of the betting analysis we use and the translation of this and other information into assessed intelligence. Where information can be translated into evidence it is. We can also focus on certain individuals. We are targeted. In the past we would gather a huge amount of information, only a portion of which might have been converted into intelligence, and even less into evidence. Now we are more sophisticated using crime-pattern analysis, and techniques that police forces use. In other words, we look at a range of activities that can then be zoned down to specific individuals and events, which we can consequently target. It helps greatly not having to throw such a wide net.'

Gunn adds: 'Today, knowing what we know from Betfair, disruption is a tactic, stopping something before it happens. If resources are short and remembering that our powers are limited, disruption is a legitimate strategy. Let them, those who are seeking to be corrupt, know that we know. Call them in, give them a formal warning. It is all part of the preventative strategy now possible.'

After overseeing in 2007 the Jockey Club handover of all responsibility for the regulation of horseracing to the BHA, Christopher Foster might be mindful that, having established a working MOU with Betfair, his empowerment lasted only a short time compared to his total years in racing. Not least as the Jockey Club was routinely criticised during the Foster years – culminating in the *Panorama* programme of 2002 – for failing to apprehend racing's wrongdoers. An understated operator, Foster allows himself some credit for establishing the original basis for today's successful collaboration. A pity not to be central to the benefits, he concedes.

Foster does not dwell too long on the counter argument to Betfair, that the ability to take bets – like a traditional bookmaker – generates fresh corruption. He is adamant that Betfair is not a catalyst for a growth in the corruption of racing. 'That was not a view we shared,' he insists. 'While the risks were heightened with the advent of Betfair and with this the ability to lay horses to lose there was the counter-balancing deterrent of greater transparency. We had the chance to deter people.'

Near the end of his three decades of service to horseracing, Foster can claim a watershed. 'Because of the level of co-operation it was an opportunity for regulators. Online operations have more information than cash operations such as traditional bookmakers. What's more, compared to betting exchanges, bookmakers take a risk with each bet. In the past, bookmakers knew a great deal more about their clients than we were ever told but that information to them is incredibly useful. A great deal of effort goes into getting such information and then assessing risk based on the information. At Betfair, other than commission, they have no financial interest in the bet. Correspondingly, they have few constraints on making information available.'

Paul Scotney is even more adamant than Foster is. 'Anyone who might cheat on Betfair would cheat whether the betting exchange existed or not,' he argues. He gives an example of an associate of the jockey, Gary Carter, who was found guilty in 2005 of passing on inside information to gamblers. Scotney's logic is that the associate of Carter, who retired before the case against him was heard and claimed that the five-year ban and £2,000 fine was 'very harsh' was a concern to the racing authorities long before

Betfair was set up yet no action would have been contemplated without the betting exchange.

Bruce Millington blows out his cheeks. 'If only ...' he mutters to no one and everyone. As editor of the *Racing Post*, and a committed gambler, he would be better paid if he received £1 for every time he heard the phrase or muttered the words, himself. In this case, the regrets are more substantial than a simple wager. In 2000, Millington was sports editor of the *Racing Post*. Today, he is overall editor. In a Canary Wharf towered office with a panoramic view of the East End, he has a view that invites him to ponder might-have-beens. He blows out his cheeks again recalling details of a phone call from Mark Davies ahead of Betfair's launch. 'He politely introduced himself,' Millington groans. 'He didn't mention his father, Barry. That might have made a difference, or if he had suggested lunch. At the time, I was being inundated by all these start-up, online bookies, all telling me they were the next big thing. Very few actually made it.'

Millington, not a man to be overwhelmed with strategic flattery, was unmoved. 'My stock answer at the time was, get yourself established, then we will have a look at the site,' he shrugs. 'They wanted publicity? They got the stock answer. It didn't win me over there and then. Sure, it sounded like a good idea but you had to wonder how they were going to generate the liquidity they were going to need.'

Lunch? The relevance of this is that Millington believes that across a table he just might have taken a personal interest in Betfair. 'I don't lie awake at night thinking, what if I had invested ten grand,' he insists. He looks out the window. 'I suppose it does cross my mind from time to time.'

Perhaps even more than most, those who work on a racing and betting newspaper are in no doubt about the benefits of hindsight. A £10,000 investment in Betfair would ultimately attain a value of £1.35 million. Millington takes another cherry from the bowl that is serving as an after-lunch snack. Along with many others, he missed the biggest fruit of them all.

The *Racing Post*, Britain's horseracing and sports betting daily paper, has a circulation comfortably into six figures on showcase days for the Turf and consistently in excess of 60,000, not to mention hits on racingpost.com; as such it has a stake in the universal maintenance of integrity. Corruption on which Betfair has shone a light is front-page news and each successful conviction of jockeys since the MOU of 2003 has made headlines in the paper.

Millington recalls the moment in 2001 that he converted to Betfair. 'We were in the office and the Lancome Trophy, a golf tournament, was on the television. Retief Goosen and Sergio Garcia were going head-to-head with the latter four off the lead. A colleague said to me, "have a look at this". Betfair was showing odds of 80–1 against Garcia winning. I thought, he cannot be 80s. We had a tenner each, and collected. Phenomenal! I wrote about it in the newspaper. From that moment on I have been a Betfair punter.'

With Millington a convert, Betfair began to establish a foothold in the *Racing Post*. Before the millennium, the pages of the newspaper – founded in 1986 before twelve years later absorbing its much longer established market rival the *Sporting Life* – were dominated by critiques of odds offered by traditional bookmakers. Today, editorial throughout the paper – and at racingpost.com – features betting on exchanges, and most specifically, as the overwhelmingly dominant player, Betfair markets. 'I don't see the point of the phrase betting exchanges,' maintains Millington. 'We are just talking about Betfair really.'

Millington recalls editorial staff grasping Betfair with both hands. 'There are some difficulties with a newspaper carrying information on Internet betting as the odds change all the time,' Millington reasons. 'What is the point about writing something when by the time it is read the story is out of date? Even today we don't print Betfair markets ahead of an event. But the transparency of Betfair was a massive aid to a sports-betting journalist, any journalist for that matter. Before Betfair, if you wanted to know the story of how a betting market had panned out you would ring a fixed-odds bookmaker and they would talk you through events in euphemistic terms. With Betfair, you could find out to the nearest penny what happened by accessing the website.'

Millington enthuses: 'Betfair gave us a narrative. We could highlight what people had bet on, the highs and lows of a market during, say, a football game. If, say, Aston Villa had come back from being 3–0 down we could show that the odds on them when three goals had been conceded reached 739–1 on Betfair before an incredible comeback. Using Betfair, the betting quantifies the story. Instead of talking about an incredible comeback it allows you to show exactly how incredible.'

How quickly did Betfair change the *Racing Post*? Initially coverage of Betfair centred on Millington's former empire, the sports section. Then with horseracing increasingly important to Betfair, the company would feature in a regular slot, 'Trading Post', at the front of the newspaper, and ultimately as front-page news. This covered opportunities to lay horses. More and more, Millington concedes, Betfair's culture and options available through the website were reflected in the coverage of sports betting and betting on horses. 'The chat among the more savvy punters who read the paper was back then, this [Betfair] is it,' Millington recalls. 'Readers' feedback reflected this to an extent, too.'

As the advertisers who help sustain the *Racing Post*, traditional bookmakers had at very least a lever to use in seeking to address any significant shift in balance of coverage away from them and towards the new innovators. Millington admits that they were not best pleased by the newspaper embracing exchanges. 'Fixed-odds bookmakers would come on the telephone saying we did this, we did that. I would always say, great, hook us up to your database and bill books and we will report what we see.'

The philosophy of MOUs sits easily within Betfair. Ed Wray explains the motivation for them was founded in the culture that underscores the company. The operation is more City than old-school bookmaking. Of course, this reflects Wray's own background. 'I worked in London's financial sector where it was unheard of that, if I did a trade, the regulator would not have all my details and accounts of what was happening,' Wray argues. 'I found the lack of transparency in the betting industry a bit odd. For me, the principle [of handing over personal information] was not an issue. Our only concern was that customers would find that they didn't like it. In fact, they loved it. They said, "great, this underlines our view that this is the place to bet".'

It may no longer come as a surprise that John Brown offers a different interpretation. He has only the one problem with Betfair. No amount of successful prosecution of jockeys found to have been betting or supplying information will change his often-stated view that the fundamental basis for the betting exchange is illegal. He argues that the integrity of betting is protected by the process of granting permits to trade as bookmakers only to fit and proper persons. Brown sighs. Now retired, he remains exasperated. 'If you take a bet you should have to have a permit. Betting exchanges such as Betfair aid and abet illegal gambling. If there are two people having a bet then one of them has to be a bookmaker.'

He adds: 'That has to be the case, doesn't it? Otherwise, William Hill never took a bet of any description for the entire forty-odd years I was with the company.'

There is something of a contradiction in Brown's view of MOUs. On one hand, he maintains that bookmakers need to be regulated, through a licensing system. On the other hand, bookmakers should be allowed then to regulate themselves. As for the impact MOUs have had on the sport's integrity, he maintains that bookmakers have always been best placed to flush out corruption (at the same time downplaying the extent). To back his belief that MOUs are an overly formal measure, he points to what he believes are the very low – less than 1 per cent incidence – of problem gamblers the betting industry acknowledges. The management of this, he points out, shows that betting has been successfully self-regulated by bookmakers for nearly fifty years.

Wray does acknowledge that his company's enthusiasm for collaboration with sports authorities did not mean an entirely stress-free implementation of what today ensures an unprecedented flow of information about betting to sports administrators. He shifts a little in his chair when recalling that Betfair first had to confront the matter of data protection. As Brown is not slow to point out, Betfair agreed to furnish the Jockey Club with betting information only to realise that this was in breach of data privacy law.

Before formally signing any MOUs Betfair had first to ask all its customers retrospectively in 2003 to agree to what a MOU would mean. Wray willingly concedes: 'It was commercially quite risky. People can be very sensitive about personal information. Look at the reaction that the introduction of identity cards can provoke. They fear the worst. People automatically assume "Police State".'

Betfair raised the commercial stakes by simply making agreement to abide by the terms of a MOU a condition of using Betfair, retrospectively for those already clients. Wray claims only one customer dissented, on a point of principle before acquiescing. 'If we had thought of MOUs when we were setting up we would have included the notion in our terms and conditions,' he explains. 'By introducing the concept we simply had to change them and hope everyone came with us.'

No one should be afraid of transparency, Wray insists (though this, it should be recorded, is not a view held universally in the City of London.). He gestures, opened palmed, as if to say, we've nothing to hide. Of course, there is a commercial side to this altruism. 'Exchanges don't work if people don't have faith in them,' Wray emphasises. 'We wanted to share information with the Jockey Club – and other sporting bodies – because we had some concerns about betting patterns. Ours is a business which requires clients to have total confidence in the regulator. We are not like bookmakers in that we are not an economic partner with either side of transactions on our exchanges so we have no vested interest in the outcome and no incentive to hide information – not to cast dispersions on others, you understand [though he does just that]. Bookmakers? Someone bets £100K and however it comes to pass, they find out or learn that the horse is not going to win, or even take part. Do they void the bet? It is a more difficult situation for them. We don't have the problem. The Jockey Club? It was just thrilled [incidentally, Betdaq rejected an invitation to join the partnership before ultimately backtracking]. I think the Jockey Club thought, before we sat down to talk, that we would be like everybody else who had come before us. They were clearly frustrated at the inability to get information out of bookmakers. Other sports I don't think had considered betting and the benefits of having an understanding of what is going on. There is always the argument that racing's different to other sports. There are rarely two-runner races. In fact, in, say, a football match, betting on A to win was betting on B not to win. Don't hide behind the complexities of the maths when the event is a seventeen-runner horseracing handicap.'

To these sort of verbal exchanges, Millington brings some understanding to both parties. Does Betfair serve as a draw to those seeking corrupt earnings from Betfair or prompt those who might otherwise have stayed straight to err? 'Floodlights failing, that happened before Betfair,'

Millington points out. 'But I don't think even Andrew Black and Ed Wray would deny that Betfair serves both as a source of corruption as well as highlighting what is going on, betting-wise, that might generate suspicion. I don't think anyone can deny that if you have a bent towards corruption Betfair is appealing. But Betfair is a huge source of transparency in the way that markets and bets can be tracked and traced, respectively. If a professional sportsman [or woman] uses Betfair it is clear that they will have their collar felt.'

He pauses, struggling to find an expression that could be universally understood. 'It is like a bank with unlocked doors and no security,' Millington decides, finally. 'The safe door is open. But steal the money and valuables and they will trace what you take all the way home. Getting to the safe is easy. But after that?'

Memorandums of Understanding send a clear message, Millington argues. He sneers at the memory of Alessio di Mauro. 'Tennis administrators might not even have known that people bet on tennis without Betfair alerting them,' he mocks. Tennis players banned for having a minuscule bet on Betfair? Millington, who is currently at the top of a profession whose business is opinions, is uncharacteristically lost for words.

Chapter SEVEN

BUSINESS
New Eyes

Opposite the carpet store on Hammersmith's King Street
– if you are local that's west of Primark – is King Street
Cloisters. For sale, on the main drag, is a mixture of elec-
trical goods, general household products and branded
items, most of which can seem like a good idea at the time
but ultimately leave you underwhelmed. That would be
all the more so when you consider that an altogether more
substantial investment is available nearby. Inadvertently,
you have come to the right place for gold bullion. Through
the cloisters' archway on King Street's north side is a prefab
building that is the latest home of Bullionvault.com. This
person-to-person website allows you to trade directly with
others keen to enter the bullion market. Of course, just as
you do not need to be in Hammersmith to gamble on
Betfair, you can trade through BullionVault pretty much
anywhere in the world. As they say, pure gold.

The credit crunch of 2008 and a collapse of public confidence in the banking system may have squeezed the life

out of many a business of late. But if your trade is gold, then you are – without wanting to muddle precious metals – the beneficiary of what represents a silver lining to turmoil in world markets. In America, the price of gold rose 32 per cent in 2007 and continued on an upward curve for the first three financial quarters of 2008. In Britain, the trend has been similar. Shrewd investors followed the market, accordingly. Take David and Maureen Somers. In 2004 they invested everything in gold, in the process selling their house to free up capital. Since closing a six-figure deal for their three-bedroom pad, then immediately investing the lot, their holdings have much more than doubled in value. When they have needed money, explains Mr Somers, a retired croupier (not a staggering surprise, that), they have simply sold a few ounces.

With panic growing in the minds of savers and investors, others have turned to one of the oldest commodities there is. BullionVault has tapped into this interest. The company creates the market by buying and holding the gold, which is then traded between those who join the exchange. With enthusiasm for other investments seemingly waning, Bullionvault.com's turnover has soared. Ahead of the financial crisis' arrival in the autumn of 2008, the company, which opened for business three years earlier, was able to boast a predicted annual churn of £200 million. In the same financial year, 2008, the likes of Northern Rock and Bradford & Bingley, for all the substance to the bricks and mortar they underwrite, required state shelter. Instead, having gone for gold, BullionVault struck it.

Across London, at Canary Wharf, the prevailing trend is on less of an upward trajectory. With a growing share of the financial sector now located here, there is little escape, a roaring gold market notwithstanding, from the anxiety about jobs and future prospects that those employed in the world of banking are facing, albeit after years of thumping bonuses.

Still, on the 20th floor of Canary Wharf's Churchill Place tower there are enough moments to lift the spirits. This level is home to Cantor Index, the spread betting company which majors in financial and currency markets. Actually, for such an operation, market volatility is pretty much a welcome companion. After all, if nothing goes up or down, on what can account holders speculate? (apart, of course, from when the stability will end).

The name Cantor Index and its holding company, Cantor Fitzgerald, resonate with a wider public to an extent greater than even more publicity-hungry market rivals such as Sporting Index for what the company went through on 9/11. With offices based at the World Trade Center, 658 Cantor Fitzgerald staff lost their lives in the attack on the twin towers. Uplifting is that today, 11 September is the company's Charity Day, when all global revenues worldwide are donated to worthy causes, resulting in the evolution of what was a sombre day of soul-searching to one of optimism with a more positive message.

So, two companies separated by the centre of London, with a journey between the two of anything up to two hours, depending on the capital's traffic. What links BullionVault and Cantor, a company that has grown back from the darkest of days and, along the way, re-established an appetite for innovation and adapting to new tastes and trends? Simply, both took inspiration from Betfair.

Cantor Index was founded in 2000, predating Bullion-Vault.com by five years. The operation's last major innovation, Spreadfair, which until December 2008 existed under the Cantor umbrella, was founded in 2004. This was, for its four-year life until financial market turmoil claimed it, the first person-to-person Internet spread betting exchange. Similarly, Paul Tustain, BullionVault's founder, also adapted Betfair's person-to-person concept to a new market, in his case, gold.

Betfair, itself, is less than a decade old. Still, this has proved long enough for the company already to have served as the mother of invention. Though the financial climate that made Canary Wharf a desperate place in 2008 claimed it at the end of that year, Spreadfair was during its four-year life, a homage to the principles of exchanges and Betfair. Likewise, BullionVault, which remains a corporate son of Betfair. Paul Tustain, the founder, mixed his personal flair for IT and the proven Betfair formula to grasp the market for gold on an impressive scale. The core of the operation mimics its neighbour, down river.

These two examples are certainly not the limits of Betfair's ability to inspire. On leaving Andrew Black's invention, where he worked alongside him at the IT coalface, Stephen Kenny had the idea of setting up a person-to-person site trading in property. Via his exchange, traders were able to speculate through buying and selling stakes in properties. Opromark launched in 2005. For as little as £1 it was possible to join the market. Opromark ultimately morphed into The Property Investment Market. Undoubtedly a better name, the company, nevertheless ceased to trade in 2007. Sometimes markets – with Spreadfair a case in point – can go against you, however strong the instinct to deal; something that anyone trading on the likes of BullionVault, and, of course, Betfair, fully understands.

Hoping to enjoy the same fortunes as BullionVault, rather than catch the cold winds that ultimately claimed Spreadfair (and Opromark, in its infancy), is Blood-Ex. In some respects the International Bloodstock Exchange, to give Blood-Ex its full billing, is even more in the spirit of Betfair. The baby of GCG Group and due to launch in the autumn of 2009, Blood-Ex will take on entrenched practices in the world of horseracing that have changed hardly at all for centuries (in other words even longer than the inertia in bookmaking). Where Blood-Ex differs from, say, BullionVault is that the company trades in living breathing matter, whereas BullionVault is a mechanism for pure speculation.

Blood-Ex exploits the longstanding habit in horseracing of multiple and syndicate ownership. On the Blood-Ex exchange, an owner places a racehorse called, by way of illustration, Shergar, for sale. Then those for whom a simple bet is too detached an involvement with horseracing can actually buy a portion of the horse in training, in this case Shergar, through the Blood-Ex website. By investing in a stake, the buyer then shares in any success and prize-money the horse brings on the track. Similarly, if the horse is sold, the investor takes a proportionate share of any proceeds. In this game, you can win twice, enjoying the excitement of a result at the racecourse and the subsequent boost to your horse's value as quantified by the Blood-Ex exchange market.

The thinking behind Blood-Ex is, according to Valentine Feerick, chief executive of the enterprise's holding company, GCG, relatively simple: racehorse owners, by and large, are wealthy individuals, have a portfolio of investments and the only one that they struggle to convert quickly, as required, into hard currency is the bloodstock. (Note here that fully acknowledged is the possibility that a horse can win nothing and fall in value.) According to Feerick, the established bloodstock market – sales at public auction, largely – is 'broken'. It is also, Feerick argues, insufficiently transparent for modern-day tastes to draw in sufficient new investment to sustain the game in the modern age.

From his high-rise office, Cantor Gaming's Andrew Garrood, managing director of Spreadfair during its best days, ponders the same notion of a broken market system except in relation to the world of gambling. 'Across London, every community is served by a local betting shop,' he muses. 'But we have seen the appetite that there is for exchanges, in both betting, and generally with companies like eBay. People like to trade directly.' He adds that his admiration for Betfair – and the principles behind Spreadfair, which sustained the company for four years – is deep. Incidentally, the extraordinary financial times, which claimed the venture, also accounted for Cantor poker and casino sites. The historical notion that gambling thrives during economic downturns is being strongly tested over the Internet.

With BullionVault, the motivation to set up was to counter boredom. Paul Tustain, the founder, maintains that, having made enough money providing the London Stock Exchange with what he describes as 'financial plumbing' – in other words, highly sophisticated software – there was no pressing need to work again. Yet he was ready for another challenge.

Today you could in theory actually reach Bullion-Vault by taking a boat from Betfair up river. It means Tustain can keep an eye on his investment. Tustain put money into Betfair a few months after the launch with the company trading, to him most satisfactory for a start-up, bets of around £200,000 a week.

'I had seen a lot of dot.com businesses which had the idea to sell something – say widgets – over the Internet,' Tustain recalls. 'But a widget has to be delivered so any profits are poured down the throats of distribution and courier companies. With bookmaking, Betfair took distribution costs – high street betting shops, essentially – through the floor. You also don't want to put money into something that is immediately copy-able. You set up, make all the mistakes, then someone else comes along and refines things, with a thank you very much for your help. Betfair was never going to be like that as once they had 30,000 customers, their rivals didn't have them if you know what I mean. And in their market the quality of the product [the liquidity giving the exchange an ability to cope with trade] is defined by the number of users. With Betfair, first-mover advantage was potentially huge. Once they had developed the ability to distribute bets of a certain size they went up to the next level. Once they were there, everyone else was effectively out the game.'

Tustain is actually Ed Wray's cousin. Bearing in mind that Betfair was reduced to tapping family and friends for seed money, odds were always short that Tustain would invest. However, he can be pretty dispassionate about this sort of thing. As he did before ultimately investing in Betfair, Tustain pauses ahead of explaining himself. 'The moment I saw Betfair, I thought, OK, I haven't put any money into any dot.com companies yet because I always found myself saying about each opportunity, "this is not a proper business model." Betfair was. Flutter? At first, Flutter was a direct person-to-person site allowing people to bet with each other on anything they liked. But that made it a clearer of debts and not an exchange. Betfair offered a genuine market.' He smiles, broadly. He sees things even more clearly now. 'At worst, I thought Betfair had the ability to get a credible product to market, where it would be spotted by a competitor. Ladbrokes, or someone would copy them, then William Hill, six months off the pace, would, rather than set up another one, offer to buy Betfair, leaving those who started the company with £20 million or so to share.'

Tustain proved to be out by a factor of seventy-five. 'Everything with Betfair looked right,' he concedes today. 'Even though they had no route to market – it was unnatural then for a person wanting to have a bet to go on the Internet instead of to the high street – they had the *Racing Post* to reach potential customers. That said, you have to remember that this was all being done by Andrew Black. The chance that Bert, who had had an idea every fortnight for the previous fifteen years, was the guy to bring this to fruition was nonexistent. Certainly not without Ed. Even with Ed, who dramatically improved the chances, the whole thing was pretty unlikely. I've got to know Bert through bridge. His ability at the game, which does require a particular type of intelligence, makes him a potential world-class player but he is also just too lazy. When they asked me at first for money back in February 2000 before the company launched in the summer, [Betfair was valued by its founders at £5 million, small in the context of what followed but still a lot for essentially no more than an idea] it was obvious to me that there was a major Internet bubble going on and which would end. So I said, no thank you, not now, even though I thought the business model was absolutely spot on.'

As we have learned, back in the early days of Betfair, Black had a distinct problem with the likes of Flutter. Copy cats was his nominated 'dislike' when, on opening an account with them, he was required to give an example of what was to his, and against his, taste. In the case of BullionVault, Black, his own venture by now firmly established, was flattered. Naturally enough. Leaving aside that Tustain is practically family, isn't imitation the greatest form of that?

Before investing, Paul Tustain's immediate thought about Betfair, once every indication suggested that the company would ultimately succeed, was, how do I apply this elsewhere?

In the end, Gordon Brown, Chancellor of the Exchequer at the time, gave him direction. 'I couldn't find the over-round, the bit in a market that would mean that I was better for the customer than anyone else,' Tustain confesses. 'Then Gordon Brown started selling gold at a rock-bottom price. My last business had taken off around the time that Margaret Thatcher, when she was Prime Minister, started selling off state assets like gas, water, and electricity too cheaply. Thinking about it, it reminded me that governments almost always sell at too low a price. So I had a look at the market for gold.'

What Tustain found was not altogether encouraging; a professional market for gold, highly efficient with a profitable 'choke' off gold bars of less than 1 per cent.

What did offer him a chance was the difference between the retail and trade markets. 'An allocated spot [professional] market, gold trade is settled in 12.5kg gold bars, which have been manufactured by a closed list of refiners and kept in accredited LBMA [London Bullion Market Association] vaults,' Tustain explains. 'A good delivery bar is likely to spend its whole life in these vaults. When finally it is withdrawn its most likely destiny is to be turned into jewellery. LBMA vaults do not deal with the general public. Nor do the professional gold dealers, as they know that all but the richest private buyers and sellers of gold cannot make or take delivery of these large bars. Therefore spot gold is not accessible to the general public.'

There is a market for gold for the general public, but it is small bars and coins, he continues. 'Typically you go into a coin/bar shop [there are a few] and buy,' Tustain explains. 'These businesses have a massively lower turnover than professional dealers do. Typically they would expect to sell a few coins and bars a day. Like any business they must allow for overheads [like staff and rent] and the cost of holding inventory. Generally speaking their costs – as a proportion of their sales – are massively higher than a professional dealer, and this is recouped in the mark-up they charge, which is typically 10 per cent on small purchases of, say, up to £2,000. The product they sell cannot be sold on the main market because it is in the wrong form, and it has been in private hands and could have been corrupted. As a result it is usually sold back to a private dealer at a discount of 2 to 3 per cent. The difference is therefore very marked. A professional gold bar is bought or sold at a cost of between 0.4 per cent and 1 per cent – depending on how many large bars you buy. A private trade is likely to be around 10 per cent.'

An opportunity presented itself. 'The chance in this situation is that to retain its value the gold must not be sent to the customer. The IT [information technology] challenge is to match [or exceed] the safety which customers feel they get with holding gold in their hand. If you can meet this challenge – and we try to do this using professional vaults, insurance, the transparency of a daily published "Audit" – then you have the Internet's ideal, which is a product, like horseracing bets, that you do not have to ship expensively to the customer.'

If Tustain could trade professionally, paying less than 1 per cent, a business generating income to cover operational costs, share dividends, and profit was possible. As for the competition, Tustain viewed what existing operations there were already in the business as poorly thought out business models.

Of course, now you can trade efficiently on computers. 'In addition we had identified – like Betfair – a disaffected retail customer base which knows that it has been getting a raw deal because of the huge differential between retail and wholesale pricing. By using an online, person-to-person Internet model you can cut out the expense of a middleman, and get the customer a far, far better deal.'

There were solutions for other issues that the idea of an exchange raised. When considering Betfair as an investment, Tustain asked where was the way to market? He worried about this in relation to BullionVault. 'Betfair had the *Racing Post* to reach the bookmakers' market in the high street shops. We had nothing similar, but equally, we did not have the competition from the equivalent of bookmakers. I figured that, with the growth and increased sophistication, our market – people who wanted personally to buy gold – would simply put into a search engine like Google, the words "buy" and "gold". If we made sure that we were top of what search engines generated in response, I had my route to market.'

All that was left was to ask, 'fancy some gold as a gift'. He explains: 'I also realised by accident how I could defeat the natural scepticism that will always exist around a venture like BullionVault. Simply, we gave new customers free gold. If they became regulars then we would get the gold back as the gold itself never left the vaults in Zurich where it was stored. We said, have a gram and see how you go with that, knowing that we could get it back.'

Financing BullionVault proved a challenge, as had been the case with Betfair, albeit for different reasons. A very wealthy man thanks to the success of his first Internet endeavour, Tustain was comfortably able to meet the initial development costs of BullionVault which came to £200,000. This went between October 2003 and March, two years later. Then Tustain sought outside investment of £2 million, ostensibly to fund the purchase of bullion the website would need to own for trading purposes.

'There was a special circumstance with the launch finance, which was that I was planning to buy gold with most of the funds raised,' he reasons. 'As this was not a wasting asset, and because I was planning to invest myself, it was possible to arrange for investors' money to be much safer than would be normal in a young business. The capital was split into three tranches; new equity, a management bond, and convertible debt. I financed the middle tranche with about £1 million. New equity – the smallest tranche at £200,000 – was simple ordinary shares, which gave the company money to sink into marketing. Both the management bonds and convertible debt were in the form of bonds to be invested in gold. Both were for £1 million. My management bond was not convertible or redeemable, but was a gold-denominated loan paying 7 per cent. The convertible debt was sterling-denominated, redeemable in two years, or at the same time convertible into ordinary shares. It paid a 6 per cent yield. For each £6 an external investor invested £1 went to equity, and £5 to convertible debt. My bonds ranked behind the convertible on liquidation. Critical to the deal was that the equity gave my middle tranche some protection, while my middle tranche gave a very high degree of protection to the convertible debt. Were we failing, it was clear I would be motivated to close the business to get as much of a redemption as possible from my £1 million, and the convertible would be completely safe. As a result the external investors were extremely likely to be able to redeem 5/6ths of their money, and get a 6 per cent yield on it, so even if things went wrong they'd get 93 per cent of their money back. And if things went well they'd get the high upside by converting.'

He says laughingly: 'Most people were so confident of me not chucking away my £1 million [which, he insists, would be very out of character], they regarded the convertible as virtually guaranteed, so they were happy to invest quite large sums.'

What Tustain had not predicted was trouble with the banking system itself. Setting out to trade in gold, integrity was a key issue for BullionVault. Like Betfair the company had aimed to be always beyond reproach. 'We could have been offshore,' Tustain suggests. 'We could have traded

silver which, offshore, would have meant deals without
any VAT which would have been an advantage. But I never
wanted to sail close to the wind. Nor would it be in my
customers' interests,' he reasons.

The Treasury seemed to be accepting. 'We got in touch
with them about a new product we were going to introduce to the market. We had a long chat about the impli-
cations of this. In the end they suggested we propose
legislation that would cover everything. We did and this
was eventually incorporated in the same year's finance act.
We were in the UK and not asking for any special favours,
just making the point that something we were planning to
do needed consideration. As a result, changes were accommodated. I am sure that would not have been the case had
we been offshore.'

The problem was that high street clearing banks were
less accepting. Initially, BullionVault set up accounts with
HSBC. The bank seemed at first to be understanding of
the website's specific requirements, a little out of the ordinary compared to more traditional clients, for sure. New
legislation covering money laundering also became law in
2003. This received due consideration and – to the relief
of Tustain who recalls about thirty-seven meetings ahead
of the crucial one with HSBC – everything seemed in place.
Until, that is, six months before the launch of Bullion-
Vault, a letter from HSBC arrived shutting down
facilities on the grounds that the business was simply not
one with which the bank wanted a relationship.

Financially speaking, Tustain was back on the streets.
'That was when the shoe leather began to wear out,' he
winces. At least today he is able to laugh. Ultimately, Bob
Smith of Lloyds TSB, came to the rescue. Bob Smith? He

laughs again at the notion that if this was an alias it was hardly inventive. Yes, his real name.

BullionVault's offices do not convey at all the sense that they represent the hub for trading which is now well into nine figures a year. On arrival across from the main office door is a deep shelf hosting a computer laptop with two barstools for those visitors curious to sit and trade using their gift of a minted gram. Behind anyone seated there is a glass case holding a gold bar. Unless you handle gold regularly, the weight and substance of this is to behold.

To the right of the bullion, hanging on the wall is a caricature of a moustached sophisticate reading from a book with jacket showing only a pound sign. Bookcases house numerous computer manuals as well as fiction and non-fiction related to BullionVault's core business. Ian Fleming's *Goldfinger* seems well thumbed. Of the eight staff on-site, all have two screens to view (with Internet companies this seems to be the fashion). The IT desk – hub of any such operation, in this instance two people – is in the furthest corner away from windows offering sight of King Street, in splendid relative isolation. Only the accounts department – at one person, 50 per cent the size of Bullion-Vault IT – is there for company.

'We started out in a garage,' Tustain recalls. 'Since then we have relocated as we have gone up the staircase; £1.6 million of trade in our first six months, then £31 million in our first full year, £42 million the following twelve months. In year three we expect over £200 million. We are not, ourselves, speculating on the price of gold. It can go down and we still make money. We have slim margins and succeed by having a big turnover. In order to win on the Internet you need to be the cheapest. We claim we are. We are also incredibly efficient. Each member of staff represents, in a year when we expect to trade £200 million, over £25 million in business.'

Tustain takes a moderately modest moment of self-admiration; having made his fortune twice over, there is an entitlement. He considers how far BullionVault has come in a short space of time. Actually, the financial crisis only helped, he notes. In trading terms, there have been many landmarks. To break through £1 million of trades in the company's first six months was significant by any measure. The leap in trade between year two and year three should go down as a conclusive step towards corporate adulthood. To hit £200 million conveys that the sky is the limit.

The first deal involving gold trading at $1,000 an ounce represented a further milestone. This one has a particular resonance with Tustain. 'A small trading company from Hong Kong bought a small sum of bullion from a private individual in Ottawa, Canada,' he recalls. At around this time (March 2008) a big fuss was made when a dealer offered to sell an ounce for four figures. Offering and actually trading are two different things, altogether, points out Tustain. Any fool can offer gold at a certain price, he argues. 'The acid test is selling it'.

He adds that recruiting a Chinese speaker was another landmark with emerging markets in mind. 'We were lucky to find her,' Tustain admits. Then a word of caution. 'You cannot deal in expectations and anticipations in these worlds. They either work, or they don't. You cannot plot a path on a graph. Where would that graph be? There is a degree of planning for success, and a big degree of hoping. But if you want a business on the Internet, there has to be a positive cash flow. There are a huge number of web businesses which have folded in the last three to four years because they never generated significant cash flow. That is something that we do and Betfair does, too.'

Like Betfair and other successful websites, sometimes the weight of trade tests the system. In the office is new hardware. 'Web servers always go down,' shrugs Tustain. 'More important, we have never lost the database. In the terms and conditions, continuous activity is not assured. But we are not Betfair, gambling on the outcome of sport. Suppose connectivity went down for two hours. The worst case scenario then is maybe a 1 per cent market fluctuation. The Stock Exchange goes down, too, you know. I do. I tried to sell some shares recently. The exchange was down.'

Tustain sometimes has to leave his office at great haste. He suffers, periodically, from Crohn's disease and, before talking, will warn you he may exit at any moment. This does not seem to break his thought process. Internet companies starting up are different, he maintains, leaning back in his chair. The conversation returns to widgets, as discussed earlier. 'If we had a production line making them and we got it wrong by just a little bit, we would think, the machines, the tools, everything costs too much to change,' Tustain argues. 'You'd most likely say, we'll just have to live with it. At BullionVault, we spend ages tinkering away.'

Andrew Garrood describes himself as a Luddite when it comes to computers. Before he joined Cantor in 2000, the Old Etonian – a scholar, which meant he was considered by the school to be worth helping to bankroll his education – was in banking. Blessed with the nickname of Shrewdy Garroody, and judging by his enthusiasm for IT, it seems fair to assume that the spread betting company wanted him for his judgement of markets rather than what he might contribute to the smooth running of what is an incredibly extensive computer services department.

A conversation about the roots of spread betting and fixed-odds betting and their relationship with Betfair is interrupted by repeated taps on the glass walls of Garrood's meeting room, high above old London and Canary Wharf. He must rule on what credit an Asian client has to guarantee for him to be able to have a spread bet on the evening's European football, playing at $500,000 a goal. Eventually, after the level of seniority involved in discussions rises to include men with ties – looking all over like financial controllers – as well as the more casual dressed coal-face operators at the start of negotiations, Garrood settles nerves by ruling that $1.6 million should be forthcoming. Though his cuff links are miniature sets of playing cards, he will not take too many chances. Clocks on the wall for New York, London, Europe, Las Vegas, Tokyo, and Sydney show that the Nevada-based Executive, whom Garrood visits at least monthly to brief of developments, is probably asleep, and not on the end of a phone to endorse his decision. 'Are the bosses up?' Garrood asks, perhaps a little hopefully.

Once order on the trading floor is restored, Garrood turns his thoughts to the world betting market as a whole. 'As a concept, I think Betfair is remarkable,' he enthuses. He admits that there are few who could have foreseen the success it has enjoyed, and includes himself in the numbers who failed to grasp what was ahead at the start of the millennium. 'I think it has helped to make sports betting markets a lot more transparent to both the provider and the consumer, and has thus contributed a high level of efficiency to the marketplace as a whole. Those who benefit from that transparency are Betfair-friendly; those who do not are Betfair-hostile. I think society as a whole is a fan of the person-to-person environment – consider eBay – and Betfair has successfully leveraged that enthusiasm, and enabled its retail users to engage in this field, without having to go to the regular high street provider in analogous fashion to eBay.'

He thinks back to his former life in the City of London with a nostalgic smile. 'The move to the exchange-traded environment is irresistible: financial markets had a similar revolution in the mid-to-late-1990s, when electronic platforms replaced armies of brokers calling transactions to each other across a pit floor.' A bit like the film, *Trading Places*, he jokes. More shouting than calling, too.

Inspired by Betfair, Spreadfair was born of Cantor Sport. In horseracing, jokes Garrood, you would say Spreadfair was out of Cantor Sport (then Cantor Index's sports spread betting division). For the four years of its life, the company traded alongside more senior, established operations. 'It grew faster than Cantor Sport ever did [in both the volume of bets taken, and revenue], and showed itself to be far more scalable [in other words, fewer staff required to administer more traffic]. As a model, it was far more attractive for us to run this one than it was to run a one-dimensional sports spread betting business.' Unprecedented market conditions claimed the business despite it, like Betfair, being based on sound principles.

Betfair was both inspirational and reassuring back before launch. 'Betfair's success gave us the security of knowing that there was a big appetite on the street for exchanges. The next question was, can this work? In fact, liquidity was pretty instant. On launching, Spreadfair attracted clients, who were not natural sports spread bettors. Size of bet? Ultimately, that was always defined by the outcome. If I buy £100 of England runs at 350, and they score 400, I have had a £5,000 bet. If they score 600, I have had a £25,000 bet. But there were solid six-figure outcomes during Euro 2004 on the eventual champions, and there were many occasions that followed ahead of closure where sums of that size were commonplace. Some of those incidents have been during high-profile events: World Cup 2006, Rugby World Cup 2007, for example. One of the beauties of spread betting is that you can never predict when the extraordinary event is going to happen. So a six-figure wager can just as easily result in a bet on a Championship football game on a Friday night as in a World Cup Final: it only needs an extraordinary result to happen.'

Spread betting on an exchange was complex (this, as well as economic downturn had some role to play in the decision to cease trading). Nonetheless, Spreadfair, on launch and during its four-year life, was a beneficiary of the educational curve clients of Betfair had experienced. Players first firmly grasped the exchange concept preparing them for grander, altogether more complex calculations trading on Spreadfair. Thanks to Betfair, the transition – or more likely the addition of an outlet to a portfolio of gambling options – to Spreadfair was consequently smoother. There is no question that this is true,

Garrood, a cautious thinker rarely prone to exaggeration or overstatement, acknowledges.

A moment to ponder the passing of Spreadfair, a profitable venture caught up in unprecedented financial market chaos, seems appropriate. The news was conveyed by a single web page effective from 4pm, 1 December 2008, with a cast-iron promise to return deposits. 'Broadly, we were dealing with a young male, quite tech-friendly, with no difficulty with the transition from one betting medium to another,' Garrood maintains. 'Some were punters, some were traders. The difference between the two is that you can only trade where the exit and entry costs are cheapest. Only if I know I can get out cheaply, am I prepared to get in. Thus, if a fixed-odds bookmaker frames prices on a football match to 108 per cent, there is an 8 per cent hurdle to surmount, if you choose to trade with him. If the prices on an exchange bet to 101 per cent, then the hurdle is only 1 per cent. The trader will migrate to the most efficient marketplace where he will enter and exit the market repeatedly. That does not mean that the bookmaker betting to 108 per cent does not see traffic. Of course, he does. But the traffic he sees is likely to be from the person who is betting on the final outcome of the event. The trader is less concerned with the outcome of the event, but more concerned with what is going to happen to the price of the asset he has just engaged, and how that price will move. These are two distinct groups of people.'

Ultimately Spreadfair needed more than just some assistance from Betfair above and beyond an early steer on how the markets are shaping up. Could Spreadfair have been set up as a stand-alone company without the backing of Cantor? Absolutely not, Garrood readily admits. The magic combination was Cantor's reserves, brains like Garrood, and some help from Betfair in broadening the average gambler's mind. 'Undeniably, Betfair added focus to this gambling space,' Garrood acknowledges.

Garrood looks out again across London. There are, he suggests, three Coral betting shops within sight. For a moment, this seems like an invitation to challenge the number and then strike a person-to-person wager in the spirit of what inspired the setting up of Spreadfair. 'A high-octane game which requires fairly high-octane pockets,' Garrood, with reverence, almost whispers. Not for the dilettante then.

The main home of Blood-Ex, in addition to City of London offices, is more rural than Hammersmith and Canary Wharf. GCG, Blood-Ex's umbrella company, an international professional services firm, is based in Bedfordshire; it is as near to Newmarket, known in British horseracing as headquarters, as to the capital.

Before you make the mistake of thinking that it must be important for an operation trading in racehorses to be near the epicentre of British bloodstock, remember that this is potentially global trade over the Internet. Like Betfair, you could be pretty much anywhere when trading.

Conceptually, perhaps Blood-Ex is actually closest to BullionVault. As gold has long been traded, so has bloodstock. Blood-Ex taps an established tradition for exchange. Blood-Ex has been innovative in recognising that historically horses have long been traded in parts so that they could be owned in partnership. Denominations can be half shares, a leg, and smaller units down to a few per cent;

even a fortieth which has been the number of shares into which colts are divided when syndicated among breeders wanting to take a stake guaranteeing them breeding privileges. In horseracing, most of what runs is for sale, in whatever portion you can buy.

With the notion of selling portions well established, Blood-Ex's invitation to an owner of a racehorse is to place a stake for sale on the exchange market the company has created. Then buyers can take a portion of that and enjoy their investment when the horse runs.

Initial interest in Blood-Ex, when the concept was road tested using imaginary markets during the week of Royal Ascot in 2008 was, according to web patterns recorded by GCG, from twenty-four countries in all. The greatest curiosity – as measured by the number of information downloads that, in all, topped six figures – came from America and Ireland. 'Horsetrading is part of their national DNA,' insists Valentine Feerick, GCG's chief executive. 'In America, there are some people who follow racing for whom a nice deal on a horse is more compelling than the racing and betting.'

Blood-Ex trial markets, which were as-if live during Ascot, showed the concept to have much potential. A stake in the then three-year-old colt called Equiano was posted for sale ahead of him taking his chance in the King's Stand Stakes. The valuation placed on him beforehand, through Blood-Ex, was £70,000. After winning the race at odds of 22–1, his valuation, after trading, rose to £750,000. Then overnight it jumped again to £1.2 million.

In further test runs around the world a private gathering of thirty people in an Arabic state without established bloodstock traditions quickly grasped the concept. In this instance, Feerick set up everyone with a trading laptop and imaginary portfolios of shares in horses, then screened some racing in which they had featured, recorded from a recent race meeting in Britain. In one of the races, a horse suffered an injury in trying to enter the stalls, cutting its head. One of the guests quickly recognised what this meant. As an imaginary stakeholder in the injured horse, he began to sell immediately. In no time, the market for shares in the bleeding colt soon collapsed.

The original idea for Blood-Ex came to Feerick in 2006. Or, to be exact, 25 November that year. He can be so precise because it was a horse race, the Hennessy Cognac Gold Cup run annually that month that prompted him to start thinking. Feerick is a highly successful consignor-seller of bloodstock. He boasts the record price for selling a 'Breeze-Up' horse (where lots gallop before being auctioned off) at Doncaster Bloodstock sales – £245,000; he also holds the record for a yearling – £270,000 – sold by the same auctioneers at the important St Leger sales. On the day of the Hennessy in 2006 he was at Tattersalls auction house in Newmarket, on this occasion as a prospective buyer. At the time of the race, a showcase event in the National Hunt jumps season, most around the sales ring exited to watch the running on televisions located in the bars and café. Feerick remained to snap up a bargain – a colt for 9,000 guineas, subsequently named Winged Cupid and ultimately sold for significant profit privately to the Dubai ruling royal family, the Maktoums. Though personally satisfied, Feerick was still left pondering the madness of how players in a market allowed distortions to value such as his purchase, which he expected to pay at least 50,000 guineas to own. The eventual price was a thought-provoking steal.

Under the planned format for launch that was tested, an owner can put up to 50 per cent of a horse on Blood-Ex. You can then buy actually as little as 1 per cent, or even less. Feerick recalls the Hennessy Gold Cup of 2006 when the race stunted the price of what proved to be a very capable colt. 'With bloodstock, if the vendor is unlucky or makes a single error in presenting his goods for sale, the market can be the end of them,' he laments. 'What's more, there is no easy way for owners to liquidise their assets quickly if required to do so. There are limits on when you can sell, as there are not auctions every day of the year. Then in many cases, the final sale price does not at all reflect value.'

As a speculator in bloodstock, himself, Feerick was able to consult more than 100 of those who are high ranking in the horseracing world about Blood-Ex. Convinced by those he consulted of the potential, he then arranged to meet with the established sales companies, like Tattersalls. An obvious concern they held was whether Blood-Ex would eat into existing market share. If Betfair met with hostility from traditional bookmakers, Feerick experienced a mixture of bewilderment – 'some in the sales companies just didn't get it' – and mild hostility sometimes rooted in ignorance or fear of change.

When he went to see the British Horseracing Authority, he sensed that some of those senior in horseracing's administration would prefer to maintain old customs rather than embrace new ideas. 'The issue is transparency,' reflects Feerick. 'The sales are not transparent enough. The Rock of Gibraltar case [a famous racehorse that raced in 2001 and the following year in the colours of the Manchester United manager, Sir Alex Ferguson, but ended up the centre of a bitter legal dispute over co-ownership and breeding rights with John Magnier] highlighted how confusion can occur. Under Blood-Ex it would need to be clear that what you were selling you also owned 100 per cent,' Feerick insists.

Around £2.5 million is what Feerick estimates would be needed for an individual to set up an operation to rival Blood-Ex. That is £500,000 for the IT and the rest for marketing purposes. He also guesses that, unable to copyright the concept – the idea of an exchange is open to all – or the software, Blood-Ex has six to nine months' head start over potential rivals. First-to-market advantage doesn't last forever.

Blood-Ex's most substantial advantage is and has been to have a corporate mother ship. Technological resources at GCG's disposal converted his idea into a slick reality. Feerick recalls: 'The IT department didn't know anything about horseracing but, after suggesting the idea, I was invited to see a presentation which showed me that they had grasped the concept.' Indeed, he adds that it may actually have been better that those who considered the concept from a technical point of view did not have preconceived ideas or notions. He borrows from Proust: 'The real voyage of discovery consists not in seeking new landscapes but in having new eyes'.

Paul Tustain's experiences at BullionVault differ in one important respect from those of Betfair and Blood-Ex. Those who make up the gold market welcomed him as an addition to the cause. Unlike betting, trade in gold cooled around the time of the millennium. From a height in the 1980s, all that was left two decades on was largely profes-

sionals trading with professionals. BullionVault brings a
new retail customer to proceedings so was welcomed, not
least because a central business aim of BullionVault was
to achieve precisely that. Pure serendipity. What's more,
this was also the brief of the World Gold Council (WGC),
originally established in 1987 by the world's biggest mine
operators. WGC members couldn't have been happier.
'We have simply widened the market,' Tustain maintains.
'All we wanted was what the dealers had to sell, which
was the best gold in the world. Everything else – retail and
distribution costs for example – we take care of.'

So what now for Tustain? 'I enjoyed launching Bullion-
Vault. More so than the first company I ran. I also enjoy
the process of overseeing things. Flotation of Bullion-
Vault? I don't want to run a public company. I have always
believed that the reasons for seeking listed status are the
kudos of PLC status, paper wealth, and the chance to
offload stock. None of which interests me, currently.'

For now at least, he has stopped looking for the next
big idea. 'Further applications of the exchange model?' he
asks himself. 'Back before BullionVault, I did really think
long and hard about where this wonderful exchange technology could be applied.' He ponders the possibility for
creating a market for 'a big slug of shares like, say, BP' to
allow trade specifically on them. He questions whether,
with rights issues and the different types of share that exist
– voting preferences, mutual funds, bonds – whether this
could ever match the simplicity of Betfair, or trade in gold.
'Gold never changes,' he points out. 'A gram of gold is a
gram of gold.'

Comparing BullionVault and Betfair – in this we need
to discount that he set up the former and merely profited

handsomely from taking a stake in the latter – Tustain moderates some of the praise heaped on what nevertheless kick-started his own endeavour. 'I knew and understood the workings of Stock Exchanges – in Betfair's case, it is more Wall Street than City of London – and I was aware of how the Internet worked. What put something like Betfair beyond me was that I knew very little at all about betting. That said, it seemed obvious that there was profit if the cost of bricks and mortar – in other words replace the betting shop with electronics – could be avoided.'

The model was, Tustain maintains, more than sound.

Chapter EIGHT

GOVERNMENT
Suited

'Io, schiavo del gioco, su Internet la nuova droga'. *La Repubblica* in Italy carried this headline on 30 November 2007. 'Slave to the Internet game, the new drug of addiction', is a summary of the menace highlighted by the newspaper. The left-leaning journal – the *Observer* or the *Guardian* would be cousins – went on to consider the *boom dell'azzardo online*, the growth in online risks to readers. Tracked was the experiences of Arnaldo, who took readers through his efforts to kick the habit of *giocatore virtuale* – virtual games – that represent, to the newspaper's mind, the latest hazard of contemporary life, alongside more established relations such as alcohol and drugs.

Italy plays host every week to an officially-blessed national lottery that in October 2008 celebrated a jackpot at the day's exchange rate worth $128 million. Such anxiety about what damage citizens can do to themselves gambling over the Internet reflects the confused thinking that often plagues societies when considering online betting. Governments are by no means free of blame for the contradictions. While lottery policy is debated earnestly by elected officials with society's wellbeing in mind, what is left unsaid is governments that sanction gambling and national lotteries, and at the same time warn of apocalyptic social problems related to betting, are potentially the biggest winners of all. From increased participation exchequers are the recipients of direct tax, and additional revenue streams – discounting the drain from ticket sales – in Britain's case from 2,000-plus instant millionaires the National Lottery has created.

British governments have historically shown plenty of caution in promoting gambling. Consensus over the years was that major deregulation would see a net-loss of votes. Like in Italy, in the past both Labour and Conservative administrations have been kept in check by newspapers and the wider media. Take the contribution of Alice Thompson in the *Daily Telegraph* in February 2008. She advised the Prime Minister Gordon Brown to 'take a long hard look at' the Treasury's addiction to gambling revenues which she estimated to be £2.4 billion a year. Online and casino gambling had risen in ten years from £7 billion to £48 billion and 250,000 people had serious gambling problems, she raged. You can almost see her wagging a finger, brow furrowed with Brown looking back, impassively, apparently silent in gratitude for what Thompson infers subsidised his Prudence policies.

The reality of online gambling's impact on the national coffers, indeed gambling as a whole, is that subsequent yields from direct taxation of betting have rarely been enough to save governments from major shortfalls in income against expenditure. William Hill, Britain's second

biggest bookmaker, registered gross profits for the first
six months of 2008 of £145.1 million. John Brown,
formerly chief executive and chairman of William Hill,
described bookmakers' contributions to the exchequer
from this bottom line as 'not even the size of a fingernail'
when assessed against the body of tax revenues as a whole.
More politically relevant as a reason for a government to
drop opposition to growth in betting might be jobs, a defi-
nite vote winner, and a source of extra tax revenues from
higher employment, always handy. For example, a start-
up company that in eight years grows to the extent that
1,350 are employed, the bulk of them in Britain, would
appeal to any government.

This is, of course, the rate of growth in staff experienced by Betfair. First and foremost, Andrew Black and
Ed Wray had good reason to repay government with a
sizeable payroll contributing to income tax revenue. The
EIS (Enterprise Investment Scheme) government initiative was, both concede, instrumental in giving Betfair a
financial leg-up during crucial early days after launching.
Black, in essence a great believer in the free market, nevertheless more than supports this refinement to survival-of-
the-fittest public economics. 'A great scheme which
thankfully, up to the Budget of 2009, the government
hadn't scrapped,' maintains Wray.

Based on what Tony Blair was saying in 2000 about the
key role of the Internet in future economic growth, it
would follow that the then Prime Minister's administration had no qualms with accommodating the company's
ambitious endeavours, whatever the core business. (Bear
in mind, also, that the government was, itself, a sponsor
of betting, through the National Lottery, the introduction

of which in 1994 was the beginning of the legitimisation of betting politically, to the mind of Westminster commentator Peter Oborne). At the start of the millennium, there seemed to be an understanding at the heart of government that the Internet was untameable. The best you could hope for would be to regulate the beast. At the launch in 2000 of the government's 'UK online' strategy, Blair made clear that he implicitly accepted this and instead saw the Internet as central to the future of the country's economy, placing Britain at the hub of the Internet. Rather than some shady operation dealing in a relatively undesirable practice, Betfair could consider itself as part of the 'knowledge economy'.

Certainly, Betfair has played its part in fulfilling some of Blair's vision. The website draws gamblers from all over the world as the odds on Betfair are attractive, because those who post them have low or no overheads, and there is no direct state involvement which would otherwise mean a take-out that precludes a globally competitive rate of return. In addition, because of the liquidity, you can get your money down. So to hedge domestic bets with this reliable, accessible international facility is, alone, reason for foreign betting interests to have a Betfair account. 'Betfair has become like a global stock exchange or clearing house for the world of gambling,' suggests Joe Saumarez-Smith. 'In this it was helped by Britain's global reputation for gambling. For example, we in Britain legalised betting much earlier than in other countries. Go to the heart of the Hong Kong Jockey Club's betting operation, or similar set-ups in Malaysia or Thailand, or indeed, an illegal operation there, and you will find British gambling experts, Ladbrokes or William Hill-trained, in

charge. Because of Britain's gambling roots and traditions
we still have more legal outlets for betting than anywhere
in the world. This is on what our reputation is based. No
other country compares.'

More than simply ensuring that Britain was at the hub
of the world's latest gambling wheel, which in 2008 was,
over the Internet, reckoned to have been heading towards
a turnover of $20 billion, Betfair has been a more active
partner with government. For example, Memorandums
of Understanding, which Betfair pioneered in 2003 helped
shape government policy on sport's relationship with
betting. Now the essence of these – co-operation with the
authorities when there are suspicious circumstances
related to betting on a match or game – are part of law,
under the Gambling Act of 2005. Perhaps most significant of all, Betfair has successfully conveyed to government that betting need not be seen as a domain full only
of caricature, pork-pie hat wearing spivs. Equally, Betfair
conveyed that the world of betting was not solely populated by victims like Steve Coogan's Bob 'Bing' Crosby
in the dark BBC comedy series *Sunshine*, drawn reck-
lessly to the local 'Cascade Bookmakers' betting shop.
Person-to-person betting is an activity undertaken by
consenting adults. There is no wicked bookmaker,
crooked finger drawing you into a betting shop. Betfair
was a most presentable operation, according to John
Healey, Labour Member of Parliament for Yorkshire's
Wentworth constituency since 1997. Healey was first
economic secretary then financial secretary to the Treasury from 2002 to 2007, including the time when Betfair
was seeking to resolve taxation matters for betting
exchanges.

GamCare's London offices certainly convey a sense of
the sort of decay that the likes of Crosby endure mentally
as their lives fall apart as a result of excessive gambling
many times beyond means. Opposite the main entrance
to Clapham Junction station – and around the corner from
William Hill, with Ladbrokes also up the road – the site
is, according to Andrew Poole, Gamcare's managing director to the end of 2008, something of a step down from the
last base in London Bridge. Nevertheless, GamCare is
better funded today, receiving more than £3.5 million in
annual grants, more than treble the resources available
earlier in the millennium. What's more, Poole seems far
from despondent about the explosion in Internet business
turnover, fuelled by the likes of Betfair. GamCare sees the
Internet betting operations as committed to addressing
problem gambling, which, after all, has never been great
for business. Gambling addicts rarely end up paying up
in full, which is why bookmakers are rarely complicit in
encouraging or nurturing pathological gamblers; that, and
the need to renew licences.

Poole, never over earnest, takes a broad view. 'Internet
gambling has brought betting into the home, and there are
fewer natural breaks in when you can bet, which is the
case at, for example, the races,' he acknowledges. 'That
said, player protection [where the bookmaker intervenes
in a case where the operator believes a gambler may be
damaging his or her life by betting] is becoming competitive between those in this market. The operation 888
[online casino betting and games such as bingo and
backgammon] set up a responsible betting site. When I
mentioned this to a competitor, the market rival was gutted
that they had been beaten to the punch with the concept.'

Poole's latest job is Head of Social Responsibility and Compliance at the satellite television gambling operation, SkyBet. He has a background in social work and arrived at GamCare in 2003 fresh to the betting industry – in his interview he told the panel that he bet 'only when it was a certainty'. At GamCare, he noted that Betfair, in particular, represented something different in attitudes to customer care, sharing a broader perspective. 'They haven't come from a traditional [betting] background so are not entrenched in the industry's ways. Certainly, to me, they seem more aware of how player protection can work for their business. I think [with audit trails and consequently the ability to monitor how much and how often clients wager] they realised early on that they were in a position that land-based operations [betting shop chains and independents] were not. They know when, on what, and how much their clients are betting. Then they can communicate directly with the individual if they note signs of gambling that could be damaging.' A refreshing approach, infectious at least with the Internet trade.

In Britain, betting has historically, with social welfare in mind, been the province of the Home Office. Of the great departments of state – the Home Office, Foreign Office, and Treasury Department – it was always the Home Office that perceived betting as a habit that should be no more than tolerated. The pitfalls of gambling were perennially and firmly to the forefront of civil servants' minds when taking responsibility for gambling now nearly forty years ago. This was not a habit to be lightly regulated.

With the arrival of Betfair that changed, too. As well as promoting the Internet, Tony Blair also inadvertently encouraged a more gentle regulatory approach to gambling. In addition to sentiment expressed in speeches around the turn of the millennium – and Betfair's launch – encouraging Internet enterprises generally, Blair changed the political landscape of betting with a departmental shuffle. Peter Oborne, himself never averse to a gamble, be it on his specialist subject of politics, or during annual visits to the Cheltenham National Hunt Festival, notes the significance of transferring in 2001 responsibility for betting from the Home Office to the Department of Culture, Media, and Sport. 'At the Home Office there was an old fashioned puritan culture against gambling,' he explains. 'The Rothschild Report of 1978 is very good in summarising this, including highlighting connections between gambling and organised crime. Through the 1980s the Treasury battled for control of betting and finally won this battle when responsibility passed to DCMS, a much smaller department that was easier to push around.'

What was the effect of this? For one, bookmakers were in general perceived more as a contributor to the state than the purveyor of a habit that needed to be closely monitored. The industry was granted a greater degree of respect. Unencumbered by a watchful Home Office, relationships between betting – and not only Betfair and exchanges – and government became more acceptable.

In this Betfair more than played a part it could effortlessly fill. The company arrived on the Treasury doorstep to talk tax in smart rather than over-flashy suits, which only helped further. Previously, it has been by virtue of muscle that bookmakers had prevailed in fiscal and regulatory matters. They had both a well-resourced and well-funded lobby group with influence throughout all political parties, according to Healey. Instead of fast talk and hired parliamentary muscle, Betfair used persuasion, even education. 'When bookmakers came to see the Treasury, there would be safety and strength in numbers; they would fill a table,' Healey recalls. Betfair? 'Mark Davies would come, usually on his own, or with one other person.' Healey, who in 2007 was made Minister of State at the Department for Communities and Local Government, adds that Chris Bell, Ladbrokes' chief executive who turned 50 in 2007, was one of the younger members of the bookmakers' parties that visited.

Of course, bookmakers expected Betfair to act the company's age. According to Oborne, they had long been accustomed to prevailing in matters that reached the Houses of Parliament. Bookmakers' interests have traditionally been well represented on the key committees when significant matters are being reviewed. Ladbrokes, William Hill, and others had always enjoyed reasonable returns from the investment made in entertaining MPs at the parties' annual conferences. 'Bookmakers have, like in 1960, managed in the past to change the law,' Oborne reflects. 'They did this to some extent by purchasing political support. MPs became clients of the bookmakers, and I suspect that remains the case. On the relevant committees, as indeed is the case for other industries, bookmaker interests are well represented.'

Today bookmaking in Britain includes a fresher-looking face. Maybe it is stretching the point to draw parallels between New Labour and Betfair. But – though the two were unaware of this – Healey and Davies, who found themselves locked together at the Treasury, might equally have bumped into each other in Cambridge at a

Christ's College alumni dinner. Both studied there, albeit during different eras.

Healey makes light of the switch in responsibility for gambling from the Home Office. Nonetheless, he was able to welcome Betfair into the Treasury's inner sanctum without inhibitions that might have been a result of the Home Office casting a long shadow. In the past, bookmakers had done their most forceful bidding via a powerful lobby, or by displays of strength. Perhaps in the spirit of person-to-person betting, Betfair was most comfortable with meetings underpopulated and informal.

Bookmakers were caught out by the quick rapport established between Betfair and the Treasury. They also took – continue to take – issue with Betfair on regulatory as well as fiscal grounds, struggling with the notion that Betfair has, as well as generating greater empathy and representing a fresh face with an alternative take on key issues, simply argued its case and received a fair hearing. John Brown maintains that Gordon Brown's Treasury essentially legalised Betfair before the due diligence to the consequences of Betfair's business had run its course. He argues that there was undue haste in an early agreement over matters relating to Betfair and tax – followed later by a ruling that those who take bets should not be subject to the same taxation principles as licensed bookmakers. According to John Brown, resolving tax issues raised by Betfair effectively settled, definitively, that the company was trading legally – despite giving customers the chance to act like bookmakers without a permit. Betting exchanges were new to the Treasury, so Brown's argument goes, and once tax issues were settled, who would argue with such an all-powerful government department? Both Healey and

Betfair contest this notion, not least because Betfair had won enough arguments, debates, and legal exchanges (before and after that) to answer anyone disputing the company's right to trade. 'The legality of Betfair was not in doubt,' points out Healey.

Depending on whether you maintain that Betfair enjoyed privileged status among government ministers, Betfair's first Queen's Award for Enterprise was either further proof of conspiracy between the Oxbridge-like-minded, or well-earned and a reflection of how a company had begun to change government perceptions. In 2003, the company collected in the innovation category. Under-scoring the approval of the Department of Trade and Industry and the office of 10 Downing Street, both involved in the awards, was the Queen's signature of approval. Undoubtedly additions to this since then with a host of other awards has made into an impressive roll call. Moreover, Betfair received a second Queen's Award honour in 2008, this time in the international category. So another Royal autograph. In the process, Betfair joined an elite group and is unique among betting industry rivals. This would seem a fair return to them for essentially bring-ing an air of respectability to the betting industry. 'You could say that Betfair has transformed betting into a central, mainstream activity,' Paul Scotney, director of Integrity Services and Licensing at the British Horserac-ing Authority, suggests.

The decision by Google in 2008 to relax a global ban on gambling advertising by allowing operators the chance to target customers in England, Scotland, and Wales suggests this view is more widespread than the British horseracing Establishment. Ed Wray hopes that both Scotney and

Google are right, respectively, to declare a new era and advocate greater acceptance of betting, in Britain and also further afield. The belief central to Betfair's future and continued expansion is Wray's view that, as well as further landmarks domestically, there remains huge potential for growth, worldwide, changing perceptions at the same time. 'Prior to the Internet, Ladbrokes was the world's largest betting company,' muses Wray. 'Back then this was an almost exclusively UK company, with a few Belgian betting shops thrown in. Yet sport today is a global market. Champions' League finals are watched the world over.'

Betfair had established a legitimate legal and fiscal footing domestically. But if they thought that everything would be plain sailing towards a path of global persuasion, they had not budgeted for the resistance to change encountered in seeking to develop Betfair internationally. If Betfair was to achieve global expansion, governments further afield needed to be convinced.

In Australia, the reason for this was largely systemic. Mark Davies relocated to Australia with Ed Wray to secure Betfair a licence to trade there legally. In Australia, they faced a betting industry different in structure to that in which they had established a foothold at home. There were bookmakers and state-owned pool betting with high street shops similar to home, and variations between states on how this was all regulated.

The importance of the state-sponsored pool betting was that this was central to generating funds to underwrite each state's racing programme. In other words, the Victoria State TAB helps towards the prize-money pool for the Melbourne Cup, run at the state capital's principal racecourse, Flemington Park. Hostility towards Betfair from

Australia's state racing administrators was based on a belief that potential contributions to racing, state and nation-wide, would be exported (overlooking Betfair's willingness to pay for licences to trade).

In the end, the establishment of a serendipitous relationship with government – in this case at state level, which ultimately opened up the market nationally – once again proved the key to Betfair securing a foothold in Australia. After an extended courtship, Tasmania granted Betfair a licence to trade on the basis that the partnership would help grow betting across the board, resulting in better funding for the sport which had much need for capital investment. What made this crucial to Betfair was that under federal law, this automatically granted a right to trade throughout mainland Australia, too, albeit without the freedom to advertise or market services in states where the company was not licensed.

This did not go unchallenged. Western Australia's state government contested the right of Betfair to trade on the back of a licence from Tasmania. This view was roundly rejected by Australia's highest courts. In the process, Betfair exposed 'draconian state laws and regulations', according to Bruce Clark, the respected East Coast horseracing broadcaster and writer. Many of these are now either being contested or will be reviewed voluntarily. As in Britain, Betfair was changing the legislative landscape of betting. 'Clearly the wagering landscape in Australia has been evolving and changing with Betfair's arrival,' Clark maintains.

So in Britain and Australia, Betfair seemingly won the argument – and in the process shaped government thinking and attitudes in both hemispheres. Ahead lie similar struggles for Betfair. To the east, much of Asia, China, and

Japan are existing and potential betting markets that would dwarf what turnover Betfair has already established. In November 2008, there was some encouragement; a first commercial race meeting in Wuhan, since Communism came to China, coupled with a breakthrough at the same time in agreeing to give Betfair access to Hong Kong betting pools. So some steps on the way to Betfair becoming a major player in Asia.

Then there is America. Of course, the arrests in 2006 of Peter Dicks, at the time chairman of the Internet gambling operation, Sportingbet, and BetOnSports' former chief executive, David Carruthers under warrants related to investigations into illegal gambling are indicative of how inflexible minds are there. Legislation passed by the then President, George W. Bush in October 2006 criminalising aspects of online betting, which resulted in the incarcerations, is a major hurdle. Yet with the illegal sports betting market – over and above the legitimate ones operating out of Nevada state – there is huge growth on offer to Betfair if the company can leverage open the world of US betting. In eventually accessing this by persuading government of prohibition's futility, David Yu, Betfair's chief executive since 2006, and Ed Wray ideally both hope to stay at large.

The purchase of TV Games Network (TVG) in January 2009 by Betfair from the Nasdaq-quoted operation, Macrovision Solutions Corporation for $50 million certainly represents a foothold. The company is the official television and interactive wagering partner of the National Thoroughbred Racing Association and, Betfair maintains, 'among the most widely distributed horseracing networks in the world and also a provider of advance deposit wagering services in the US'.

If America is a work in progress, closer to home there is France and other European Union member states. The struggle to secure overall freedom to operate throughout the European Union mirrors the battle in Australia. There a licence in one state gives rights to trade nationwide. Under EU law, a licence to trade in one member country should mean the same privileges throughout the community unless individual countries choose to licence no one in which case no one profits. Betfair has encountered some difficulties with the so-called common market (just as the company did in Australia with interstate disputes), not least at the French tennis championships of 2008 when those suspected of trading on Betfair were removed from Roland Garros. The French tennis federation protested that on Betfair €230 million in bets were traded, yielding nothing to fund development of the game, nationally. At least proposed deregulation in 2010 of domestic French law may help Betfair address this.

Are any of the obstacles insurmountable? Not if Betfair continues to impress government and shape official thinking. Bookmakers in Britain would have given long odds on Betfair clearing legal hurdles ahead of launch in 2000, let alone establishing a working relationship with government that, partly because of what Betfair represented and partly through the company's persuasion, has contributed to wholesale changes to thinking on betting. Proof of which alone is in the Gambling Act of 2005. The latest battleground is the Netherlands. In 2008, Betfair's case against the Dutch government preventing the company from taking bets from there was referred to the European Court of Justice. Betfair maintains that the Dutch Council of State has asked for key rulings on whether it is legal to refuse Betfair a licence to take bets online when a state monopoly is free to do so.

Back in 2000, before the era of exchanges, Andrew Black had told friends, family, indeed anyone who would listen that 'we are going to the moon'. World domination is presumably part of that journey. So far, Betfair has made it halfway round the globe to Australia and, in the process of changing perceptions of those in power, now has licences in Germany, Austria, Italy, and Malta, as well as site users in more than eighty countries. Colour these domains on a map in pink and you have a landmass spreading further than the old British Empire enjoyed in days gone by. Not a bad base from which to press ahead.

The Houses of Parliament have a presence about them, which means that, whatever your opinion of individual politicians and however cynical you might be about their nature generally, you cannot contest that this is a true seat of power.

At its heart is the central lobby. Here Members of Parliament and those with peerages sitting in the House of Lords gather to greet visitors. A similar concentration of elected and nominated public servants can also be found during the summer recess in the corporate box that Betfair has at Lord's cricket ground. (Politicians like their cricket and Betfair, though a relative novice to lobbying games, is delighted to accommodate them). Otherwise, this is a unique space, between the Upper and Lower Houses.

Since John Healey was elected as an MP along with a host of other hopeful Labour Party candidates in 1997, he has passed through this space on an almost daily basis when the House of Commons has been in session. Andrew

McIntosh feels even more at home. He took up a seat in
the House of Lords as Baron McIntosh of Haringey in
1983, having crossed swords with the former Mayor of
London, Ken Livingstone, during the latter's struggles to
rule the capital from his Greater London Council power
base. That is a quarter century at the capital's real seat of
power, and counting.

Both acknowledge the power of the bookmakers' lobby
in Parliament. 'Confident', Healey suggests. For the reasons
behind this, he suggests a look at the register of members'
interests, which lists allegiances that MPs have with worthy
or constituency-relevant causes. Ladbrokes, William Hill,
other bookmakers are all well represented. The MP George
Howarth, a former junior government minister under Tony
Blair, has earned £30,000 a year advising William Hill. His
party colleague Gareth Thomas enjoyed the 2008 FA Cup
Final courtesy of a Ladbrokes invitation. Others involved
with the betting industry include Alan Meale (Labour) and
John Greenway (Conservative). Traditional bookmakers
have always invested heavily in political capital. (Incidentally, Healey has no consultancies or interests outside his
brief, McIntosh receives a weekly payment for a day's work
at the Gambling Commission and Betfair did ferry the then
Sport Minister, Richard Caborn, to the 2007 Rugby World
Cup Final in Paris).

From 2002 to 2007 Healey was part of Gordon Brown's
Treasury team and took responsibility for resolving issues
related to the taxation of betting exchanges. 'Betfair was
something completely knew to us,' Healey recalls. 'The
business model was different to traditional bookmakers.
The Betfair model [with the churn of betting exchanges]
could not sustain betting duty [based on turnover]. It

would have driven them out the business. Another tax scheme was needed.'

Healey maintains that the Treasury is where the sharpest brains in government go, though sometimes without the most deep knowledge of the brief. 'Brighter, younger, often serving in a number of jobs within the Treasury,' Healey sums up the common profile of those in his old department. In conversation, he leaves no doubt that the team was greatly impressed by Betfair's approach to regulatory matters. About the fixed-odds traditional bookmakers, he is little more than diplomatic.

As political persuaders, Healey's assessment of Betfair in the company's early days is that 'they learnt as they went along'. They grew in confidence, he adds. What did strike him was a general openness in dealing with Treasury officials whom Healey instructed to 'drill down' in search of information that would ensure fair fiscal treatment. 'We had access to the books, and access to client accounts, as needed.'

A compelling element of Betfair to a government minister in the midst of changing attitudes to betting was the company's commitment, against a backdrop of bookmakers having set sail to Ireland and Gibraltar, to remaining in the UK. Healey refutes the notion held by, among others, Alice Thompson, that the Treasury saw gambling as a cash cow. To illustrate his conviction, he highlights, based on official returns, that the change in casino betting duty for smaller houses in 2007 was officially estimated to be worth £30 million a year in 2007/8 rising to £35 million in the two following financial years to the Treasury, small beer. Instead, he identifies job creation as a motive for supporting the deregulation of betting. It was not so much that bookmakers leaving Britain hit tax yields, more that this put locals out of work. A company broadly committed to the UK and doing exactly what was most appreciated by creating jobs was likely to be better placed to compel government to change minds about betting.

Healey recalls being very struck by first impressions of Betfair. 'The company came across as enterprising and dynamic, having created something that was generating immediate popularity.' He believes that government motivation for deregulating the gambling industry through the Gambling Act of 2005 was to allow those involved to offer more sophisticated, innovative forms while, at the same time, ensuring that the public was protected from the unscrupulous. More sophisticated and better monitored betting – note here the views of GamCare's former managing director Andrew Poole – could be a catch line for much of what Betfair had at very least aimed for since launching in 2000.

Lord McIntosh, at the Department of Culture, Media, and Sport, remembers how impressive Betfair was in contributing to the examination of issues covered by proposed legislation that would ultimately become the Gambling Act of 2005. 'A very professional operation, reasoned debaters and impressive through the rigour of argument,' he recalls. McIntosh remembers that perhaps the greatest curiosity in the Betfair model was the creation of MOUs. 'In particular, there was great interest in the ways that Betfair could detect irregularities in betting,' he recalls. 'The Memorandums of Understanding which Betfair established were of particular interest to us.' John Brown had lost the argument. 'We had no concerns about the ability to take bets – to lay – on Betfair,' McIntosh

assures. 'There has always been layers. In the past, they
had been bookies. Now they were not on their own.'

It was fortunate for Betfair that those politicians who
were most responsive to the company were of the party in
power. Along with Ed Wray, Mark Davies attended a string
of meetings at the Treasury and Select Committee inquiries,
on occasions experiencing the inquisitions alone. 'Labour
MPs have engaged much more than the Conservative Party'
he suggests. 'The guys in power have seemed to have had
more time to listen. The natural predisposition of Tories
would seem to be to start off listening and then try to finish
your sentence for you, without necessarily getting it right.
Labour MPs listen to the end of your sentence, then ask
questions which hopefully can be addressed.'

He adds that Betfair's representative, right-leaning
politically, at the European Parliament has more joy talking to the socialists. Gambling of the people, for the people,
perhaps.

Today Davies maintains that he has never met anyone
in authority or power who has looked at the business in
depth and hasn't come round to Betfair's way of thinking.
By that he means those who have taken at least time to
read a five-page document – be warned, not for those
whose interest is only passing – on risk which outlines
how Betfair is just the next phase in the evolution of bookmaking.

At the start of Betfair's exposure to the political game,
Davies did have a chastening experience, ahead of bringing the company's philosophy to bear. He was at his first
Interactive Betting, Gambling, and Gaming Association
conference when a professional lobbyist came up to him
and asked: 'What do you make of the Joint Scrutiny

Committee line-up?' Davies admits today that back then
he didn't know what the JSC was.

On visits to the Treasury it was always best to be
prepared and to have handy the aforementioned five-page
document on risk management, either to use offensively
or defensively. To illustrate, Davies recalls discussions over
whether person-to-person betting required all Betfair
customers to be taxed like fully-fledged bookmakers.
'Truthfully, I couldn't believe we had so many debates
about something so simple over time. I became really
worried that they would come out against us. I would go
to meetings and their economists would argue, argue,
argue, and argue. I'd be left thinking, how can they argue
that point?' Now he laughs about it. 'In the end they ruled
in our favour. "How do you feel, delighted?" an official
asked. "Relieved," I answered. I explained that it seemed
to me that the economists and civil servants arguing with
us every time just didn't get it. I was then told, that, in fact,
the one who was most argumentative had to be reminded
before meetings that he was there to argue against us in
order to get to the bottom of our case. He had grasped the
concept after the second of many meetings and decided
there and then that, chances were, there was no case to
answer. This was the man who – meetings could get quite
heated – I'd leave thinking that all I wanted to do really
was punch him!'

Peter Jones has squared up, metaphorically speaking,
to his share of government advisors and civil servants. With
over a decade as chairman of the Tote – dealing with the
Home Office for half that time, then DCMS, and facing
the Treasury for all ten years – he saw ministers and secre-
taries of state come, and go. Likewise, Treasury officials,

including those specialising in devil's advocacy. 'The Treasury? How could they hammer Betfair once the company picked up a Queen's Award?' he asks, incredulously. 'The Department of Trade and Industry would not have stood for that.'

He allows himself a quiet chuckle. 'You know,' Jones laughs. 'I was never absolutely sure that government understood Betfair in the first place.'

Peter Jones asks an interesting question about Betfair and America. If the company was a product of US thinking, would a licence be more acceptable? He suggests the answer is yes. He is probably right. Making the case for Betfair currently is Rudi Giuliani. Or at least the lobbying firm the former Mayor of New York set up on leaving civic office (to run, albeit unsuccessfully, for president).

A win for John McCain in the 2008 Presidential election rather than Barack Obama might have helped Betfair accelerate the company's entry to America and licence to trade there. McCain has extensive connections with gaming in the US. The Betfair case is founded on the belief that a state of prohibition is temporary and in America undermined by a belief in freedom of citizens to do as they please. Betfair's hope is that this will in time include the liberty to have a bet online, which is currently legally restricted.

In winning over politicians, Betfair generally suffers from the largely short-term approach to law making. Politicians don't think ahead by ten years on the basis that, most likely, they will have left the political stage by then. The error of this is that by using the law and blocking access to websites an opportunity passes to establish a partnership before the market drifts to other parts of the Internet, legal or otherwise. Also lost in the drift are potential tax revenues. Protectionism is not usually a long-term solution and more often than not reflects an outlook gripped by fear more than anything.

The example of India is a case in point. As Jockey Club Keeper of the Match Book, Christopher Foster has always been very much on the right side of the law. Likewise in the international duties he conducts on behalf of British racing, which include a number of posts with the International Federation of Horseracing Authorities.

The Memorandum of Understanding that Betfair signed with the Jockey Club in 2003 gave Foster every reason to believe that the new company was a force for good or, as has been noted already, in his words, an 'interesting concept'. Naturally enough, on this basis he felt compelled to share the concept with other senior administrators of principal racing domains that he regularly encountered. Accordingly, he asked Ed Wray to produce an explanatory document.

'Ten pages in all, distributed to all the CEOs of racing administrations, worldwide. I said, along with the document, you should really think seriously about doing this for yourselves. One or two were quite interested at first. India was keen to harness the idea. They had and still have real trouble with illegal betting.'

Ultimately, an overriding fear stalled Indian plans and gripped many other domains before the matter had been given anything like a serious consideration. 'Most were totally driven by a fear that the market, overall, would be reduced,' Foster reflects. In other words, they feared for their ability to sustain their own racing industry, as they had done in the past on the back of gambling.

Foster adds that most countries preferred to take issue with the integrity aspect of exchanges. 'That was to cover up what was the real reason, which was commercial,' he argues.

Ed Wray and Tim Levene, at the time head of Betfair's international business division, learnt the hard way that reservation in the likes of China was going to take a while to break down. When the pair arrived at Happy Valley racetrack in Hong Kong, where the local Jockey Club enjoys a gambling monopoly, neither expected that the first conundrum they would have to solve would extend beyond finding the winner of a trappy handicap in which every runner was a potential winner. Instead they had to ponder first, how they could extricate themselves from the Security Room. Levene laughs: 'Within twenty seconds of arriving we were whisked away, apparently because our mobile phones were in breach of some local rule.'

After a decade of corporate start-up stress, beginning with a fruit juice bar chain in 1998, which numbered ten outlets when he cashed in his stake, Levene took the guts of 2007 off. He had earned a leisurely shot or two of vodka in his tomato juice, not least for having advised the Russian government in the Nineties about privatisation.

Levene brought to Asia experience of working with Flutter, joining Betfair after the merger. He had also worked in the betting sector in both the UK and Australia. According to Levene, the main difficulty with online enterprise in Asia is government control of the web. In September 2007, the *Guardian* newspaper reported: 'Thai government tries to shut down 400 websites'. This was achieved under article 20 of Thailand's Computer Crime Act and resulted in the blocking of an additional 1,200 sites on the grounds that they 'disturbed the peaceful social order and morality of the people' or threatened national security.

As well as this sort of obstacle, Betfair may have handicapped itself in Asia. Levene concedes that Betfair's approach there was perhaps more gung-ho than with domestic politicians. 'Maybe we were perceived as arrogant? In Hong Kong, for example, we said "you are ripping off customers by taking 20 per cent out the pool. We are launching Hong Kong racing on our website." That was a mistake. Next time, we went in, doffed our caps, and said, "we shouldn't have done it, can we begin a new relationship?"'

Subsequent approaches were more collaborative (though in Hong Kong, where gambling funds a host of worthy causes, as well as contributing more tax than any other single body, Levene was accused of proposing to take food out of underprivileged children's mouths). Emphasised was the potential of an exchange, licensed and paying corporation tax like any other bona fide business, to mop up illegal betting. 'China has betting of £1 billion a weekend. Singapore, Malaysia, Indonesia, Thailand, Taiwan, Hong Kong; they also all have huge illegal markets,' Levene maintains. 'Our pitch was, you cannot prohibit it as prohibition doesn't work, so you have got to regulate it. Existing government-run gambling monopolies will be uncompetitive, compared to illegal betting, and, if the only option, will fuel the illegal market. To this, we are the obvious solution, a partnership tapping into global liquidity. You cannot put your head in the sand.' An agreement on

Betfair routing bets from Betfair.com to Hong Kong Jockey Club pools is the beginnings of a foothold.

The business sense of collaboration is undeniable. The difficulty is that within these arrangements there needs to be consideration for cultural and social concerns. In Malaysia, Betfair was ruled out on socio-political, cultural, and religious grounds. In Thailand, there is Buddhism to reconcile with the concept of gambling. China had the Communist Manifesto, which is quite clear on the evils of betting.

The absence of unequivocal legislation prohibiting online betting in some parts of Asia, can give the illusion that you can trade already. In Singapore for example, where Levene reckons Betfair made good progress in persuading government to license an exchange, online betting is legal according to Betfair counsel. That said, what if you invite three friends around and all play together? Potentially, this could amount to organised gambling, which is, of course, against the law. At least for now.

Maybe it is exactly because there is such a huge appetite for gambling that betting in Australia is tightly regulated. A nation which seems not to have imported the mother country's historically prudish attitudes to gambling does, nevertheless, require those who bet to do so within parameters that range from restrictive to verging on repressive. Outlawed throughout Australia, for example, is online casino and poker wagering widely available elsewhere and flourishing in Britain.

In Australia, nationally there are also some puzzling anomalies. Take betting-in-running. This is allowed over the telephone but on the Internet is restricted to only horseracing. The logic is that the narrative of sport could be interrupted if betting was encouraged. However, cricket, something of a national pastime, fits perfectly into the in-running model with the narrative sometimes enhanced by up-to-date odds on the state of play. Furthermore, the rules within which punters have to exist also depend on exactly in what state you seek to chance your luck. In Victoria, for example, bookmakers at racecourses can use computers and laptops to have bets in order to hedge positions. Yet they cannot take bets through this software. At the same time, racegoers can do both. Tracks in New South Wales make things a bit more straightforward, if different from elsewhere. At Sydney and country tracks, bookmakers are forbidden from using computers at all.

Over and above all this, Betfair found Australia immensely hostile to the arrival of the concept. Ed Wray and Mark Davies relocated in 2004 in order to establish their company in this ripe domain. The logic was that they would be more respected and heard for having committed to travelling thousands of miles and taken out lodgings to deal with matters in person. In this, bear in mind that there was nothing stopping Betfair simply setting up and trading offshore, which was the option taken initially by many (though this meant restrictions on advertising and taking offices on the mainland).

Wray recalls: 'In Australia when we arrived everyone seemed to know who we were already. In the UK, we sailed in under the radar. People thought, nice chaps, albeit a bit deluded. When they realised we were not so deluded they took us on. In Australia, the first time I went to see a TAB operator, I saw an email in front of my host. All it said was, they [Betfair] are coming.'

Betfair, which set up in partnership with James Packer, son of the late and legendary gambler-businessman, Kerry, was pretty much hindered in its pursuit of a licence from the moment Wray and Davies stepped off the plane. In particular Victoria and New South Wales states found Betfair's mere presence almost too much to bear. 'In the end we put out a press release saying, it is time to play fair dinkum,' Davies shrugs.

Tasmania was the state where Betfair established a partnership with government that was, in fact, even deeper than the working relationship with government back home. The state has always been strongly regulated as far as betting was concerned. What was persuasive about Betfair's approach was that the company proposed effectively a joint venture with the state, to the mutual benefit of Tasmania, Tasmanian racing and, of course, Betfair. More than this – as state-run betting pools had long been the primary source of income for state racing – Betfair pledged that the exchange model would grow betting – responsibly – in conjunction with existing betting arrangements. In other words, Betfair's ambition was not to take the whole cake, but share, modestly, of course, in an even bigger one.

Ahead of the arrival of Wray and Davies, Paul Lennon had been Tasmania's racing minister. He would go onto become the state's Prime Minister. Lennon is proud of the tough regulatory approach to gambling in Australia and in particular his home state. 'We didn't have the first casino in Tasmania but we did have the first one that was legal,' he maintains.

Soon after their arrival in Australia, Lennon met with Wray and Davies, which began what he describes as a two-year courtship. During this, Lennon's anxieties about Betfair – financial and ethical – were addressed satisfactorily. After a further ten months of ironing out details that emerged in drafting the necessary legislation, betting exchanges were made legal. Then on successfully applying for a licence, Betfair became an Australian legal entity in February 2006.

Now out of politics, having resigned as Tasmania's Prime Minister in 2008, Lennon wanted to set the finances of state racing on the best footing possible, aware that online betting, offshore, would leave Tasmania with potential shortfalls in revenue. 'A major consideration was the effect that Betfair could have on Tasmania's ability to participate in the Australian racing industry as a whole,' Lennon explains. 'I was trying to find a new source of income to fund racing. Betfair was an opportunity.'

Since being granted a licence, Betfair has contributed over AUS$14 million to the coffers of Tasmanian racing interests and the government. 'I also had to take into consideration the issues of taxation, probity and integrity, and the funding of racing,' insists Lennon. 'But I had no problem with the probity [because of Betfair's ability to provide audit]. Lay bets?' Lennon asks. 'Isn't that what bookmakers have always done?' he concludes.

Lennon was taken by Ed Wray, whom he describes as 'very impressive'. Wray gave him 'great confidence' in the principles on which the company was based. Further reassuring was Betfair's pledge that if Tasmania's overall income from racing went down as a result of licensing betting exchanges, Betfair would make up the difference, including an adjustment for inflation. Betfair aimed to operate in tandem with the state's pool betting which had previously funded the Tasmanian racing industry. 'Punters could alternate between the two,' Lennon explains.

As a fellow native Tasmanian and racehorse owner and breeder, Rod Thirkell-Johnston was as concerned as Lennon about the integrity and general health of the state's racing and bloodstock. As Tasmania's representative on the Australian Racing Board (ARB) and while maintaining a relatively open mind about betting exchanges, he found himself at the heart of organised opposition to the concept. ARB board meetings got 'pretty heated', he reflects. Remember in this that New South Wales still blocks the use of computers on-course. 'I was caught in the crossfire,' Thirkell-Johnston shrugs.

Personally, he admits to reservations, at first, about Betfair. Today, he heralds the partnership as 'an essential part of Tasmanian racing's future'. A long-time public servant, Thirkell-Johnston maintains: 'I have won and lost a lot of arguments. My view has always been, if things go against you or go the other way to how you were thinking, you still have to get behind the measures. With betting exchanges, I can see that the state partnership with Betfair has yielded better prize-money and also funded capital developments.'

In confronting issues raised by Tasmanian government officials during talks, Ed Wray had British bookmakers to thank. The arguments thrown at him were pretty much what he had experienced at home. This was especially true in relation to concerns over integrity and using inside information for profit. 'In Tasmania, the lower house of the Parliament is government-controlled and they had made their decision [to support us]. The Upper house was independent, so we had an open session. I was asked about criticisms we had received in the UK. I was able to pull out a quote from the individual who had been critical which said, inside information is the lifeblood of racing. Then I could say, I disagree, we should all have the available information. As for backing to lose, I took them through what that actually means and what laying is. For that there is always the Stock Market analogy. If you want to sell shares, it doesn't mean you want that company to go bankrupt or, worse still, that you will make it go bankrupt. You are selling the shares simply because you believe them to be too expensive.'

The reasons for Betfair seeking a foothold in Australia – and in the process reshaping government thinking – are more than just the nation's appetite for betting. As former City of London men of finance, Black and Wray understood the notion of following the sun, like banks. 'We wanted to function round the clock and with the best will in the world people do not perform as effectively at four in the morning as they do during the day,' Wray explains. 'So we needed to go as far away from the UK as we could. Australia has some similarities with Britain in terms of racing and betting, with a few big players, albeit predominantly pool betting. Plus, of course, Australia is English-speaking. Our international phone system is sufficiently sophisticated to reroute calls during the night in the UK to where someone is at work during normal hours. With disaster in mind, we now have a contingency for if something happens in the UK that means we cease to operate. In the face of such a catastrophe we can run things from Australia.'

To date, Betfair's prize for prevailing in Australia barely seems worth the effort. According to Andrew Twaits, chief executive of the company's venture there, Betfair has achieved market penetration of less than 1 per cent. Indeed the company name is better known for litigation towards a licence than for the product on offer. Nor will it be able to make an impression by offering online casino and poker while these remain banned.

That will change, eventually. Already being addressed is the general awareness of Betfair. In November 2008, Twaits announced a deal with Sandown Park racecourse in Victoria. The venue has been renamed Betfair Park.

Chapter NINE

BOOKMAKING
High Net-Worth Individuals

Tim Levene epitomises how Internet betting has drafted in a whole new class to an age-old trade. Educated at City of London School and Manchester University, he speaks fluent Russian, along with acceptable German and, by virtue of marriage, passable – according to Mme Levene – French. At Luciano's in St James's Street, Marco Pierre White's current London flagship eatery, his entrepreneurial mentality takes him away from the selection of coffees, some of the best in town, to the range of fruit juices on offer. He may have sold the bulk of his founders' stake in Fresh n' Smooth, the chain now called Crussh he established in the last decade before cashing in around the millennium, but he cannot leave the market entirely alone (partly because he retains a small interest in his creation). This, and Russian privatisation, a specialist area of Levene's when living and working there in the last decade, are not the usual concerns of traditional bookmakers.

Bookmakers? Ah, he says. His expression alone is indicative of a cultural divide. Having worked in Australia on the privatisation of TABCorp, the state and national pool betting network – and the flotation and acquisition, respectively of the British bookmakers, William Hill and Coral – Levene experienced worldwide exposure to them before he took up with Flutter in 2000. Then he joined Betfair when the two exchanges merged two years later.

During his time with betting exchanges, Levene recalls that bookmakers in Britain seemed fixated on the legality of this new market threat, that a company could facilitate the taking of bets by unlicensed individuals spared all the hassle of applying for an official permit. Of course, at the same time, whatever the substance of the gripe, businesses had to be run, and areas certainly existed for collaboration. Indeed, co-operation might have led to mutual gain. Instead, to Levene's mind, bookmakers simply hammered away at Betfair's right to exist. When he did find himself chatting, usually informally to senior management of traditionally-minded gambling houses, the conversation would inevitably come round to the same old, same old – namely whatever was the ongoing litigation or inquiry of the day into Betfair's right to be.

Levene recalls a casual exchange that for him, now out of the betting world again and restored to the wider corporate domain, seems like another age. To him, moments like this represented the chance to talk informally to bookmakers and try and better understand their mindset amid regulatory battles and conflict in government inquiries that were ongoing between the traditional industry and Betfair. 'Bookmakers had lost about what seemed to be ten hearings in a row,' Levene recalls. 'I found myself talking to a CEO of one of the big players in British betting. I asked, "so, 10–0, is that it?"' He shakes his head. 'The response was along the lines of, yes, you are right, 10–0. But after the next one, if it is 10–1, we actually win. So we keep going. In other words, let's not simply compete when we can shut betting exchanges down.' Institutions like Ladbrokes cannot lose to operations like Betfair, Levene concludes. 'They would always say, look we have been lobbying Parliament for years. We have spoken to MPs. They agree that it is outrageous.' So on we went, he adds.

Levene laughs. 'At Betfair board meetings, I would report this, that they were not giving up. Everybody would say, great. Our biggest fear? That would have been that one of the major bookmakers was starting up an exchange, themselves. Or all together? That would have made it even worse. Every time we thought that might be happening we were scared.'

Levene left Betfair in 2005. To an extent bookmakers remain pre-occupied with the legality of betting exchanges, which effectively means the right to exist of the dominant market force in Betfair. Victor Chandler is universally recognised by the betting industry as one of the more innovative operators. In 1996, after two years of searching for the ideal location, he took his family firm's head office – something of a bespoke gentleman's bookmaker amid nationwide and increasingly interchangeable high street brands in Britain – to Gibraltar, ahead of completing the company's relocation by 1999. This ensured that generations of clients built up over years of traditional bookmaking enjoyed tax-free betting and positioned the firm – set up in 1946 by Chandler's grandfather, William – to exploit fully the Internet which in 2002 became the predominant source of turnover superseding telephones as a means of trade. Today, Chandler is personally based in Gibraltar overseeing an operation claiming 500,000 customers in 160 countries betting over £1 billion a year. 'Betfair?' he ponders for a moment. 'You know, I still cannot understand how Betfair and betting exchanges can be legal,' he reasons. 'If I am sitting on a bar stool in the pub taking your bet that is illegal. So what is the difference?' More accepting than most, he adds: 'I'm still jealous I didn't think of it first.'

John Brown, formerly of William Hill, doesn't even concede at least that the idea was a good one (maybe, privately, in a quiet moment of contemplation). For him, 100–0, or even 1,000–0 in the courts is not going to change anything. 'If two people are having a bet then one of them must, by anyone's logic, be a bookmaker,' he reasons. 'Otherwise, William Hill, the rest of us, what have we been doing exactly if we haven't ever taken a bet.'

Brown still grumbles about the taxation of exchanges which he maintains gave an advantage to Betfair in the company's early months then cushioned their growth once turnover-based betting tax became a gross-profits duty in 2001. 'Betting exchanges were aiding and abetting unlawful gambling. We felt that government should act. But no one brought the exchanges to account. Rates of duty and tax were agreed. By agreeing to those, companies like Betfair were legitimised.' He also takes issue with the relevance to the business of Betfair's pioneering Memorandums of Understanding that give sporting associations and federations access to betting information when market moves hint at – or scream – the possibility of corrupt practices affecting outcomes. Betfair claims the ability to deliver meaningful audit trails allowing the authorities to locate and then, as needs be, confront and ultimately prosecute. 'Perfect audit trails,' Brown snorts. 'When someone in Asia today – illegal most likely – tries to lay bets of £10 million with them? They are going to find him, are they?'

According to Joe Saumarez-Smith, who has experience of a wide range of Internet gaming operations, Betfair audit trails mean that the company is 'reasonably accurate' in claiming that bets can be traced, even allowing for the existence today of accepted ways to mask your address and details when using the Internet. 'You have to get your money into the system somehow and that has to come by way of a recognised source,' he argues. He bases this on a decade of working in the field and contests Brown's opinion that money in Betfair is potentially from some mystery, untraceable source. 'You cannot take a bundle of used fivers down to Betfair's Hammersmith offices,' Saumarez-Smith insists. 'Even if you did, that is not how you will be paid out. Once in the banking system, these days you practically have to produce your first born as well as your passport.'

It is a bit rich the bookmakers squealing, Saumarez-Smith suggests. 'In one instance, they have been told off in an English court because some manager of a building society has nicked millions in order to go next door to the bookies. Bundles of cash with the society's tag still on them. Obviously the money should not have been accepted. Then there is the guy, maybe Chinese, who comes into his local betting shop and loses eight grand or so. They don't go to much effort to find out where that money comes from or if the cash is being laundered. They know what is going on, and they don't always stop it.'

In the opposite corner to Brown, Andrew Black and Ed Wray observe bookmakers with a mixture of respect – limited, on occasions when attacks on their creation have exceeded acceptable boundaries of corporate competition – and occasional bewilderment.

Wray admits: 'One of the biggest concerns we had early on was that one of them would look at the idea of betting exchanges and think, great thinking, we should do this, too.'

Black identifies the limits of the bookmakers' business model as reasons for their reaction to a new force arriving in the market. 'When I first told people about the Betfair model, the first reaction was, typically, why has no one else done this? The answer was that the bookmakers could not. They are this inflexible and immovable object. They might want to copy the Betfair model but they cannot. Imagine, Ladbrokes re-inventing themselves as a betting exchange? They couldn't. There was no halfway step for them.'

The problem bookmakers faced was that within the betting exchange model was the germ that would most likely destroy them. This was, after all, person-to-person betting. Players operated without the vast overheads of running a high street shop chain. As a result, the market on Betfair featured better odds than bookmakers could sustain. Individuals at home operating with computers don't face the cost structure of a highly-developed retail network. If a bookmaker had set up an exchange – offering odds similarly unburdened by costs – and running alongside an extended off-course chain of high street betting shops the exchange odds would most likely also be more attractive. In the circumstances customers might rightly ask, 'in my shop the odds are 3–1. But on the exchange they are 5–1. Why don't I have a bet at 5–1 along with everyone else on the Internet?' Only if these markets could be kept separate – and there are some grounds for believing this could be achieved – could a traditional book-maker add an exchange to the corporate portfolio.

There was, over and above the difficulties of simply copying Betfair – industrial plagiarism – an altogether more serious aspect to bookmakers finding themselves simply confronted by low-cost competition. Betting shop prices – the Starting Price – are actually determined by what happens in betting at the racecourse. A market there forms and trading produces prices – the odds – which are relayed back to betting shops. Also 'returned' is an official Start-ing Price (SP), which is the market at the time the race begins. Again back at betting shops this is used as the general odds at which the majority of bets are settled. Under this antiquated system (whereby the much larger off-course market is served by a tiny derivative on courses wherever the racing happens to be taking place), prices don't reflect all the money being bet, just a small portion. The arrival of Betfair constituted a new competitive element giving, at very least, both customers and clients self determination, the freedom to set their own markets, and a consequent wider choice. Betfair's presence in the market lengthened odds. If bookmakers didn't follow and increase the odds they were offering the alternative was reduced turnover. Then bookmakers started bringing their own laptops to the races – after swift deliberation, or in John Brown's view, undue haste, this was allowed – which meant racecourse markets began to reflect, even more the punter-friendly exchange markets. In turn, this meant that Betfair began to influence the Starting Prices directly, tilting the market in the gamblers' favour, again. All together, the effect was to eat into bookmakers' margins.

At the same time, bookmakers found their ability to steady the market compromised. In the past, a company like Ladbrokes could, through the telephone, engineer odds more favourable to profit – by channelling money into the on-course betting market. The weight of Betfair money seeping into racecourse betting greatly diluted bookmakers' ability to shape markets in their favour. Betfair's arrival, with prices determined by a pure market, too big for Ladbrokes to influence significantly, meant bookmakers were disempowered.

Andrew Lee, business analyst for Dresdner Kleinwort, saw the dilemma bookmakers faced not least when William Hill was about to be floated and potential investors were expressing concerns about this new market rival. He considered the issue of betting exchanges as being wholly one of profitability. 'People were negative about William Hill because of the idea that Betfair would cannibalise customers,' reckons Lee. 'That was on the basis that all customers are price discriminatory, which is absolute nonsense. The biggest impact – which we at Dresdner Kleinwort were, I believe, actually the first to publish – was via the Starting Price. By increasing SPs (which meant bigger payouts to punters) was how Betfair hit them.'

Much as William Hill and Ladbrokes might want to start up betting exchanges, they would collapse their own profit margins, Lee concludes. 'Ladbrokes, William Hill, they very aggressively put down Betfair.' He adds, 'They wanted to do it for themselves. But couldn't.'

So that's that, then? All over for Britain's bookmakers, after a place on high streets, nationwide, for nearly fifty years? Betfair might well have ultimately been the end, or at least the beginning of the end, were it not for book-makers' deep-rooted instinct for survival. That and their ability to recognise that Betfair's emergence did not contain only negative elements.

It would be very hard to estimate but Betfair's success must – even John Brown would surely concede this – have brought fresh blood into the world of betting previously underwhelmed by betting shop interiors and general offer-ings. Inevitably, some of this will have leaked out into the wider bookmakers' domain. Bookmakers may not admit to Betfair's quality as a recruiting sergeant publicly. Privately, they cannot rule out that new customers and clients might just be as a result of the individuals spend-ing a bit of time on the Net. Bookmakers have Betfair to thank, at least for *some* new business.

More tangible, Betfair, as well as eating into profits, supplied information to bookmakers that had the oppo-site effect. Historically, bookmakers would produce a first market for races on which they were taking bets. This 'tissue' was often very inaccurate. On occasion, book-makers had simply to guess. Shrewd investors could then jump in early to place their bets – in betting you either take the SP or the odds showing at the time you bet – and watch the odds tumble, their own business concluded. With Betfair beginning to trade on races twenty-four hours before they were due to run, by the time of the raceday 'tissue' the following day there was often enough of a market for bookmakers' first odds to reflect accurately the respective chances of the field. In effect, Betfair became the 'tissue'. The result of this is betting coups – when punters have information ahead of bookmakers and take advantage of the extended odds bookmakers offer in ignorance before realising what is going down – are today fewer and fewer. This is thanks to, as Andrew Black puts it a 'free and totally reliable source they would be idiots not to use and which saves them millions'.

Black has a point. There is altogether something much more important to consider, at least for now. Fundamental to a bookmaker is his betting shop customer. Operations like Ladbrokes – with 2,300 locations in Britain, Ireland, and the European mainland – and William Hill, Britain's second largest operation, really need not have viewed Betfair as the plague. They have a loyal betting shop clientele, which your average retailer would die for. Many punters who visit the companies' betting shops are, in countless instances, doing so as much out of habit and for the companionship contained within – however limited and restricted this is – as they are chasing the odds available. Visit any betting shop in Britain and you will see signs of a community, for whom the notion of price discrimination is at best incidental. Many betting shop punters are ultimately too set in their ways. Simply, people like betting shops, especially their own.

Perhaps most important of all, faced with a formidable adversary with the potential to undercut their core market, bookmakers responded with improved products. Bookmakers have also now more than embraced both the Internet and concepts such as betting-in-running. In sports such as golf, bookmakers today are able to bet right through, uninterrupted from start to finish on for example, the four days of Britain's Open Championship, or the Masters. Betfair inadvertently helped bookmakers overcome reservations about this, helping profitability as had happened with the 'tissue'. That is because underscoring any bets the traditional bookmakers offer is Betfair's up-to-the-minute market. If a company like Ladbrokes wants reassurance that offering odds on Tiger Woods to win is not to allow a golf insider the chance to exploit some nugget of information about the player not in the public domain, they can at least check on Betfair what the odds are trading. The odds there, which they can duplicate, reflect weight of money and are close to a true market.

A reflection of Betfair's reach and the range of the Internet, of course, is that bookmaking has become less and less a home for the technophobe. In October 2008, William Hill announced an alliance with Playtech, the gaming IT specialists, that has bolstered its under-performing Internet operations. Playtech took a 29 per cent stake in a new online gaming and sports betting operation, William Hill Online, in return for an interest in affiliate businesses with a strong supply of customers as well as 'marketing and customer-retention expertise'. Ralph Topping, William Hill's chief executive, added: 'We could not stay the way we were, it was not an option – we were weak. This deal strengthens us. It was the right thing to do; we will have a much, much stronger business over the course of the next four years.'

Maybe it is a generational shift. Attitudes to Memorandums of Understanding – albeit with them now enshrined in law – seem to be shifting, too. 'Bookmakers are moving,' Ben Gunn, of the Gambling Commission and the British Horseracing Authority, maintains. 'I have seen a distinct change in the last three or four years. Historically, they have always looked after themselves, dealing with matters internally. I am not saying whether they did a good job at that or not. They might claim, for fifty years we have looked after ourselves. In fact, they have begun to sit up and take notice. It is perhaps not that they co-operate more. They always were co-operative. No, the co-operation is just sharper.'

An epiphany? Bookmakers' attacks on Betfair in the company's early days were relentless. So much so that the attitudes to the company became like a dogma and were out of kilter with what might be expected of, say, a Stock Market listed company which William Hill became after the millennium and which Ladbrokes has long been. Yet, for all this, bookmakers, during moments of introspection as opposed to time spent questioning Betfair's legality, have risen to the market challenge. Certainly, that is the view of Bruce Millington, editor of the *Racing Post*. 'Ten years ago?' he remembers. 'A hell of a job to get satisfaction. Now, punters have never had it so good. You have to give credit where credit is due. Bookmakers have fought back since the emergence of Betfair. There are, today, a vast array of markets on everything, prices quoted which would not have been available in the past. The size of bet that is accepted? Sure, that remains an issue, which is not the case on Betfair (if the liquidity is good). But credit due.'

Millington does suggest that the almost renaissance in British bookmaking could be something to do with age. 'A new generation is growing up with Betfair. With book-makers, the issue will be not how they crush this but how

they deal with it.' He looks momentarily perplexed, recalling the early days of betting exchanges. When Betfair
launched, William Hill market makers were at first reputedly banned from using the site and markets not only at
the office but also in their homes. Turning your back on
that sort of information? 'That is just bizarre,' Millington
reasons.

There is almost an art-deco quality to the building on
Imperial Drive, off Rayners Lane that is home to
Ladbrokes, perhaps the most recognised name in the
gambling world. Such a style would place the company
around the period from 1925 up to the beginning of the
Second World War. In fact, we have to go back even further
for Ladbrokes' roots, to the 1880s when the operation
began life as a commission agent for horses stabled at
Ladbroke Hall in Worcestershire; it wasn't until 1902 that
the current brand name crystallised from these origins.

In the foyer, there is no effort to hide this extended
history. The betting account card of the Duke of Windsor
– briefly Edward VIII before abdicating in 1936 – is
displayed in a glass cabinet. As for more contemporary
items, a photograph shows a man, broadly smiling, having
just drawn a huge pay-day courtesy of a lottery-style scoop
card. A smattering of casino chips decorate the glass case
to give the display some colour. These generic gambling
symbols remind anyone who arrives of the building's main
function. Lest there be any misunderstanding, this is the
headquarters of a network of high street betting shops
throughout Britain, Ireland, and mainland Europe
employing more than 10,000 staff. In addition, telephone
and Internet businesses take the payroll over 14,000, that

in all generated profits of £154.4 million during the first six months of 2008.

High above this reception area on the executive floor sits John O'Reilly down the corridor from Chris Bell, Ladbrokes' longstanding chief executive, with Mike Dillon, Ladbrokes' highly respected master of communications and public relations on the same level. A director and fellow board member of Bell's, O'Reilly joined the firm in 1991, and today boasts the title, Managing Director of Remote Betting and Gaming. On the walls of his office is a poster for the Montreal Olympics in 1976, some iconic Rolling Stones artwork, and a framed old bank note. More history, and, in showcasing the world's oldest rock and rollers, a homage to longevity.

O'Reilly has three sons. One of his gifts to them is a passion for the Tour de France both as a spectacle and a betting proposition. This illustrates that for all bookmakers' seeming inflexibility, there is an appetite for fresh worlds and different takes. Betting on the tour when O'Reilly joined Ladbrokes wouldn't exactly have been high on the corporate agenda. The latest O'Reilly generation likes to watch sport, with a laptop to hand, O'Reilly Senior confesses. Father, from another era, is possibly just a little bit more comfortable with his telephone account. 'I do sometimes ask what the odds are on their screens,' he confides.

Mention betting exchanges and O'Reilly shifts uncomfortably in his chair. The arms of someone who is overall warm and open company fold, while his shoulders hunch. His foot also starts to tap. As well as the Tour de France, he has a passion for poker. The foot seems to be his telltale sign that gives away that he is about to play a weak hand. 'Yes, I sometimes bet with the exchanges,' he admits. The betting exchange concept, and, in particular Betfair, remains a difficult subject for him, indeed for the majority in the fixed-odds world of traditional bookmaking.

Ladbrokes was slow to the Internet, O'Reilly confesses. He cites a number of endeavours that occupied him – O'Reilly is a natural volunteer – such as Ladbrokes' purchase, then enforced sale in the face of government monopoly concerns, of market rivals, Coral, before he was asked to turn his attention to the Internet. Ladbrokes went live in 2000. It could have been sooner. O'Reilly has a story, culminating in a 2am phone call from a colleague who couldn't wait until the morning to discuss the news that his proposal to take Ladbrokes to the web had been deferred. The tale's punch line is that if the company had been swifter, there might be no Totalbet.com (the Tote's Internet arm) and no Blue Square online bookmakers, which the caller ultimately went on to help establish.

A reference by O'Reilly to West Germany, instead of the more up-to-date united republic, hints that the company still occasionally seeks refuge in a pre-Internet past. Yet since the web's emergence and the arrival of Betfair the company has made up lost ground. The change is evident from O'Reilly's revelation that Ladbrokes.com had just taken more than £1 million in bets on volleyball. Betting with Ladbrokes in 2000 was a relatively one-dimensional affair, compared to today. The emergence of a new medium coupled with the birth of a genuine market shaker in Betfair galvanised Ladbrokes to offer a wide range of new enticements at Ladbrokes.com. Today, take your pick from sports betting, poker, casino and other gaming, bingo, lotto, backgammon, and so on. In addition, there is a thriving market betting on 'financials' – in other words, the Stock Exchange, Dollar v Pound v Euro, the Nasdaq and the Dow Jones, which at the very least offers City traders another chance to hedge. In 1999, Ladbrokes' trade – based on gross win, which is the money you and I leave behind on settling up – was split 85 per cent betting shop, 15 per cent telephone betting. In 2007, Internet betting was 21 per cent and rising, displacing telephone betting which had dropped to 6 per cent and betting shops, down to 73 per cent.

New products are supply-led more than demand-driven, O'Reilly maintains. 'With the Internet we can fly faster with changes, compared to betting shops, where something new has to be implemented at 2,300 different places and can be expensive to introduce. Financials? They are a developing area, getting bigger and bigger. People seem to like to take a view. As for the volleyball, that shows how the Internet has enabled us to break from these [UK] shores. It is quite big in Latvia!'

We came late to the game, O'Reilly concedes. 'From last place to first, or at least near first. First, certainly in product development. That has been our focus.'

Andrew Black describes betting-in-running, with the security of knowing what the odds are trading in Betfair's parallel world, as 'his gift' to bookmakers like Ladbrokes. In the past this sort of high-octane gambling was, leaving the technological aspects aside, considered too risky for Ladbrokes leaving them vulnerable to someone better informed on the ground. Exchanges are a consistent indicator of market demand, so you can see where and when there is real demand, O'Reilly shrugs. Demand for bets always exceeds supply a bookmaker can manage, he maintains, a little argumentatively.

O'Reilly is certainly reluctant to acknowledge any debt Ladbrokes might owe for the ability to take relatively unexposed bets on any in the field contesting Britain's Open Championship while they play, or on Rafa Nadal and Roger Federer during their epic Wimbledon final of 2008. Nonetheless, this is big business now for Ladbrokes' Internet arm. The figures tell the story. Suffice to say, 62 per cent of all Ladbrokes' bets taken during Wimbledon fortnight over the telephone or Internet were mid match. Indeed in all sports, around 30 per cent of total bets via the website are 'in-running'.

The corporate line about Betfair at Ladbrokes is that, as O'Reilly puts it: 'Taxation helped create exchanges, for sure.' He explains: 'Up until 2001, the betting consumer paid tax [6.75 per cent], not the bookmaker. In 2001 Gordon Brown abolished betting tax and replaced it with a gross profits tax [GPT at a rate of 15 per cent of revenues] on the bookmaker. He did this to "persuade" bookmakers like Ladbrokes, William Hill and others to relocate their telephone and Internet betting businesses back to the UK. The big retail operators agreed. Now imagine an exchange on which you had to pay tax on your stake. It simply would not work. The key window for the exchange model was the abolition of betting tax'.

He unfolds his arms: 'Take this a stage further. If you were a budding bookmaker today what would you do, set up shop as a licensed, regulated bookmaker under the Gambling Commission with all that that entails or play on Betfair and pay no tax? That is why the exchanges have proven popular and, frankly, it is a supply-side advantage they have over the traditional bookmakers.'

O'Reilly maintains that the mass market, which frequents his betting shops, has yet to discover Betfair. 'They were not the first betting exchange, were they?' he points out. 'Lots have heard of Betfair, identified them, then decided that the concept is not for them. All too much like commitment.' He makes the point as if to bring discussions about betting exchanges, generally, and Betfair, in particular, to a conclusion.

Betfair's substance today cannot be ignored by someone as intelligent as O'Reilly. What he does accept is that Betfair is a profitable home for those who gamble semi-professionally. 'Where Andrew Back and Ed Wray got it right was that they played to the trade,' O'Reilly does acknowledge. 'They wanted to get serious committed players in their bid to establish acceptable levels of liquidity. At the start of Betfair, plenty thought that they could have a shot at becoming an online bookmaker (taking bets). They proved to be cannon fodder [for highly sophisticated, professional and semi-professional players] and did their money pretty quickly. In truth, there are two types of Betfair player, those who offer and the taker. There are a pretty large number of takers who think they can get better odds on Betfair than with bookmakers like us. That said, the offering side is driven by [the bookmaking] trade.'

Overall, O'Reilly believes that bookmakers and Betfair exist symbiotically. Those who play big on Betfair hedge with Ladbrokes, he maintains. 'They all have accounts with us,' he smiles, knowingly. 'As said, players on Betfair divide up into those who offer [those who put up the lay side and those who put up bets they are willing to accept] and takers [ditto in reverse]. The former are market makers, relatively few in number [certainly in terms of the provision of liquidity] and, by want of another name, the trade players. The latter typically are consumers who believe they can get better value from the exchanges than they can from a bookmaker. The key issue is liquidity and players who take a position on the exchanges, as for all bookmakers, need a facility whereby they can hedge their position or liability. This requires an account with a book-maker who will lay a decent wager. Big exchange players need a hedge and we provide it.'

A Ladbrokes betting exchange? O'Reilly expects the question and has been asked a good few times before. The arms fold again. 'There is only one successful exchange,' he notes. 'Lots have tried to rival Betfair, and lots have failed. That doesn't mean Ladbrokes could not try and even succeed. Ultimately, elements suggest that the market is a natural monopoly,' O'Reilly concludes. The conversation tails off.

After a moment, O'Reilly has a second thought. To rival Betfair, an exchange would have to generate better prices, he maintains. O'Reilly then questions whether anyone could set up an exchange that might compete. This sounds like he considers Betfair to be either too good at what the company does, or too expensive to emulate then surpass in the market. If today the expense of contesting Betfair's grip on the market is what holds Ladbrokes back then the company missed a trick. Back before the merger with Flut-ter when – as Bullion Vault's Paul Tustain suggested might have happened – what is now worth $3 billion-plus might have been secured for a fraction of that amount. A tidy solution to what has grown into a major issue.

If there is shared turf between Betfair and Ladbrokes it is Hammersmith. As well as this being home to the creation of Black and Wray, Ladbrokes is strongly represented with, as well as a brace of outlets on King Street, a premier shop looking out at the Broadway shopping centre and transport complex. The last of these shows how betting shops have evolved since the 1960s. As you walk in, on your right is Café Direct with the encouraging words of Vince Lombardi: 'If winning isn't everything, why do they keep the score?' To the left is a wall of television screens showing live feeds from racecourses, greyhound tracks, Sky television. Clear windows offer passers-by a view of those indulging. Spotlights ensure that the place is well lit and laminated wood floors ensure that each morning the premises is ready to receive regulars and new trade with a clean slate below. As far as betting shops go, this is the higher end.

Highest of all is Ladbrokes' Curzon Street shop in Mayfair. This services an altogether different market to the one in Hammersmith. The former is separated from its nearest rival, a William Hill outlet, by a pair of casinos, Crockfords and Aspinalls, both to the west a few doors down. In fact, these are the competition, rather than William Hill which has – in addition to smoked windows – an interior that smacks more of the old Eastern Bloc than this high rollers' neighbourhood. Whales are what the biggest players are called in Las Vegas. Those beached in Mayfair are more likely to expect facilities of the standard downstairs at Ladbrokes' Curzon Street shop; this is the bespoke area, carpeted and comfortable with reserved tables and other creature comforts, not least privacy.

Betting shops are expensive to run. All the more so if the competition – such as market makers on Betfair – has in effect no retail outlets. Yet betting shops remain part of Ladbrokes' business model, even with growing numbers switching over to online betting. 'Shops are fully integrated,' O'Reilly explains. 'If you open an account with us you can collect and deposit money through shops. With 2,300 shops that is really important.'

The changes reflect the customers' different demands today. 'In 1991 [when O'Reilly joined Ladbrokes] betting shops existed simply for the purpose of people having a bet,' O'Reilly maintains. 'Internet customers have new demands on our shops, as well as different demands to what they were in 1991.'

There are some customers who bet on the Internet and couldn't bet without it, O'Reilly maintains. These include clients who initially seemed without any inclination towards the web, he adds. 'There has been some retail-to-Internet movement. Going to a betting shop is a cash-driven, social activity, which is not replaced by gambling over the Internet.'

O'Reilly shrugs. In the end, it all comes down to business. Has Betfair undermined Ladbrokes? 'Betfair, betting exchanges, they take market share,' confirms O'Reilly (which is not exactly saying much). 'Customers find their way to the exchanges and think, hallelujah. That said, a lot of people who play on the exchange can find themselves in a position where they need someone to take a decent bet.'

He gives a big smile. He is by nature both enthusiastic about life and generous with his time and thoughts, the antithesis of the bookmaking caricatures with which so many are familiar. He gives a nod to Andrew Lee who believes there is more to betting than simply chasing the best odds. 'You know, Internet customers are not as price sensitive as you might think. Most customers of ours have on average 3.3 betting accounts, and maybe a default traditional bookmaker whose shops they would visit or they would call. People shop around. Some use a free bet if that is a marketing offer, check the odds with a couple of sites, then that is it. In some cases, it is all about having a bet quickly, before a race, or the start of a match. They can have gone online to browse and end up having to have the bet quickly.'

O'Reilly laughs: 'I think that is what is known in retail as a stress purchase!'

Victor Chandler's Mayfair betting shop on Deanery Street is just around the corner from Ladbrokes' Curzon Street branch. William Hill is closer but to Ladbrokes, Victor Chandler, along with the casinos, is the competition. Both Ladbrokes and Chandler are aiming for the highest end – the right end at which to aim – of the market. In the shadow of the Dorchester Hotel, Victor Chandler achieves a balance between the modern and the old school. The windows of the betting shop are clear yet the view inside is a little obscured. This way, Chandler keeps everyone happy. Welcoming you in is a jockey figurine about 4ft tall, more often seen in the gated communities of Berkshire and Suffolk, front of house in the racing silks of the property's owner. Once past that token to Turf history, strip out the television screens and shop counter – incidentally, there is no glass front separating customer and staff – and put in some music decks and you could be in a Studio 54-style space. This is a place for pleasure. Betting shops' pens are notoriously cheap and of a length that fits behind your ear. Here, we have an altogether better writing implement fit even for your jacket pocket. A healthy supply of the *Racing Post* newspaper fill a rack attached to the wall. At £1.60 a copy this is not the same as a stack of free sheets.

At the back of the shop is a separate annexe. The main body of the space has a relaxed ambience. Somewhere for fun. The back annexe is more for serious business. Tables can be reserved in the public area but access to this VIP zone is further restricted. In the main space there is a water cooler round which clients can gather. In the VIP zone, there is a different sort of camaraderie. The intimacy is more quiet and understated. The more you bet, the more involved with the self you become. Gamblers can become pretty self-absorbed.

Few if any who come to this place for a bet have insufficient funds to cover the outlay for satellite television coverage of racing, and online facilities to wager away the day. Yet, for reasons over and above the bowls of free boiled sweets on the shop counter, they come anyway. 'They have credit accounts with us, sure, but still they come to shout home a winner, to criticise a jockey, or to have a go at a trainer,' Chandler explains. A relatively late convert to the state of marriage and first-time father at 52, he jokes: 'In betting shops people listen to you in a way that your wife never will.'

It is an old line, and still entertainingly delivered. Nonetheless, Chandler accepts that the betting shop world has changed for ever, as retail chains exist in the growing shadow of Betfair. 'The majority of the high street sites are in a different business now,' he nods. 'Many are supported by Fixed Odds Betting Terminals.'

FOBTs, as they are known in the gaming industry – slot or fruit machines, one-armed bandits if they have an arm – have been identified as a reason for expecting betting shops to suffer more during economic downturn. Historically gambling holds up well during hard times on the basis that punters have even less to lose. In addition, those who bet are creatures of habit who make the journey to the betting shop whatever the climate, economic or weather-wise. According to market research, the FOBT user is a more discretionary customer, with other options, which makes him or her a much less dependable client with habits that are less ingrained and certainly affected by general economic buoyancy. 'A couple of quid on a horse or £10 or £12 at the weekend, it's part and parcel of the fabric of UK life – I don't think people will give that up,' summarises Ralph Topping, chief executive of William Hill.

Chandler's of Mayfair is indeed a home from home. It also has FOBTs – more state of the art than the ones that in the past graced local pubs, or indeed those in the Ladbrokes and William Hill shops nearby – with a sort of B-flick sci-fi style. Having never had an extensive chain of shops, Chandler doesn't dwell greatly on the possibility of an overall decline in off-course betting. He headed offshore – and more importantly into cyberspace – now well over a decade ago. Since then, with the explosion in Asian gambling, he's given not so much as a backward glance. 'I just saw the Internet as another way of showing what prices I was offering,' he shrugs. Chandler does not shirk from competing on unfamiliar turf.

If Chandler does have a major regret about Betfair's emergence it would be the impact the exchange has had on his old world, before relocating to Gibraltar. Betfair has had a dramatic effect on bookmakers who trade at Britain's now sixty-one racecourses, the best of which served as offices for Chandler to shout – or whisper, if you wanted such a consideration – the odds. Today those who stand in front of the grandstand in all weathers are fewer and fewer in number. It was not only punters who were taken by the virtues of Betfair. Bookmakers, themselves, increasingly opt to trade from home online instead of standing in the pouring rain and cold taking racegoers' money and establishing market prices that fed back to the betting shops as SPs. Even Coral, Britain's third biggest bookmakers, announced cutbacks to racecourse operations at the end of 2008.

At the racecourse, Chandler's sense of style and understated personality long seemed to rise above the hectic betting fray at the likes of the Cheltenham National Hunt Festival, Royal Ascot, and Epsom on Derby Day. In 2008, Chandler, after having spent most of his adult life taking bets at the track before relocating to the Mediterranean, brought to an end the proud Victor Chandler family tradition of on-course bookmaking and wrapped up that end of the business. 'I should have done it earlier,' he sighs. 'I kept things going because I loved it. It got too much when I was down to taking just eight bets a day. Racegoers would walk up and see what prices we were offering and then compare them with what was online. It is emotional for me. I miss the racecourse – certainly as it used to be. I spent my youth there, and then my early middle age. I made good friends, some of whom became clients. It is gone now. That's for good.'

Ultimately, for Chandler, he probably did hang on for too long. In 2002, Mickey Fletcher described on-course betting as in a 'terrible state' and sold the majority of pitches from where he traded for two decades alongside Chandler. Fletcher, known universally as 'the Asparagus Kid' – he once sold asparagus to fellow bookmakers trading at Cheltenham – quit after taking less than £5,000 in a day at Epsom. 'Betfair is now a really dominant force as well,' Fletcher said then before taking a month-long holiday in Spain. 'All the action is there, they are taking plenty of money and, at the press of a button, you can get your money on.'

Chandler's deep bookmaking roots meant he hung on to the past. Yet, the longevity of the Chandler family in bookmaking reflects the generations' adaptability. The current Chandler figurehead enjoyed first-to-market advantage in Asia thanks to his early decision to relocate to Gibraltar and then commit to Internet betting ahead of all his major competitors.

Chandler was at least ready for Betfair. Within two years of the millennium, Internet became Chandler's principal source of bets. Broadband's arrival was a tipping point. Settled offshore, just as Betfair began to pick up serious momentum newly merged with Flutter, Chandler has long now been more than comfortable with the web. He was able to offer customers from his offshore base tax-free betting, coupled with streamlined costs – to begin with the operation had eight landlines and as many mobile phones as the staff could muster – which meant that the fall out from Betfair was perhaps less drastic than for rivals. Certainly not as big a shock.

Chandler is not one to fish for compliments. He will not take credit for being settled with the web, ahead of his major competitors. 'Plenty of customers still prefer the phone,' he reveals. 'Certainly, the high rollers. Why? Because they like to negotiate their own prices. These are customers with whom we have personal relationships. Many have been with us for years.'

Chandler chuckles: 'They used to be called high rollers. These days? High Net-Worth Individuals! We have a separate office to deal with their needs. We have special relationships with these customers.' Ladbrokes still takes a big bet, too, he adds.

Bookmaking is a lot more complex than in the past, Chandler confides. He is upgrading his whole Internet service. 'Instead of Java, something called, at least I think so, Ruby on Rails,' he laughs. That's more likely to be a curry on wheels than elaborate software to some of Chandler's City of London clients. He winces at the cost he is incurring in upgrading his own IT service. Betfair's own IT costs run into hundreds of millions. The market dominance that Betfair enjoys, coupled with the outlay that a potential market rival would incur in contesting the betting exchange throne, together makes the emergence of a new, previously unconsidered rival highly unlikely, according to Chandler. He also believes that the chances of a new global bookmaker emerging anywhere any time soon are pretty much zero. 'There may be some new names; companies currently operating out of places like the Philippines and Taiwan but which have yet to register to a wider audience,' he shrugs. 'Other than that, I don't expect to see a new presence in the market now. The costs of entry are simply too high.'

Chapter TEN

SOCIETY
Impossible Steps

There is something a little old fashioned about the editor's office of Bruce Millington in the corner of the *Racing Post*'s editorial floor up high on Canada Square, Canary Wharf. Piles of old newsprint and paper shape the landscape regardless that today the production of daily journals involves more high-tech computer equipment than paper, ahead of the latter becoming wrapping for tomorrow's fish 'n' chips. On a side desk to the right of Millington's work space, a study in organised chaos, is an old trophy awarded to horseracing tipsters for proving masters of selecting winners ahead of printed rivals, both daily, Sunday, weekly, national, and local. A copy of Millington's book *The Definitive Guide to Betting on Sport*, a seminal tome published in 2004, reflecting the extent to which the author has long been in command of his world, is close to hand. A bunker mentality prevails.

In many ways, Millington is very much at ease in this space. By mid afternoon, there is a growing sense that the definitive hour is soon upon him. Tomorrow's news is beginning to take shape. Metaphorically, at least, he has his sleeves rolled up and sports a visor, the look favoured by Hollywood when portraying old-style print men. In the chair now for over a year, Millington may not yet have had the opportunity to shout the traditional editor's cry, 'Hold The Front Page'. Anyway, with today's printing process, such moments are more likely to feature the request, 'Don't Hit That Key'. He remains hopeful that a chance will come, an optimistic state of mind generally important with newspapers under fierce assault from the web as sources of information.

The *Racing Post* is unique among newspapers in that it looks relentlessly forward, much more so than any other daily paper with a greater responsibility to report rather than predict. The previous day's horseracing, other than Blue Riband days such as the Cheltenham Gold Cup or the Epsom Derby, rarely supplies the main headlines.

Millington was raised in a world of the most traditional, fixed-odds gambling in south east London's many betting shops. Looking even further ahead, he has no doubt that he is witnessing, first-hand, while presiding over the bookmaking trade's paper, an era when the grounds beneath are shifting. 'I have friends who have never had a traditional betting account but they all bet happily with Betfair,' Millington reveals. 'Say for the FA Cup Final, they will be on the phone after the game to say, "I backed the first goalscorer. The odds were 5.2." They talk in the decimals of Betfair. The traditional fractions of the bookmaker, 7/2, 100/30, would leave them puzzled. They would just not get it. Definitely a struggle.'

Back in 2000, Flutter went with fractions. Betfair pioneered decimals. 'These punters I know who are more comfortable with decimals, they are the final generation of penetration,' Millington suggests (his choice of phrase, a headline in the making, further endorses the view that there is much of old-school print culture in him. He must hope the game still has legs). Millington continues: 'They see television advertisements for Betfair, that is how the new population grows,' he argues. 'The marketing department at Betfair has every right to say, we are attracting virgin players who make Betfair their first account, our work is done. As for someone like me, I would see Betfair as the Oxbridge of punting, something to which you graduate via the other ways that there are to bet.'

The language of traditional betting today extends way beyond the world in which it is used. Even those who never bet might well talk about the possibility of an occurrence being 'odds-on', or someone being 'favourite' for a job. If Betfair achieves a still wider audience, some of the chat room slang will ultimately also spill over into the wider, popular domain. This would confirm the generational change to which Millington refers.

Millington shakes his head. He recalls his own formative years betting when racecourse bookmakers relied on a hand-signals code called Tic Tac – today, they use two-way radios – to keep up to speed on changes in the market, and chalked up odds on blackboards. 'Those who have grown up with Betfair, the old ways would just bamboozle them,' Millington mutters. 'Some old bloke in a Trilby hat shouting 15/8!'

Beneath Millington, based high up the Canada Square tower, and a few hundred yards away to the northwest, is

Docklands' Museum of London. If this is a home to the
past, then nearby, no more than an amble past some of
Canary Wharf's many eateries and bars, and within view
still of the *Racing Post's* elevated location, is perhaps the
future. Canon Drive remains part of the West Quay dock,
which in the past was where goods shipped from the
Caribbean were unloaded. Today, at the centre of what
is called the City Bunker, is the Canary Wharf Sports
Exchange, a licensed betting premises, Gambling Commis-
sion-approved location where all-comers are free to test
themselves against anyone else in play on the Internet.

Walk in and, above a certain eye line, you might think
you are in a standard betting shop. A bank of twelve
screens shows a mix of horseracing, greyhounds, and other
betting odds. A further four others carry whatever live
sport tops the bill at the same time. Yet, look up and you
see old beams that reflect the premises' listed status under
the English Heritage umbrella. Below, instead of an open
area for punters to mingle, floor space is taken up by rows
of cubicles each with two screens hooked to the Internet,
along with headphones for some privacy. Watching over
them is a wall-size poster of Muhammad Ali in his pomp.
Also hanging, adjacently, are heroes of the immediate era
such as Manchester United's Wayne Rooney, Andrew
Flintoff and assorted Ryder Cup golfers, all in European
colours.

For £40 a day – or the preferred rate of regulars, £900
a month – to access state-of-the-art technology you can
come here to trade over the web, which of course means
Betfair. On an ordinary Tuesday afternoon in November,
a crowd of ten bet (or should that be speculate?) on the
day's racing and greyhounds. They are sustained by snacks

from City Bunker's golf simulator centre – so a one-stop
shop for some – from 10am to 10pm. Etiquette rules such
as silence throughout a race are impeccably observed.
Between betting opportunities, the crowd chats among
itself, using a lexicon of IT and trading jargon you would
never hear in a traditional betting shop.

The facility went live in October 2007. This was four
years on from a night back at Chiswell Street's Old Brewery, one of the locations Betfair chose when taking the
betting exchange concept out on the road. Could any of
those there that night who were employed in the old City
of London financial sector now, having been relocated to
Canary Wharf, find their way to Canon Drive, preferring
to make their money trading sport rather than foreign
exchange or stocks and shares? Richard Redmond, the
founder, has three categories for customers. 'I split them
into three types,' he explains. 'The horseman, with twenty
years of gambling who uses Betfair because the prices give
him an edge; City traders, who because of fire walls are
finding it difficult to bet at work – they often go for the
executive package where we customise your computer
station ahead of arrival; and then the recreational punter.'

Redmond previously worked in publishing. That is
when he wasn't playing poker professionally. 'To me,
Betfair has created another type of magazine altogether
for the shelf,' he suggests, drawing an analogy from at least
one of his past endeavours. He has no doubt that the
company has changed betting forever. As for his own innovation, he boasts that others have already copied his own
template, albeit without the creature comforts he has
installed. There are bookmakers who set aside a designated
old room for his type of customer, Redmond explains. His

bespoke, ultra-fast Internet-connection destination is the real future, he insists. Regulars sitting back in their comfortable, black PVC executive chairs really do seem like regulars. Furniture certainly fit for those with illusions of control.

Back at Hammersmith, those in the flagship Ladbrokes betting shop have access to a computer of sorts. A single terminal invites customers to go online to learn about their favourite football teams' fortunes in the context of betting opportunities. Comprehensive surfing is beyond whoever is at the screen. Certainly, don't think that you can check your emails here. This is one of Ladbrokes' most important shops, in a well-populated part of the capital and fitted to reflect the millennium. Still, it would be too much to suggest that there are *all* mod cons available on the premises. For now, just the very basics.

Computers in betting shops (with, whisper it, access to Betfair markets)? John O'Reilly of Ladbrokes, who oversees the company's web endeavours, looks a shade underwhelmed at the prospect. 'Difficult,' he suggests, frowning just a little. 'Regulatory issues make this so. Dedicated terminals are a bit of a problem with the Gambling Commission. Under current regulation we are permitted to give access via the Internet [dedicated terminals] or machines [self-service betting terminals] to betting on real events – in other words, not virtual events. So you could bet on Alejandro Valverde to win a stage in the Tour de France [O'Reilly's devotion to this event is no affectation] but not on a virtual event, a casino game, a hand in Texas Hold'em. We are not permitted to give access to Ladbrokes.com but can offer restricted access to sports betting/event betting such as *Big Brother* or something like a by-election.'

He pauses to think for a moment. 'Changes to the regulation?' he asks himself. Anyone in the traditional betting industry hesitates before promising swift legislative change. 'Well, I think this is an uphill struggle. On the one hand we would like to offer a broader range of Internet offerings in licensed, regulated betting shops. On the other, neither we nor government would want to see Internet cafes offering dedicated gambling facilities without licensing (and therefore regulation).' It will come, O'Reilly assures. 'We are massively in favour of it. Once a premises is licensed then the place should be able to do exactly what the management likes. Albeit the concern is that Internet cafes open and represent simply online betting joints.'

Now retired from chairmanship of the Tote, Peter Jones belittles his otherwise forward, progressive thinking during a decade in office by questioning whether there is, culturally, a fundamental ceiling to Betfair. 'Computers and betting?' For a moment, he considers whether there is an ingrained preference for good old-fashioned cash across the betting shop counter, or a phone call. 'There will always be a degree of paranoia about pressing the wrong button,' Jones concludes. 'With Betfair in mind, laying something which you meant to back is what will be a source of anxiety. That is because there is a big difference, financially, to betting £20 at 8/1 and laying at 8/1. It is a bit like when you book a flight there are points in the process when you are asked to check your itinerary to ensure you are making the transaction you want to make. With Betfair, there is more pressure to conclude your trade. That is not pressure from the company. More of time, when the horses are going behind the stalls. Even more so if you are betting-in-running.'

People make mistakes, Jones argues. 'I have done it myself,' he confesses. He makes himself sound more of an old timer than he actually is. He continues: 'Today on Betfair, I think that there is a warning if the odds involved are more than 100–1. You have to confirm that, yes, you do want to trade at those odds. Otherwise, a slip can be quite expensive.' He adds: 'This is one of the limits to the rate of growth. That said, new generations will be more familiar and nimble when using the keyboard. Younger, with more dexterity.'

If Jones and O'Reilly represent industry views, Andrew Lee, senior leisure analyst for Dresdner Kleinwort, is a detached observer. He sits back in a chair, round a conference table at the City firm, which according to the group's website: 'Advises clients, provides financing and supplies liquidity' (the same old concept, yet again).

Dresdner Kleinwort boasts: 'Our activities range from helping clients raise capital and execute their most strategic moves to offering straightforward loans, structured finance or delivering asset liability driven transactions.' On the basis of this expertise, Lee ponders the idea of betting exchanges on British high streets in Internet-style cafes against which O'Reilly warns. 'In thirty or forty years' time, maybe that is how we might end up,' Lee says. 'Bookmakers bet with a margin of 15 per cent so, assuming the same cost base, you would, with exchanges profiting at around 2.5 per cent need at least seven times the volume.' Such general growth in betting is feasible. Bookmakers, he adds, having hypothetically in the future spent two decades kicking themselves for not thinking of exchanges first, will have to think somehow about changing the retail format in the next ten or twenty years to reflect more person-to-person culture. 'The next generation may just prefer that, and to bet online,' he warns.

Lee maintains that he was a little surprised with the expansion to the business that Betfair achieved following the merger in 2002 with Flutter. As for the future, though, he maintains that growth rates can only decline. They are, he insists, not sustainable. 'Is Betfair going to be reporting profits in billions over the next five years?' Lee asks. 'The answer is probably, no.'

Of course, with any company it is pretty much inevitable that growth rates slow. As an entity becomes bigger, percentage increases can become smaller even when, in absolute terms, greater market gains are being recorded. This is no more than simple mathematics. As important as the quantitative is the qualitative. In this, Betfair's domination of the market has grown, year-on-year. In 2008, revenues were £239 million, up from £185 million in 2007. Profits for the financial year were £29.73 million with the amount of site investment reflected in the fact that gross profits were £193.46 million.

So, is Betfair unstoppable? Amid continued growth and strength of power base, along the way, and with the blessing of hindsight, some situations might have been played differently by the company. The appointment of Stephen Hill as chief executive in 2003, with Ed Wray taking up an international role, culminated two years later in Wray's brief restoration, after Hill's exit, ahead of David Yu taking the chair in early 2006 to the present day. This was a period when the company seemed to lose sight of its founders' ambitions. JoJo Primrose, head of marketing in Betfair's early days, recalls a phone call from Andrew Black letting her know that a 'coup' was being hatched. This was intended to restore much of the old philosophy eroded by Hill who, for all his corporate gifts, was not shy in high-lighting how little he understood fundamentally about betting.

Since Hill's departure, Betfair has had to contend with a range of issues, some of which have dented the company's corporate armour. In 2007, Betfair introduced a 'Starting Price' for some markets. Not only did this perhaps dilute to an extent the greatest appeal of person-to-person betting – namely self-determination – the concept backfired horri-bly on betting for the following year's Grand National, horseracing's biggest day of the calendar, betting wise. 'Fiasco' said the *Racing Post*. The concept 'failed embar-rassingly', prompting a 'hold up our hands' moment, admitted Betfair.

An even more catastrophic public relations episode was the introduction in 2008 of 'premium charges'. Accord-ing to Betfair, this punishing commission, above normal commission rates of up to 5 per cent, was aimed largely at countering 'Robots', computer systems set up to identify moments of arbitrage then automatically take market posi-tions of guaranteed profit. A good Robot means that its creator can pretty much leave profit making to the soft-ware, which will trade automatically when a position offer-ing profit regardless of outcomes presents itself. Of course, Betfair was not created to bankroll enhanced lifestyle choices of IT masters, not least if they clogged up the markets and in the process diluted the element of skill to Betfair so revered by punters.

The problem was that in the process of disabling Robots with targeted charges, some real, live punters also claimed to have become embroiled in the consequences of the innovation. The Premium Charge was insufficiently accurate in identifying Robots. Hence, customers who had earned their winnings without electronic assistance, suffered a reduction in profits they had made using their skills in the spirit of person-to-person betting to the best effect. Chat rooms exploded, including Betfair's Forum, with criticism of this move. The *Racing Post* gave these opinions the prominence they warranted and also carried details of a Betfair Forum exchange between senior management and clients that didn't seem to capture the true extent of the dissatisfaction with the decision.

WBX, along with Betdaq, the main competition to Betfair – though millions away in liquidity from mounting a sustained challenge to market domination – followed this up with adverts in the *Racing Post*; they parodied Betfair's name, mocking the billing for the very reasons that it was chosen in the first place. 'Pay even more commission? How's that bet fair', asked WBX, along with offering new clients a free soccer shirt to switch camps and answer in the affirmative to the well-crafted corporate slogan 'are you in?' The *Guardian* newspaper took particular issue with Betfair's claim that only half a per cent of customers – as opposed to Robots – would be affected. A complete contradiction to the company's boast that winners are welcome, Greg Wood, racing correspondent, noted. 'Betfair was started by punters for punters and has transformed the betting landscape in less than a decade. The news of premium charges, though, could spark the moment when it stopped being a plucky start-up and turned into just another faceless corporation'. The subtext was that this indicated flotation for Betfair couldn't be that far off (though Wood did not predict stock market chaos that was to follow and that has most likely postponed any flotation plans).

An inevitable consequence of corporate maturity? Andrew Black concedes that a number of additions to the Betfair core service such as poker are no more than 'me too' developments. In other words, nothing like the towering innovation that Betfair represented in 2000. A strangely corporate sounding Black maintains they are additional revenue streams, in the next breath admitting that Betfair might as well just have bought an existing website for poker, instead of setting up in 2005. Perhaps it is unavoidable that levels of innovation recede after a big breakthrough. Indeed. Tradefair Spreads, unveiled in 2008, was in essence a copy of the Cantor Index exchange spread betting, Spreadfair, launched in 2004 and profitable for four years, and spread betting, itself, dating back to the 1970s. The Betfair arcade, offering the chance to bet on a host of games such as virtual slot machines, amounts to little more than the sort of games that bookmakers have successfully translated to the web from the casino. 'Betfair's transformation from thinking punter's playground to giant online fruit machine continues apace,' *Racing Post* commentators observed, dismissively.

Andrew Lee considers Betfair's introduction of its own Starting Price to be a sign that miraculous rates of corporate growth are over. He dismisses the description of the concept as revolutionary. 'Going from not having Betfair to having Betfair is undoubtedly a dramatic step,' Lee maintains. 'Having no Betfair SP to having a Betfair SP? Not quite so revolutionary. I have read how it is calculated three times and still do not understand it. How is it calculated? That is crucial. What is the difference with the bookmakers' version? Most important, is it better than what Betfair has always offered, anyway?'

The difficulty with new markets is that ascendancy in them is not guaranteed to reflect core success. Lee warns that there is no certainty that Betfair will become a dominant player in areas where it seeks growth. He also cautions against the expectation that every punter will ultimately switch to online person-to-person betting with technological difficulties relating to multiple bets, such as Doubles, Trebles, Yankees, the most popular fare of betting shops a hindrance. 'What's more, some online gamblers are pretty price discriminate,' he notes, implying that Betfair must always be aware of meeting the needs of its core customers. 'It is a relatively more mature gambling market.'

What areas of growth there are, Lee identifies as being abroad. These could be both east, towards Asia and west, where America waits. Analysts in his field envisage that the American market could open up within five years. The US presidential election of 2008 was almost a no-lose contest for Betfair. For the Republicans, John McCain had well-established gambling industry credentials. For the Democrats, Barack Obama represented, at very least, a change from George W. Bush, the architect of anti online-wagering legislation that was shaped largely to satisfy a section of his support opposed to betting on moral grounds. President Obama may have been elected to office on the back of some nods towards protecting domestic markets from competition, but that is easier said than done when it comes to the web. The Betfair pitch for a licence is, the trade will simply be illegal so in maintaining effectively prohibition you are missing out on revenue, which the Federal Reserve could certainly use right now.

The paradox of America is indicative of confusion that grips governments about betting. In the *New Yorker* magazine of 25 September 2006, James Surowiecki highlighted the stop-go history of lotteries and racetracks in the US – established, banned on moral grounds, revived to meet revenue needs – and considered 'America's love hate relationship' with gambling. 'Americans have been avid gamblers from the start – Jamestown, itself, was funded via a lottery and the nineteenth century saw a boom in gambling on cards and horses – but a powerful puritanical streak has led to periodic clampdowns,' Surowiecki observed. According to his analysis, thirty-eight of America's states had lotteries generating $16 billion in revenues through 2005, with South Dakota dependent on gambling for 15 per cent of tax receipts. He also noted that David Carruthers had prior to incarceration been lobbying for regulation so *bona fide* operators could trade legitimately, and not just in the grey legal area of 'underenforced law'. (Carruthers, formerly chief executive of BetOnSport.com, was arrested ahead of Bush signing legislation largely outlawing Internet betting on sports, other than horseracing.)

At home, Betfair has certainly played a major part, as far as gambling goes, in meeting the government's expectations at the start of the millennium that Britain becomes the hub of the Internet. In 2003, *The Economist* magazine, ahead of the *New Yorker*'s take on its home market, was encouraging that this wish would be met. An article quoted Leighton Vaughan-Williams, an economist who then headed the Betting Research Unit at Nottingham Trent University. 'Britain is the natural world centre of gambling. There is nowhere else that has the size, the tradition, the market and the probity'. The article identified significant progress in the first three years of the new century and also the contribution of Betfair to this. Betfair was commended for achieving growth of 15 per cent a month and further praised for having successfully thrived in attracting cross-border trade. Once again we are back to our old friend, liquidity. As Joe Saumarez-Smith explains, Betfair correctly identified the path to market domination as being based on high rollers rather than mass market. Better 500 people betting £100 a time than 5,000 who each stake £10, he suggests.

The Economist speculated that Betfair might team up with the Tote 'and establish a really powerful international brand'. Today, Betfair does allow those using the website to channel money into Tote pools – 'Tote-ally covered' is how Betfair puts it in advertisements – both in Britain and Ireland. The article also featured speculation that book-makers might collaborate and set up their own betting exchange, swallowing their pride in having at first questioned the legality of exchanges. 'No strangers to risk, the biggest bet they are now making is on their own future,' *The Economist* concluded. So far, bookmakers haven't accepted the gamble. Their preference remains for offline customers with online ones forcing their way into the picture. 'They go to the betting shop in their lunch hours, or between shifts' John Brown, formerly of William Hill insists. 'They don't play at home. The type that do, online, are watching racing all the time.' Hardcore punters, he suggests.

An altogether different kind of gambling was behind the original investment in Betfair. Those who bet initially on the company by bankrolling it through its formative years had the chance to collect in 2006 when 23 per cent

was sold to SoftBank. The sale was partly respectful of
their initial support, allowing those who wished to cash
in some of the shareholding they had taken out during
Betfair's three rounds of corporate funding. The move was
also an alternative to flotation (which, incidentally, had
previously been the source of serious and divisive debate
contributing, by consensus, to the departure of Stephen
Hill in 2005).

Looking back, Ed Wray, who stepped in as chief executive briefly ahead of David Yu taking the chair having
served as chief operating officer, is phlegmatic about the
times. 'The sale to SoftBank was important for our shareholders. People running a business can sometimes forget
whom they are running it for. Some of our investors have
been in even before we started [for example the investors
in Flutter, who became investors in Betfair when the
companies merged, have stakes held effectively even longer
than first-time investors in Betfair]. We allowed people to
de-risk. There comes a point when you must de-risk as
otherwise you make irrational decisions.'

He shrugs: 'We looked at floating in 2004/5 and decided
against it. Either way, I like to think when I am discussing
the future of Betfair that it has always been clear the
company is in it for the long haul and not just to get rich
quick.' He notes the multibillion dollar valuation now
placed on Betfair and takes from it reason not to panic at
this time. 'Not matched by many other companies of our
generation, is it?' he asks, rhetorically. 'If we run a good
business, the exit will take care of itself,' he adds.

Wray is not a naturally sentimental or philosophical
man. He takes a little while to suspend his micro management of Betfair and ponder the greater magnitude of his

involvement in a company that has gone from nothing but two heads banging together in a business park office in Wimbledon to a global brand.

Of course, before then was the cookery course. 'Did I do it to meet women?' he protests. Wray is a little incredulous. This suggestion, often repeated, apparently seems to be an issue. 'Everyone says that. It simply isn't true. I wanted to cook. Now I accept that sometimes you have to acknowledge that there are some things at which you are always going to be no good.'

You might say that Wray has shown just a smidgen of ability in setting up companies. Recalling the early days of Betfair is, for him, a mixture of nostalgia and reflection. And yet he seems reluctant to enter the fray again from scratch. 'Another one?' he asks, with just a little bit of circumspection in his voice at the suggestion that a new start-up concept might occur in the future. 'I am ten years older, I am married, I have children.' The early days of Betfair nearly put paid to all that. 'The office in Parson's Green was about 200 yards from my house,' Wray confides. 'I used to arrive at 9am and often wouldn't manage to return home before midnight. At the weekends, I was already looking forward to going back to work on Monday. The company very nearly killed my relationship.'

In terms of courtship, things weren't so much better in Wimbledon, where it all began. 'Go to Skillion Business Park in South Wimbledon, our first office,' Wray suggests. 'A window that did not shut during cold snaps and would ice up on the inside, two desks, and that was pretty much it. We arrived at the end of the summer of 1999. Bert continued to build a prototype on his computer and I started to put together a business plan. If we are honest, the early days were not that productive. We had started off working from home but in many respects that was even worse. We were a real business – we had to have our name on the door – so we needed offices.'

Usually more comfortable talking about the company, generally, than about himself, Wray is on this occasion a bit more open. 'I suppose a large part of starting Betfair was to prove that we could do it. We made a lot of mistakes, huge ones. I cannot tell you the number of times I went to bed thinking, that's the game up then, all that time, money and effort wasted. The next day we would look at the problem again. By bedtime we might well have found a solution. Even today, we have our moments. I am very conscious that if you can go, as we have done, from nought to whatever we are now, there is no reason why we cannot go all the way back again in four years, three, two, maybe even one year.'

Would he do it all again? Yes or No? Wray admits that he would be dependent on someone else coming up with the inspiration. 'You always need a creative thinker,' he argues. 'With that you also need someone to challenge the thinking and where necessary say, "you what?" In other words, someone dogmatic enough to say, "sure, that is a pretty good idea, but how are we going to push it?" Never in a million years would I have had the creative thought, the breakthrough idea that Bert had. Me? I would have to be honest enough to say that Betfair would never have happened without Bert but it might have done without me.'

Perhaps Wray is wise not to contemplate a repeat. 'No, unless I was dealing substantially with the same group of people, I am not sure,' he muses. The question is framed, in as much as it can be, with the money he has made out of Betfair left to one side. 'Betfair has been outstanding,' Wray enthuses. 'I would always worry about making comparisons.' He laughs at his own expectations. 'I am also an awful investor. I look for the kind of returns you enjoy only with projects like Betfair.'

He adds: 'To those friends and family I approached about investing, I would say, "I am going to talk you through this once, then I am going to leave you a copy of the business plan if you like, then after that I will never call you again about this. If you are interested, all the details are in the plan. You are friends and family first and foremost. So I am not going to badger you. You have to be prepared to lose all your money." In other words, a complete under selling because I didn't want people coming back to me and saying, "you said that this was going to be worth it".'

As well as sound advice, this represents an insight into Ed Wray's way of thinking and perspective. The original funding of Betfair still troubles him. In some respects, raising money back in 1999 and after the millennium was harder than it should have been. 'We were never interested in a joint venture or deals with existing bookmakers, we were trying to create new markets,' Wray confirms. 'One of the problems we had was that I don't think Bert or I really knew how much money we needed. We had a business plan [note again, the one for which he has forgotten the password] but we had no implementation plan. We would go in and see people to say, "we have this great idea". To be honest I doubt if I had been on the other side of the table I would have invested. We were chaotic. I didn't sense it at the time but I did afterwards. Bert never doubted that we would raise enough money. I did sometimes think, how are we going to raise this as some seriously smart individuals are turning us down? What are we doing wrong? We certainly had to re-evaluate the business plan. This did mean that we had to think very carefully about how we were going to spend what we had. We hadn't exactly raised much. Ultimately, it did instil a discipline in the company from day one. That was no bad thing, at all. Internet businesses are ultimately no different from any other business. You have to generate cash flow and turn that into a profit.'

Andrew Black had few doubts. And certainly not about money. On the second and third fundings ahead of the Flutter deal, those who had come in on the first round were approached again. 'Yes, I suppose we had run out of money,' he acknowledges. 'That said, the business was going well. The numbers were up. Growth was so rapid, for a time doubling every fortnight. Plus we received critical acclaim. This didn't happen very often but when it came it was fantastic. In truth, there wasn't a single bad word written about us. We had a lot of investors who had jumped in first time around without actually seeing the website, without numbers or hard evidence that the idea would work. Yet they had still jumped at the chance. For the second and third fundings we explained, the world had changed, Internet companies had been everybody's darling and everyone wanted to have one. Now the same names were mud. But you believed in us from day one and we delivered as we said we would.' Look at the numbers, Black simply suggested.

Today Black remains supremely confident. He has virtually no fear that, for example, Betfair could through markets or technology going against the company, be reduced back to the two-man start-up business that grew into a respected, award-winning commercial operation with worldwide reach (capable of sustaining a five-year sponsorship deal backing Ascot's prestigious King George VI & Queen Elizabeth Stakes). If this came from anyone else it would seem pretty arrogant (it should be noted here that he insists that trying to create Betfair without Wray would have been 'a complete disaster'). Rather than arrogant, you are more likely to consider Black simply to have been methodical in concluding that Betfair is copper-bottomed against a competitor making a breakthrough in say, software that would enable them to seize the market. 'I can't see it,' he insists. 'I know that they say in boxing the punch that gets you is the punch you don't see but I spent years thinking through the idea of Betfair. No, I cannot see it.' He shakes his head.

For all his talk of being a 'visionary', Black, like Wray, is a modest man. Still, in respect to Betfair he is, he admits, pretty confident generally. 'Slightly arrogant even. As I know how difficult it was to come up with the idea. Ultimately, when we launched, ours was not a version-one website. It was more like a version two or three, even. The thinking behind the site by me had not been in one go but had happened over a period of time. I am a very hard thinker and I had run this through my mind. Over time, I saw a picture of the site, how we would get from A to B, to C, to D and so on. It had taken ages but I had all the answers. I also knew that our rivals didn't and were not from the right background, either. They had not had the thinking time that you needed. With Flutter, for example, the company was basically a couple of US consultants who had had this idea over a beer. How could they be at my level? Not possible. I simply could not accept someone else coming up with something I had come up with in the time available to us.'

Black is much more open than Wray in airing the emotional attachment he has to Betfair. He is candid in admitting that as the company has grown, for all the continued innovations in marketing – for the London Mayoral elections, Betfair paraded two huge plastic *It's a Knockout*-style balloon heads of the main candidates, Ken Livingstone and Boris Johnson – Betfair has become a corporation rather than simply the pure concept he started. Rather darkly, he talks about the forces of capitalism. A subscriber to many free-market philosophies, Black also knows that competition has consequences. 'I worry most about the forces of capitalism turning Betfair into a company with a short-term outlook,' he confides. 'Also the corporate situation of the company needing more money to develop and shareholders refusing to provide the funding.' For a few moments he considers the path of corporate growth and the theory that along the way what has been established has to be destroyed for renewal. 'When smashing things up, relationships break up, too.'

This sombre notion – a general observation rather than a specific remark relating to Betfair – is displaced by a more upbeat thought. Black is an ideas person. For him, Betfair is the translation of an idea into reality. If he found a project with the same potential to achieve that for a second time? 'I would love to do something else amazing again,' Black enthuses.

To be sure, there is still some hesitation. This is not because two of his investments since Betfair have been Silverjet (the now insolvent airline) and Swindon Town (hovering near the relegation zone, March 2009, Coca-Cola Football League Division One). 'Sure, I know that expectations have altered,' he shrugs. 'With Betfair I thought I will go and do that and it will be very easy. Now? I have lots of possible things that I want to do. But with each one, I have a lot of reticence against pursuing them. A fear of failure? Yes, that could be a factor. The consequences of failing, whatever they might be? Becoming more pessimistic about things generally from my experience of starting a company from nothing? You know, in some ways, I am not sure that I could live Betfair all over again. Would I like another idea as good as Betfair and to start from scratch with the knowledge that everything might not work out? Of course Betfair was always going to work! Still, there were very stressful and difficult times.' Better ideas haven't made it, Black concedes. He attributes much of Betfair's success to execution and the strength of the idea. 'Of course, a significant portion was also simply down to luck,' he notes.

'I still think in the same way,' Black reflects. 'I'm always thinking of ways to do other businesses. What I lack is energy, to some extent the time; I have all sort of business interests to amuse me. And family. When I started with Betfair, I had no children. Now I have four.' He pauses to consider the cost/benefit of launching himself back into an entrepreneurial world, having taken a step back from Betfair at the end of 2007. 'Net Net?,' he asks, contemplating both the toll on any endeavour taken by the tax man and also that on himself and those around him. 'That is pretty difficult. If I was divorced from Jane, away from my children, sold all my business interests, loads of money in the bank and a void in my life? Would I go out there again? Bloody hell, yes. Absolutely.'

In the rural setting of family-seat, embryonic stud lands, Black has the open spaces and views that often inspire great thoughts. He is adamant. 'I think I was a visionary,' he repeats (as well as, countless times, that he is a buffoon). 'I had a vision, I could see clearly how things were going to be. It was in my mind. I had run the idea through my mind many times, I had got it right. I had told lots of people about it but no one believed in me and they didn't because on the surface I am not a credible person. That was the problem. I didn't have a history of success. Not the sort of person who would come up with the next brilliant idea'.

The family kitchen today is bigger than the original room in which Black and Wray first started work together on Betfair back at Skillion Business Park, South Wimbledon. Black readily acknowledges that he was far from house trained, something made worse by having to share a confined room. 'Wimbledon was pretty miserable,' he confesses. 'Ed sort of took charge in a way that, at the time, I did not like at all. Never mind during winter, when it was freezing, the office was sometimes so hot I couldn't concentrate. So I'd sort of do a bit of work, while Ed worked away, go outside for a cigarette, play some games, play some more games. I wasn't working very hard and in truth was probably more working myself out of IT contracts for clients that I had signed. I wasn't really sure about where it was all going, and I wasn't that comfortable with Ed. He would only say that I needed to work harder.'

This was Black's baby. 'In the most part, certainly in Wimbledon, the ideas were just mine. Ed would ask me about the business plan he was working on. To an extent I was his sounding board. As for the website, itself, there was really only the one idea that Ed had which ultimately got through to the final version. It is quite complicated.'

Black pauses. Then he frowns just a little. 'Ed has not always appreciated how hard it was to come up with the website, and how much of myself went into it. I just told him, this is the way it is meant to be. I sometimes thought that he had the idea that I would grind out these ideas which were fairly straightforward. Maybe that was because Ed was, in gambling terms, more a regular punter. Make no mistake, Betfair was a very difficult concept. At the same time, Ed saw that here was this giant company called Flutter, which raised millions, achieving all that he wanted to achieve where as we were reduced to going to family and friends; if we failed we were losing mates' money. Once we had raised the money from family and friends, Ed became even more difficult than before. I think he felt the pressure of the investment whereas before the fundraising it was a project that on which he had spent a bit of time, a few months of his life, learnt a few things, no big deal either way. The financing meant that it had to work for him. Otherwise he could look like a complete idiot. That was a lot to carry on his shoulders.'

Amid this, Black did his best to manage what is a seemingly chronic condition. 'One of my problems is that I suffer from terrible headaches,' he reveals. 'I have done all my life. If you come to see me, either I have one, am just about to have one, have just had one, or am momentarily – not for long – without one at all. I am always in one of those four states. I know that when I am about to have a headache I am a very difficult person to be with and cannot think at all. In the main, I am a pretty clear-thinking person. But I am always liable to do some pretty silly things when my head is not quite right. Because of this there will always be moments when I let myself down pretty badly. I have real off days, which other people cannot always understand. I expect that will continue.'

Back in 1999, when Betfair began its journey to the Internet's global top ten, Black was mourning his father, Tony, who contracted MRSA. He tells the story very movingly of sitting in his chair, days before the funeral, composing a speech, making the speech – even though his throat was bone dry – then returning to his chair. Tony was his hero for many reasons.

'I had enormous admiration for my father,' Black confides. 'He was quite an entrepreneurial spirit in his own way as well as being a quiet man, very clever. Somehow, he was a rock. When he was alive I never thought I would ever be in trouble. If I needed some money, I would ask, can I have some? I actually didn't need to do anything, or certainly didn't feel that. Maybe I also didn't want to challenge him. He really bought into Betfair. "A good idea," he would say. "You should do something with it." I think if he was alive I would still have developed Betfair but at a very slow pace. When he died, I thought, I need to do something with my life, I cannot sit around twiddling my thumbs, which I had done for a long time, and notwithstanding the work I had done for various people. Some of that was quite impressive. Some really good stuff. But I did always feel justified in what I was doing as I was working towards a big idea while at the same time thinking, I am kidding myself, I am not really working on anything at all. Then my father died. I thought, well, this is the time.'

Before his father, Black also lost his brother, Kevin, from the effects of a brain haemorrhage. This was shortly after Black had 'fallen out of University'. He concedes: 'My whole life was a mess'. Betfair followed his father's death. 'Of the three males in the family – I have three sisters – I was the only one left,' he reasons today. 'Suddenly, I felt I had to bring in the bacon. If nothing had happened to my brother or father I probably would not have done anything with my life.'

Yet another shrug. With Black, as his mind processes a situation before arriving at a conclusion there are many staging posts. 'You know, I could have done everything differently. If things had not happened the way they happened I would probably have had a very boring life.'

Black goes back to the very beginning. It is an observation he never spares from repetition. 'I was telling people, I had this idea. The typical reaction was, if this is such a good idea, surely someone else would have done it. The bookmakers? But I would say, can you imagine it? Ladbrokes as a betting exchange? They just could not do it.'

Black stops himself. 'I think that might be it,' he suggests. At times like this it is very hard to be convinced that Andrew Black has not temporarily left the conversation in which he was participating fully to take a different path with his own thoughts. 'You know, that might be exactly where the best business ideas lie.' He smiles. 'When the step that needs to be taken is impossible.'

INDEX